CIM
PRACTICE & REVISION KIT

Diploma

Integrated Marketing Communication

BPP Publishing
September 2000

First edition September 1999
Second edition September 2000

ISBN 0 7517 4913 3 *(previous edition 0 7517 4928 1)*

British Library Cataloguing-in-Publication Data
*A catalogue record for this book
is available from the British Library*

Published by

BPP Publishing Limited
Aldine House, Aldine Place
London W12 8AW

www.bpp.com

in association with
Nottingham Business School
Nottingham Trent University

Printed in England by DACOSTA PRINT
35-37 Queensland Road
London N7 7AH
(0207 700 1000)

All our rights reserved. No part of this publication may be reproduced, stored in a retrieval system or transmitted, in any form or by any means, electronic, mechanical, photocopying, recording or otherwise, without the prior written permission of BPP Publishing Limited.

We are grateful to the Chartered Institute of Marketing for permission to reproduce past examination questions. The suggested solutions to past examination questions have been prepared by BPP Publishing Limited.

Authors
Chris Fill

Series editor
Paul Brittain, Senior Lecturer in Marketing and Retailing at Nottingham Business School, Nottingham Trent University

©
BPP Publishing Limited and Chris Fill
2000

Contents

Page

CONTENTS

Question and answer checklist/index	(iv)
About this kit	(vii)
Revision	(viii)
Question practice	(ix)
Exam technique	(x)
Approaching mini-cases	(xii)
The exam paper	(xviii)
Syllabus	(xxii)
QUESTION BANK	**1**
ANSWER BANK	**25**

TEST YOUR KNOWLEDGE

Questions	171
Answers	172

TEST PAPER

June 2000 paper questions	179
June 2000 paper suggested answers	185

TOPIC INDEX	203

ORDER FORM

REVIEW FORM & FREE PRIZE DRAW

Question and answer checklist/index

The headings indicate the main topics of questions, but questions often cover several different topics.

Tutorial questions, listed in italics, are followed by **guidance notes** on how to approach the question, thus easing the transition from study to examination practice.

A date alone (6/99, say) after the question title refers to a past examination question.

Questions marked by ★ are **key questions** which we think you must attempt in order to pass the exam. Tick them off on this list as you complete them.

		Marks	Time allocation mins	Page number Question	Answer
PART A: STRATEGIC MARKETING COMMUNICATIONS					
1	*Tutorial question: Defining marketing communications*	-	-	4	27
★2	Marketing communications strategy	20	32	4	27
3	Different mixes	20	32	4	34
4	*Tutorial question: Strategy and objectives*	-	-	4	36
5	Illustrated integrated communications	20	32	4	38
6	Integrated marketing communications	20	32	4	42
7	More integration	20	32	5	47
★8	Implementing integrated communications	20	32	5	50
9	*Tutorial question: Technology*	-	-	5	52
10	Objectives (12/99)	20	32	5	53
PART B: DEVELOPING A THEORETICAL UNDERSTANDING					
11	*Tutorial question: Consumer buying behaviour*	-	-	7	55
12	*Tutorial question: Organisational buying behaviour*	-	-	7	57
★13	Two practical models	20	32	7	60
14	Life cycle	20	32	7	62
★15	Changing attitudes (6/99)	20	32	7	66
16	Perceived risk (12/98 & specimen)	20	32	7	68
17	Client needs (12/98 & specimen)	20	32	8	69
PART C: MANAGING THE MARKETING COMMUNICATIONS PROCESS					
Segmentation, targeting and promotional opportunities					
18	*Tutorial question: Auditing, segmentation and positioning*	-	-	10	71
19	Segmentation, targeting and positioning	20	32	10	73
★20	Toothpaste positioning	20	32	10	79
21	Promotional mix (specimen)	20	32	10	81
22	Promotional mix and branding (specimen)	20	32	11	84

Question and answer checklist/index

		Marks	Time allocation mins	Page number Question	Answer
Strategy formulation					
*23	Plan links (6/99)	20	32	11	86
24	Analyse the current situation	20	32	11	88
*25	Marketing communications objectives	20	32	11	91
26	Markets and strategies	20	32	11	95
27	Internal communications	20	32	11	100
28	Internal marketing communications (12/98 & specimen)	20	32	12	102
29	Planned communications (12/99)	20	32	12	103
30	Internal marketing communications: technology (12/99)	20	32	12	105
Branding					
31	Brands hatch	20	32	12	107
*32	Branding and marketing communication	20	32	12	109
33	Internet	20	32	12	111
34	Business-to-business branding (12/98 & specimen)	20	32	12	113
Budgeting, media and external resources					
35	*Tutorial question: Promotional budgets*	-	-	13	115
36	*Tutorial question: Inter- and intra-media decisions*	-	-	13	116
*37	Budget process (6/99)	20	32	13	117
38	Evaluate repositioning	20	32	13	119
*39	Evaluate effectiveness (6/99)	20	32	13	121
40	Measuring effectiveness	20	32	13	123
41	Marketing communications expenditure (12/98 & specimen)	20	32	14	125
42	Competitors' advertising spend (specimen)	20	32	14	127

PART D: SUCCESSFUL MARKETING COMMUNICATION STRATEGIES

		Marks	Time allocation mins	Page number Question	Answer
43	Current campaign	20	32	16	129
44	Public interest	20	32	16	133
45	An actual student's answer	20	32	16	136
46	*Tutorial question: Branding*	-	-	16	137
*47	Examples of PLC (6/99)	20	32	16	138
48	Loyalty schemes (12/98 & specimen)	20	32	16	141
49	Customer retention (12/99)	20	32	16	143

PART E: CROSS-BORDER MARKETING COMMUNICATIONS

		Marks	Time allocation mins	Page number Question	Answer
50	*Tutorial question: Differences*	-	-	18	145
51	Two countries in the kitchen	20	32	18	146
52	With or without	20	32	18	148
53	Global campaign	20	32	18	151
*54	Advantages and disadvantages of international agencies	20	32	18	152

Question and answer checklist/index

	Marks	Time allocation mins	Page number Question	Answer
PART F: MINI-CASES				
★ 55 British Gas Recycling Company	40	64	19	154
★ 56 Car Communications (6/99)	40	64	20	159
57 Netline Technologies (12/98 & specimen)	40	64	21	163
58 Dutton Engineering (12/99)	40	64	23	166

ABOUT THIS KIT

You're taking your professional CIM exams in December 2000 and June 2001. You're under time pressure to get your exam revision done and you want to pass first time. Could you make better use of your time? Are you sure that your revision is really relevant to the exam you will be facing?

If you use this BPP Practice & Revision Kit you can be sure that the time you spend revising and practising questions is time well spent.

The BPP Practice & Revision Kit: Integrated Marketing Communication

The BPP Practice & Revision Kit, produced in association with Nottingham Trent University Business School, has been specifically written for the syllabus by experts in marketing education, Valerie Youngson and Brian Searle.

- We give you a **comprehensive question and answer checklist** so you can see at a glance which are the key questions that we think you should attempt in order to pass the exam, what the mark and time allocations are and when they were set (where this is relevant)
- We offer **vital guidance** on revision, question practice and exam technique
- We show you the **syllabus** examinable in December 2000 and June 2001. We **analyse the papers** set so far, with summaries of the examiner's comments
- We give you a **comprehensive question bank** containing:
    - *Do You Know* checklists to jog your memory
    - *Tutorial questions* to warm you up
    - *Exam-standard questions*, including questions set up until December 1999 and the new syllabus specimen paper
    - *Full suggested answers* - with summaries of the examiner's comments
- A **Test Your Knowledge quiz** covering selected areas from the entire syllabus
- A **Test Paper** consisting of the June 2000 exam, again with full suggested answers, for you to attempt just before the real thing
- A **Topic Index** for ready reference

The Study Text: further help from BPP

The other vital part of BPP's study package is the Study Text. The Study Text features:

- Structured, methodical syllabus coverage
- Lots of case examples from real businesses throughout, to show you how the theory applies in real life
- Action programmes and quizzes so that you can test that you've mastered the theory
- A question and answer bank
- Key concepts and full index

There's an order form at the back of this Kit.

Help us to help you

Your feedback will help us improve our study package. Please complete and return the Review Form at the end of this Kit; you will be entered automatically in a Free Prize Draw.

BPP Publishing
September 2000

To learn more about what BPP has to offer, visit our website: www.bpp.com

Revision

REVISION

This is a very important time as you approach the exam. You must remember three things.

> **Use time sensibly**
> **Set realistic goals**
> **Believe in yourself**

Use time sensibly

1. **How much study time do you have?** Remember that you must EAT, SLEEP, and of course, RELAX.

2. **How will you split that available time between each subject?** What are your weaker subjects? They need more time.

3. **What is your learning style?** AM/PM? Little and often/long sessions? Evenings/ weekends?

4. **Are you taking regular breaks?** Most people absorb more if they do not attempt to study for long uninterrupted periods of time. A five minute break every hour (to make coffee, watch the news headlines) can make all the difference.

5. **Do you have quality study time?** Unplug the phone. Let everybody know that you're studying and shouldn't be disturbed.

Set realistic goals

1. Have you set a **clearly defined objective** for each study period?
2. Is the objective **achievable**?
3. Will you **stick to your plan**? Will you make up for any **lost time**?
4. Are you **rewarding yourself** for your hard work?
5. Are you leading a **healthy lifestyle**?

Believe in yourself

Are you cultivating the right attitude of mind? There is absolutely no reason why you should not pass this exam if you adopt the correct approach.

- **Be confident** - you've passed exams before, you can pass them again
- **Be calm** - plenty of adrenaline but no panicking
- **Be focused** - commit yourself to passing the exam

 (viii)

QUESTION PRACTICE

Do not simply open this Kit and, beginning with question 1, start attempting all of the questions. You first need to ask yourself three questions.

> **Am I ready to answer questions?**
> **Do I know which questions to do first?**
> **How should I use this Kit?**

Am I ready to answer questions?

1 Check that you are familiar with the material on the **Do you know?** page for a particular syllabus area.

2 If you are happy, you can go ahead and start answering questions. If not, go back to your BPP Study Text and revise first.

Do I know which questions to do first?

1 **Start with tutorial questions**. They warm you up for key and difficult areas of the syllabus. Try to produce at least a plan for these questions, using the guidance notes following the question to ensure your answer is structured so as to gain a good pass mark.

2 Don't worry about the time it takes to answer these questions. Concentrate on producing good answers. There are 21 tutorial questions in this Kit.

How should I use this Kit?

1 Once you are confident with the Do you know? checklists and the tutorial questions, you should try as many as possible of the exam-standard questions; at the very least you should attempt the **key questions,** which are highlighted in the **question and answer checklist/index** at the front of the Kit.

2 Try to **produce full answers under timed conditions**; you are practising exam technique as much as knowledge recall here. Don't look at the answer, your BPP Study Text or your notes for any help at all.

3 **Mark your answers to the non-tutorial questions as if you were the examiner**. Only give yourself marks for what you have written, not for what you meant to put down, or would have put down if you had had more time. If you did badly, try another question.

4 Read the **Tutorial notes** in the answers very carefully and take note of the advice given and any **comments by the examiner**.

5 When you have practised the whole syllabus, go back to the areas you had problems with and **practise further questions**.

6 When you feel you have completed your revision of the entire syllabus to your satisfaction, answer the **test your knowledge** quiz on pages 171 to 177. This covers selected areas from the entire syllabus and answering it unseen is a good test of how well you can recall your knowledge of diverse subjects quickly.

7 Finally, when you think you really understand the entire subject, **attempt the test paper** at the end of the Kit. Sit the paper under strict exam conditions, so that you gain experience of selecting and sequencing your questions, and managing your time, as well as of writing answers.

Exam technique

EXAM TECHNIQUE

Passing professional examinations is half about having the knowledge, and half about doing yourself full justice in the examination. You must have the right approach to two things.

> **The day of the exam**
> **Your time in the exam hall**

The day of the exam

1 Set at least one alarm (or get an alarm call) for a morning exam.

2 Have something to eat but beware of eating too much; you may feel sleepy if your system is digesting a large meal.

3 Allow plenty of time to get to the exam hall; have your route worked out in advance and listen to news bulletins to check for potential travel problems.

4 Don't forget pens, pencils, rulers, erasers.

5 Put new batteries into your calculator and take a spare set (or a spare calculator).

6 Avoid discussion about the exam with other candidates outside the exam hall.

Your time in the exam hall

1 **Read the instructions (the 'rubric') on the front of the exam paper carefully**

 Check that the exam format hasn't changed. It is surprising how often examiners' reports remark on the number of students who attempt too few - or too many - questions, or who attempt the wrong number of questions from different parts of the paper. Make sure that you are planning to answer the right number of questions.

2 **Select questions carefully**

 Read through the paper once, then quickly jot down key points against each question in a second read through. Select those questions where you could latch on to 'what the question is about' - but remember to check carefully that you have got the right end of the stick before putting pen to paper.

3 **Plan your attack carefully**

 Consider the order in which you are going to tackle questions. It is a good idea to start with your best question to boost your morale and get some easy marks 'in the bag'.

4 **Check the time allocation for each question**

 Each mark carries with it a time allocation of 1.6 minutes (including time for selecting and reading questions). A 20 mark question therefore should be completed in 32 minutes. When time is up, you must go on to the next question or part. Going even one minute over the time allowed brings you a lot closer to failure.

5 **Read the question carefully and plan your answer**

 Read through the question again very carefully when you come to answer it. Plan your answer to ensure that you keep to the point. Two minutes of planning plus eight minutes of writing is virtually certain to earn you more marks than ten minutes of writing.

Exam technique

6 **Produce relevant answers**

Particularly with written answers, make sure you answer the question set, and not the question you would have preferred to have been set.

7 **Gain the easy marks**

Include the obvious if it answers the question and don't try to produce the perfect answer.

Don't get bogged down in small parts of questions. If you find a part of a question difficult, get on with the rest of the question. If you are having problems with something, the chances are that everyone else is too.

8 **Produce an answer in the correct format**

The examiner will state in the requirements the format in which the question should be answered, for example in a report or memorandum.

9 **Follow the examiner's instructions**

You will annoy the examiner if you ignore him or her. The examiner will state whether he or she wishes you to 'discuss', 'comment', 'evaluate' or 'recommend'.

10 **Present a tidy paper**

Students are penalised for poor presentation and so you should make sure that you write legibly, label diagrams clearly and lay out your work neatly. Markers of scripts each have hundreds of papers to mark; a badly written scrawl is unlikely to receive the same attention as a neat and well laid out paper.

11 **Stay until the end of the exam**

Use any spare time checking and rechecking your script.

12 **Don't worry if you feel you have performed badly in the exam**

It is more than likely that the other candidates will have found the exam difficult too. Don't forget that there is a competitive element in these exams. As soon as you get up to leave the exam hall, forget that exam and think about the next - or, if it is the last one, celebrate!

13 **Don't discuss an exam with other candidates**

This is particularly the case if you still have other exams to sit. Even if you have finished, you should put it out of your mind until the day of the results. Forget about exams and relax!

Guidance from the senior examiner

APPROACHING MINI-CASES

What is a mini-case?

The mini-case in the examination is a description of an organisation at a moment in time. You first see it in the examination room and so you have 64 minutes to read, understand, analyse and answer the mini-case.

The mini-case (Part A of the paper) carries 40% of the available marks in the examination.

As mini-cases are fundamental to your exam success, you should be absolutely clear about what mini-cases are, the CIM's purpose in using them, and what the examiner seeks; then, in context, you must consider how best they should be tackled.

The purpose of the mini-case

The examiner requires students to demonstrate not only their knowledge of the fundamentals of marketing, but also their ability to use that knowledge in a commercially credible way in the context of a 'real' business scenario.

The examiner's requirements

The examiner is the 'consumer' of your examination script. You should remember first and foremost that a paper is needed which makes his or her life easy. That means that the script should be well laid out, with plenty of white space and neat readable writing. All the basic rules of examination technique discussed earlier must be applied, but because communication skills are fundamental to the marketer, the ability to communicate clearly is particularly important.

An approach to mini-cases

Mini-cases are easy once you have mastered the basic techniques. The key to success lies in adopting a logical sequence of steps which, with practice, you will master. You must enter the exam room with the process as second nature, so you can concentrate your attention on the marketing issues which face you.

Students who are at first apprehensive when faced with a mini-case often come to find them much more stimulating and rewarding than traditional examination questions. There is the added security of knowing that there is no single correct answer to a case study.

Suggested mini-case method

You have about 64 minutes in total.

Stage		Minutes
1	Read the mini-case and questions set on it very quickly.	2
2	Read the questions and case again, but carefully. Make brief notes of significant material. Determine key issues in relation to the questions etc.	5
3	Put the case on one side and turn to your notes. What do they contain? A clear picture of the situation? Go back if necessary and concentrate on getting a grip on the scenario outlined.	4
4	Prepare an answer structure plan for question (a) following exactly the structure suggested in the question, highlighting your decisions supported by case data and theory if appropriate. Follow the process outlined for question (b), etc.	3
5	Prepare a timeplan for each part of the question, according to the marks allocated.	1
6	Write your answer.	44
7	Read through and correct errors, improve presentation.	5
		64

A good answer will be a document on which a competent manager can take action.

Approaching mini-cases

Notes

(a) It is not seriously suggested that you can allocate your time quite so rigorously! The purpose of showing detailed timings is to demonstrate the need to move with purpose and control through each stage of the process.

(b) Take time to get the facts into your short term memory. Making decisions is easier once the facts are in your head.

(c) Establish a clear plan and you will find that writing the answers is straightforward.

(d) Some candidates will be writing answers within five minutes. The better candidates will ignore them and concentrate on planning. This is not easy to do, but management of your examination technique is the key to your personal success.

(e) Presentation is crucial. Your answer should be written as a final draft that would go to typing. If the typist could understand every word and replicate the layout, then the examiner will be delighted and it will be marked highly.

Handling an unseen mini-case in the examination

The following extract is taken from a Chartered Institute of Marketing's Tutor's/Student Guide to the treatment of mini-cases.

Tutor's/Student Guide to the treatment of mini-cases

'It needs to be stated unequivocally that the type of extremely short case (popularly called the mini-case) set in the examinations for Certificate and Diploma subjects cannot be treated in exactly the same way as a long case study issued in advance. If it could there would be little point of going to all the trouble of writing an in-depth case study.

'Far too many students adopt a maxi-case approach using a detailed marketing audit outline which is largely inappropriate to a case consisting only of two or three paragraphs. Others use the SWOT analysis and simply re-write the case under the four headings of strengths, weaknesses, opportunities and threats.

'Some students even go so far as to totally ignore the specific questions set and present a standard maxi-case analysis outline including environmental reviews through to contingency plans.

'The "mini-case" is not really a case at all; it is merely an outline of a given situation, a scenario. Its purpose is to test whether examinees can apply their knowledge of marketing theory and techniques to the company or organisation and the operating environment described in the scenario. For example answers advocating retail audits as part of the marketing information system for a small industrial goods manufacturer demonstrate a lack of practical awareness. Such answers confirm that the examinee has learned a given MIS outline by rote and simply regurgitated this in complete disregard of the scenario. Such an approach would be disastrous in the real world and examinees adopting this approach cannot be passed, ie gain the confidence of the Institute as professional marketing practitioners. The correct approach to the scenario is a mental review of the area covered by the question and the *selection* by the examinee of those particular parts of knowledge or techniques which apply to the case. This implies a rejection of those parts of the student's knowledge which clearly do not apply to the scenario.

'All scenarios are based upon real world companies and situations and are written with a fuller knowledge of how that organisation actually operates in its planning environments. Often the organisation described in the scenario will not be a giant fast moving consumer goods manufacturing and marketing company since this would facilitate mindless regurgitation of textbook outlines and be counter to the intention of this section of the examination.

Guidance from the senior examiner

'More often the scenarios will involve innovative small or medium sized firms which comprise the vast majority of UK companies which lack the resources often assumed by the textbook approach. These firms do have to market within these constraints however and are just as much concerned with marketing communications, marketing planning and control and indeed (proportionately) in international marketing, particularly the Common Market, as are larger enterprises.

'However, as marketing applications develop and expand and as changes take root, the Institute (through its examiners) will wish to test students' knowledge and awareness of these changes and their implication with regard to marketing practice. For example in the public sector increasing attention is being paid to the marketing of leisure services and the concept of "asset marketing" where the "product" is to a greater extent fixed and therefore the option of product as a variable in the marketing mix is somewhat more constrained.

'Tutors and students are referred to Examiners' Reports which repeatedly complain of inappropriateness of answer detail which demonstrates a real lack of *practical* marketing grasp and confirms that a leaned by rote textbook regurgitation is being used. Examples would include:

- the recommendation of national TV advertising for a small industrial company with a local market;
- the overnight installation of a marketing department comprising Marketing Director, Marketing Manager, Advertising Manager, Distribution Manager, Sales Manager, etc into what has been described as a very small company;
- the inclusion of packaging, branded packs, on-pack offers, etc, in the marketing mix recommendations for a service.

'It has to be borne in mind that the award of the Diploma is in a very real sense the granting of a licence to practice marketing and certainly an endorsement of the candidate's practical as well as theoretical grasps of marketing. In these circumstances such treatments of the mini-case as described above cannot be passed and give rise to some concern that perhaps the teaching/learning approach to mini-cases has not been sufficiently differentiated from that recommended for maxi-cases.

'Tutors/distance-learning students are recommended to work on previously set mini-cases and questions and review results against published specimen answers. They are also advised to use course-members' companies/organisations as examples in the constraints/limitations of marketing techniques and how they might need to be modified.

'Students are also advised to answer the specified questions set and if for example a question was on objectives, then undue reference to market analysis and strategies would be treated as extraneous.'

Approaching mini-cases

GUIDANCE FROM THE SENIOR EXAMINER

The Senior Examiner

The current Senior Examiner, Chris Fill, was appointed in September 1997. He has set exams from June 1998 onwards.

The following comments were made in the light of the June 1998 exam.

Examiner's comments

'(1) This question signals that the minicase will in future draw on a range of contexts. Students will be required to use material that reflect a variety of circumstances and that global brands can no longer be expected to be the base material.

(2) Students are advised that *this* question format will not necessarily be followed in future. Students must be able to prepare marketing communications plans for products and brands in the consumer and business-to-business sectors. In addition, students may be asked to prepare a plan for a major global brand, a small industrial product or for any type of product or service in unfamiliar contexts. **It does not follow that students will always be expected to produce a marketing communications plan.**

(3) The answer that follows contains elements that for some students are new or only vaguely familiar. I did not receive many answers with the content as set out here, although most followed the same structure. '

The solutions in this Kit

Chris Fill has written the majority of the answers in this Kit, and his answers also include notes on various matters indicating how the emphasis of questions might change in the future.

Here is a brief summary of the main points. See the suggested answers for further details.

Comment

Integrated marketing communications will not necessarily feature regularly in a separate question in future, but may be relevant to a number of questions in the paper.

Where models feature in questions, practical application and examples will be required. Students should feel free to criticise models, not accept them blindly.

'Context analysis' not 'situation analysis'.

Justify media and promotional tools selections.

Budgets and the need for quantitative material.

Students should be aware of the structure of a marketing communications plan without being told.

Plans should be *justified*, based on the student's context analysis and understanding of aspects of customer behaviour.

Comments on an actual student's answer

Question 45 in this Kit, *An actual student's answer* (6/97), is (as you can probably guess!) a verbatim reproduction of an answer to a June 1997 question written by one of the candidates in that exam. Below are Chris Fill's comments and suggestions for improvements.

We suggest that you read the answer itself right through, now, and then read the comments below. They are set out *here* (rather than directly beside the answer), because they are potentially relevant to any questions that might appear in the future.

Guidance from the senior examiner

'There are a number of good elements about this answer and there are a number of flaws. All answers are invariably a mixture of the two and the trick is to get more good elements than flaws. You will probably have noted some points yourself as you read it through.

What we cannot reproduce here is the clarity in which the answer was penned and the style and confidence with which it was presented. The answer covered five pages, was neatly written and was easy to read. The student had obviously prepared for this type of question and tried hard to adapt their knowledge to the question. Indeed, the structure of the response is to be applauded as it follows the points asked for in the question.

Structure

The structure is straightforward as per the question. There are other ways of structuring an answer that still meets the requirements. The question asks for an outline report and so the following structure would have been an improvement.

To:

From:

Date:

Ref: The RSPCA's Marketing Communications Campaign

1.0   Executive summary

2.0   Introduction and background

3.0   Target audiences

4.0   Promotional objectives

5.0   Campaign strategy and tactics

6.0   Evaluation of effectiveness

The student numbered each of their paragraphs which indicates an awareness of the report format. A more complete format, as set out above, would have been even better.

Content

In addition to the stated requirements the student had the good sense to provide an *introduction*. However, the material included describes the campaign contents and materials whereas this should have been relocated to the section entitled campaign strategy and tactics. The *background* section could have been used to introduce the campaign by setting the scene and providing relevant information as background for the reader (the examiner in this case). I am also looking for the *rationale for choosing* the selected campaign, to try to understand any motivation or particular interest the student has in the case. In addition, I am looking for students to recognise particular strengths within the case and hence a strong reason to use it, in order to make certain points.

The section on *campaign objectives* needs to separate the goals into its two main parts. I prefer to see a headline of *Promotional Objectives* and then two subtitles, *marketing objectives* and *marketing communication objectives*. It is important that students recognise and use these two types of objectives at all times, not just in the examination but when working with marketing communications back at work.

The section on the *target audience* is correct but *in need of invigoration*. This is segmentation in practice and the process of target marketing needs to be brought into play. What, if any, are the particular *characteristics* of these segments, how big are they and of what value are they to the campaign, as they cannot all be of equal value? Perhaps lifestyle and demographic data would have been of use for message and media deployment.

The role of objective setting is not to just set up a means for the strategy to be derived but to provide the main means by which the *effectiveness* of the campaign is determined. This point was missed by this student. I expect to see the objectives reiterated or at least referred to as being met partially, totally or not at all. Recognition of the need to set *quantitative* and *qualitative criteria* is invariably a sound inclusion in all work of this nature.

One of the strengths of the student's answer is that they have been prepared to be *critical* in a positive way. The feelings and judgements of the student have been brought out particularly towards the end of the campaign. Many students rely solely on descriptive accounts of campaigns and here *it was the critical comment that helped make this a pass answer.*

Overall this student displayed a sufficient level of knowledge in answering the question and presented their response in an adequate manner. Please note once again that the student was *prepared to pass an opinion* and this matters a great deal. I want students to demonstrate their willingness and ability to make critical assessments in addition to the need to display knowledge and understanding.'

The exam paper

THE EXAM PAPER

Format of the exam

	Number of marks
Part A: one compulsory mini-case study	40
Part B: three questions from six (equal marks)	60
	100

Time allowed: 3 hours

Analysis of past papers

June 2000

Question number in this Kit

Part A (Compulsory, 40 marks)

1. Preparation of an Integrated Marketing Communications Plan

Part B (Three questions from six, 20 marks each)

2. Opinion leaders and opinion formers
3. Development of internet-based marketing communications
4. Brand development
5. Influence of competition and other external forces on branding
6. Developing media strategy
7. Corporate identity

December 1999

Part A (Compulsory, 40 marks)

| 1 | Dutton: Internal report on the key strategic issues facing the company | 58 |

Part B (Three questions from six, 20 marks each)

2	Perceived risk and risk reduction	-
3	Planned communication with channel members	29
4	The role of objectives in the communication planning process	10
5	Corporate identity and the use of ethical issues to differentiate OR external events effects on corporate identity	-
6	Customer retention schemes	49
7	Internal marketing communications	30

Examiner's comments

There was an overall improvement in the answers to this paper.

Candidates need to know what a strategic issue is. Message, media strategy, marketing segmentation, positioning and branding are all strategic issues.

Many candidates did not know what a marketing channel was. Strong subjects included internal marketing communications, loyalty and perceived risk. Students should avoid Tesco as an example of a loyalty scheme, though!

Candidates should avoid reproducing diagrams in answers unless they are relevant. They are usually too time-consuming to draw. Again, many candidates failed to relate their answers to the context of the question or give examples when required.

The exam paper

June 1999

Question number
in this Kit

Part A (Compulsory, 40 marks)

1 A car manufacturer is to launch a replacement for a long established brand   56

   (a) Promotional strategy supporting the launch
   (b) Key strategic features in allocating financial resources

Part B (Three questions from six, 20 marks each)

2 Positioning a brand of toothpaste   20
3 The product life cycle and promotion   47
4 Changing the attitudes of the target audience   15
5 Marketing communications plan   23
6 Setting budgets for marketing communications   37
7 Campaign effectiveness   39

Examiner's comments

This paper contained strategic issues relating to marketing communications. Some candidates were not strong on strategic issues and the majority were weak on the financial aspects in the exam.

Many candidates' knowledge base was not broad enough. Students need to work on decision making and buyer behaviour. It is not enough to reproduce a marketing communications plan when strategic issues are called for.

The Specimen Paper

The specimen paper for the December 1999 and June 2000 examination sittings is almost identical to the December 1998 paper, which is detailed below. However, questions 2, 6 and 7 have been supplemented by the following optional elements to reflect the new syllabus in the Specimen Paper.

2 Strategic significance of promotional mix   21
6 Consumer and business-to-business promotions   22
7 Competitor advertising spend   42

All other questions remain identical to those set in December 1998.

December 1998

Part A (compulsory, 40 marks)

1 Netline: Short internal report covering strategic issues regarding the launch of a new product. (*Note.* A marketing communications plan was *not* required.)   57

Part B (three questions from six, all 20 marks)

2 Buyer behaviour and perceived risk   16
3 Retention and loyalty schemes   48
4 Advertising agencies' failure to restructure   17
5 Internal marketing communications   28
6 Branding   34
7 Strategic value of marketing communication   41

The exam paper

> *Examiner's comments*
>
> There was a mixture of good and poor answers. Some candidates failed to read the question properly which led them to fail to answer the question in its entirety. Other candidates failed to go through the paper and select the questions they can best answer. Errors were common in graphs and charts. Candidates continue to use incorrect formats for reports, memos and letters, etc.
>
> Another area which needs attention is to adopt the correct tone and relate answers to the context set out in the question.

June 1998   *Question number in this Kit*

Part A (compulsory, 40 marks)

1	British Glass Recycling Company: Prepare a strategic marketing communications plan	55

Part B (three questions from six, all 20 marks)

2	Repositioning campaign	38
3	Communications mix in consumer and business markets	3
4	Technology and communications	-
5	Brand strategies	32
6	Integrated communications	8
7	Analysing the current situation	24

> *Examiner's comments*
>
> Overall results were encouraging. As a general point, diagrams are welcome but students should *refer* to them in their answers. An area for improvement is students' understanding of the *context* of the communication message.

December 1997

Part A (compulsory, 50 marks)

1	Pepsi Cola: outline marketing communications plan for 1998 and 1999	-

Part B (three questions from six, all with equal marks)

2	Internal marketing communications	27
3	Marketing communication methods and the product life cycle	14
4	Pros and cons of advertising bans	-
5	Digital TV	-
6	Marketing communications agencies and business strategy	-
7	Integrated marketing communications	7

> *Examiner's comments*
>
> UK students did well. Although overseas students were less successful than UK students, their performance improved. In general, students demonstrated a reasonable level of knowledge but failed to elaborate on standard knowledge. Many anticipated IMC but failed to relate it to the context of the question. Many students also had developed a good range of examples – in future they must explain how these relate to the models they are trying to explain. In general, students need to improve their understanding of situation analysis. Assembly of the promotional mix is sometimes divorced from objectives and the situational analysis.

The exam paper

June 1997

Question number in this Kit

Part A (compulsory, 50 marks)

1   Australian Tourist Commission: marketing communications plan for the years leading up to the Olympic Games in 2000   -

Part B (three questions from six, all with equal marks)

2   Integrated marketing communications   6
3   Communications models   13
4   Brands and marketing communications   31
5   Describe and evaluate any charity/government campaign   45
6   Cultural and social trends, end users, retailing structure and media appropriate when entering the hot beverage market of a country of your choice.   52
7   The Internet and business communications   33

Examiner's comments

No comments were made about students' performance in this exam in general. Comments on individual questions are included at the beginning of each suggested solution in this Kit.

Syllabus

SYLLABUS

Aims and objectives

- To develop students' understanding of the formulation and implementation of integrated marketing communication plans and associated activities

- To enable students to appreciate and manage marketing communications within a variety of different contexts

- To encourage students to recognise, appreciate and contribute to the totality of an organisation's system of communications with both internal and external audiences

- To enable students to be aware of the processed, issues and vocabulary associated with integrated marketing communications in order that they can make an effective contribution within their working environment.

Learning outcomes

Students will be able to:

- Determine the context in which marketing (and corporate) communications are to be implemented in order to improve effectiveness and efficiency, understand the key strategic communication issues arising from the contextual analysis and prepare (integrated) marketing communications plans

- Determine promotional objectives, explain positioning and develop perceptual maps, and suggest ways in which offerings can be positioned in different markets

- Formulate marketing communications strategies with particular regard to consumers, business-to-business markets, members of the marketing channel and wider stakeholder audiences such as employees, financial markets, environmental groups, competitors and local communities

- Determine specific communication activities based upon knowledge of the key characteristics of the target audience. In particular, they will be able to suggest how knowledge of perception and attitude, levels of perceived risk and involvement can impact upon marketing and corporate communications

- Select, integrate and justify appropriate promotional mixes to meet the needs of the marketing communication strategies

- Determine appropriate levels of marketing communications expenditure/appropriation

- Evaluate a variety of promotional campaigns drawn from different sectors

- Be aware of the impact and contribution technology makes to marketing communications. Be appreciative and sensitive to uses associated with cross-border marketing communications

- Advise on the impact corporate communications can have on both internal and external audiences and their role in the development of integrated marketing communications

1 Strategic marketing communications *(study weighting 20%)*

1.1 A definition and appreciation of the scope and dimensions of marketing and corporate communications.

1.2 A contextual analysis understanding and justification for marketing and corporate communication strategies.

1.3 The strategic significance and impact of integrated marketing communications.

1.4 The appreciation and recognition of the importance legal, ethical and technological impacts have on promotional activities.

2 Developing a theoretical understanding of marketing communications *(study weighting 20%)*

2.1 Understanding the key drivers associated with information processing and buyer decision making processes.

2.2 Communication issues for internal and external audiences.

2.3 The role of personal influences on the communication process.

3 Managing the marketing communications process *(study weighting 40%)*

3.1 The determination and appreciation of the prevailing and future contextual conditions as a means of deriving and developing promotional strategies and plans.

3.2 The target marketing process as a means of identifying significant promotional opportunities.

3.3 Determining promotional objectives and selecting positioning opportunities.

3.4 Identifying, selecting and formulating promotional strategies.

3.5 Selecting appropriate promotional mixes.

3.6 Determining message styles and key media goals.

3.7 Deciding upon the level and allocation of the promotional spend.

3.8 Managing internal and external resources necessary for successful promotional activities.

3.9 Managing and developing product and corporate brands.

3.10 Evaluating the outcomes of promotional activities.

Syllabus

4 Evaluation of different types of marketing communication campaigns *(study weighting 10%)*

4.1 Knowledge and understanding of different campaigns from different context (including FMCG, business to business, services and public sectors, and not for profit organisations).

4.2 Consideration of the competitive conditions, available resources, stage in the product life cycle and any political, economic, social or technological factors that might be identified as influencing the development of a campaign.

5 Cross border marketing communication *(study weighting 10%)*

5.1 Cultural, social and media influences.

5.2 Organisational type and communication approaches.

5.3 The adaptation/standardisation debate.

5.4 Agency structure and support

Note: the words 'promotional' and 'marketing communications' are used interchangeably

Question bank

DO YOU KNOW? - STRATEGIC MARKETING COMMUNICATIONS

- *Check that you know the following basic points before you attempt any questions. If in doubt, you should go back to your BPP Study Text and revise first.*

- The word *strategy*, in very broad terms, can be seen as a natural follow-on from objective setting and as a process of providing a short-term guide to the specific actions of the marketing plan. Alternatively, strategy is concerned with the long-term plans for the organisation's positioning, growth, profitability and so on. It is helpful to accept that there are *multiple* definitions and qualify each more carefully, as Mintzberg does.

- Marketing communications strategies cannot be formulated and analysed in isolation from the strategies of the organisation as a whole or from its marketing strategies. Marketing activities can be defined in terms of the 12Ps of the extended marketing mix and each of the 12 elements can be linked directly to marketing communications - each of them says something about the organisation.

- Marketing communications strategy must be integrated with the overall strategy of the business, and with all the other aspects of the marketing strategy. The promotional tools used for communication must also be used in an integrated way.

- The integrated approach will be adopted by organisations in the future because of pressure on expenditure, fragmentation of the media, client sophistication, the higher profile of marketing communications itself, and increasing market segmentation.

- The marketing communications process as a whole must be properly planned, implemented and controlled.

- There are three main marketing communication strategies: pull, push and profile.
    - Pull strategies are those marketing communications directed at consumers. Push based strategies are aimed at members of the marketing channel and supply network. Both push and pull strategies tend to be product orientated.
    - Profile based communication strategies are aimed at a wide array of stakeholders, both internal and external to the organisation. The message tends to have a corporate (rather than product) orientation.

- Integrated Marketing Communications is about blending all forms of communications which are directed at different stakeholder audiences.

Question bank

1 TUTORIAL QUESTION: DEFINING MARKETING COMMUNICATIONS

(a) Define marketing communications.
(b) Define marketing communications in terms of its constituent elements.

Guidance note

For (b) you may like to reproduce the 'promotional tool kit' diagram shown in the BPP Study Text *Marketing Communications Strategy*.

2 MARKETING COMMUNICATIONS STRATEGY 32 mins

Prepare an outline of a talk you are to give to a group of Marketing Managers on the subject of Marketing Communications Strategy. Describe the key elements of the communications planning process, showing how marketing communications strategy is distinguishable from, though part of, overall marketing strategy. Plan to illustrate your talk with examples of strategy drawn from your experience. **(20 marks)**

3 DIFFERENT MIXES 32 mins

The characteristics of the marketing communications mix for consumer markets are significantly different to those mixes normally designed for business-to-business markets. Making reference to examples, examine these characteristics and comment on how you feel these two types of marketing communication mix are likely to evolve in the future. **(20 marks)**

4 TUTORIAL QUESTION: STRATEGY AND OBJECTIVES

(a) Mintzberg suggests that there are five definitions of strategy: plan, ploy, pattern, position and perspective. Explain what each definition entails.

(b) A marketing communications strategy involves decisions about what, in outline?

(c) Suggest three objectives for each element of the promotional mix (advertising, sales promotion, public relations, personal selling).

Guidance notes

1 You may be able to answer (a) from your studies for other Diploma papers. The point is to remind you that, like those, this is a *strategy* paper. *Apply* this knowledge when you see the word 'strategy' in an examination question.

2 Answer (b) in the form of a flow diagram if you can. This is a *communications* paper too, and visual presentation is a highly effective method of communicating.

3 For (c) suggest *more* than three objectives if you can.

5 ILLUSTRATED INTEGRATED COMMUNICATIONS 32 mins

State what you understand by the term 'integrated marketing communications' and describe with the aid of diagrams how an integrated strategy may be successfully implemented. Illustrate your answer by reference to your own organisation or an organisation of your choice. **(20 marks)**

6 INTEGRATED MARKETING COMMUNICATIONS 32 mins

In a memorandum to the managing director of an organisation of your choice explain the concept of 'Integrated Marketing Communications'. In particular you are asked to describe, with a diagram and with examples, how marketing communications strategy should be integrated into the organisation's business strategy. **(20 marks)**

Question bank

7 MORE INTEGRATION
32 mins

Saatchi and Saatchi, the international advertising agency, has decided that to serve its clients effectively it needs to provide expertise in integrated marketing communications. The agency has appointed a Senior Manager with responsibility for this area of business. Assuming the role of this Senior Manager, write a short paper addressed to clients describing the advantages of integrated marketing communications and setting out methods to accelerate its adoption by the agency's clients. **(20 marks)**

8 IMPLEMENTING INTEGRATED COMMUNICATIONS
32 mins

As marketing manager, for an organisation of your choice, prepare a briefing document for the chief executive.

(a) Explain the strategic importance of integrated marketing communications

(b) Explain the actions you feel the chief executive should take to encourage the successful implementation of the concept. **(20 marks)**

9 TUTORIAL QUESTION: TECHNOLOGY

(a) Explain how telemarketing may be used as an integrated marketing activity.

(b) What impact are the Internet and digital TV likely to have on marketing communications?

Guidance notes

1. We list seven areas in which telemarketing has an important role. Just think about an average telephone conversation with a (potential) customer.

2. Technological developments are good meat for exam questions and, more importantly, they are *your* future. Communications is by far the most exciting area of technological development in the 1990s and you should be an avid consumer of any media coverage of the subject.

10 OBJECTIVES (12/99)
32 mins

You have decided to speak to your marketing team in order that they better understand the role of objectives in the integrated communication planning process.

Prepare notes for your presentation explaining the role of objectives, and identify which of the different elements of the communication process might be influenced by the objectives set. **(20 marks)**

DO YOU KNOW? - DEVELOPING A THEORETICAL UNDERSTANDING

- *Check that you know the following basic points before you attempt any questions. If in doubt, you should go back to your BPP Study Text and revise first.*

  '**Marketing communications is a management process through which an organisation enters into a dialogue with its various audiences. To accomplish this, the organisation develops, presents and evaluates a series of messages to identified stakeholder groups. The objective of the process is to (re)position the organisation and/or its offerings in the mind of each member of the target audience. This seeks to encourage buyers and other stakeholders to perceive and experience the organisation and its offerings as solutions to some of their current and future dilemmas.**' (Fill, 1999)

- Marketing Communications has a number of roles. It can be used to **D**ifferentiate and organisation or product, it can be used to **R**emind or **R**eassure past or current customers. It can be used to **I**nform customers and stakeholders or it can be used to **P**ersuade people to take particular actions. This can be memorised as DRIP.

- Models can be used to help simplify and provide a framework for the understanding of complex processes, such as consumer buying behaviour. The overall aim of marketing communication is to reach and influence those individuals or groups that have been defined as target customers. In order to reach and influence these target customers the marketing communicator must have as clear an understanding of their attitudes, beliefs and motives as possible.

- It is vital for marketers to have an understanding of the processes that customers go through when buying a product, whether this product is being bought by a consumer for individual consumption or by an organisation for production of other products or for resale. The thought processes of the buying process, both organisational and consumer can be simply summarised as follows:

  - Recognition of problem/need
  - Information search
  - Evaluation of alternatives
  - Purchase decision
  - Post purchase evaluation

- The extent to which a consumer engages in all these stages will depend on the size complexity and specific circumstances of the buying situation and a range of influencing factors can be identified which could possibly affect the process. Such factors need to be recognised by marketers in order that they are taken into account in marketing and promotional activity.

11 TUTORIAL QUESTION: CONSUMER BUYING BEHAVIOUR

(a) Describe the general stages in the buying process.

(b) What makes a new product successful?

Guidance notes

1 The stages identified by Kotler and described in our answer are need recognition, information search, evaluation of alternatives, purchase decision, and post-purchase evaluation. We have answered at some length.

2 For (b) we identify and briefly describe five characteristics, following Rice.

12 TUTORIAL QUESTION: ORGANISATIONAL BUYING BEHAVIOUR

(a) Identify and briefly describe four types of organisational market.

(b) How does the American Marketing Association explain the main influences and participants in the process of organisational buying behaviour?

Guidance notes

1 PRIG is a good acronym for Dibb *et al's* types of organisational market. What does it stand for?

2 The AMA framework deals with influences within or outside the organisation, and within/outside the department.

3 Other frameworks are also useful, for example Kotler's four forces (environmental, organisational interpersonal, individual); the DMU; Dibb *et al's* six stages (recognise the problem, develop product specifications, search, evaluation relative to specifications, select and order, and evaluate product and supplier performance) and so on.

13 TWO PRACTICAL MODELS
32 mins

Write a short report on the practical use of two communication models in developing marketing communication plans. Illustrate your answer with examples. **(20 marks)**

14 LIFE CYCLE
32 mins

With the aid of diagrams, suggest and justify the most effective mix of marketing communication methods for each stage in the product life-cycle of a named consumer product of your choice. **(20 marks)**

15 CHANGING ATTITUDES (6/99)
32 mins

Many marketing communication campaigns are designed to change the attitudes held by the target audience towards a product or product category. Explain four methods that might be used to achieve a change in attitudes, using examples to illustrate your answer. **(20 marks)**

16 PERCEIVED RISK (12/98 & Specimen)
32 mins

The level of perceived risk a consumer might experience when purchasing products and services can vary significantly across product categories. Knowledge of these risks can impact on the design and implementation of promotional strategies.

Using examples from both the consumer and business-to-business sectors to illustrate your answer, explain how marketing communications can be used to reduce different types of perceived risk. **(20 marks)**

17 CLIENT NEEDS (12/98 & Specimen) — 32 mins

It has been noted that many advertising agencies have failed to adapt and restructure themselves in order to keep pace with the increasing demands and international communications strategies of their clients. What are the reasons for this apparent incompatibility and suggest how agencies might adjust to better meet their client needs.

(20 marks)

DO YOU KNOW? - MANAGING THE MARKETING COMMUNICATIONS PROCESS

- *Check that you know the following basic points before you attempt any questions. If in doubt, you should go back to your BPP Study Text and revise first.*

- Before it can formulate a marketing plan and a complementary communications strategy an organisation must regularly carry out a comprehensive, systematic and independent examination of its marketing environment, objectives, strategies and activities. Much marketing planning is based on the concepts of segmentation and positioning.

- The main requirement in today's modern markets is better *targeting*. To determine whether a segment is worth pursuing the marketer needs to consider its size, measurability, access, uniqueness of response and stability. The basic options in targeting are undifferentiated or mass marketing, differentiated marketing, concentrated marketing and customised marketing. *Positioning* is concerned with how products create and establish an image in the minds of consumers and how they are evaluated against competing products.

- Marketing communication strategy starts with a thorough understanding of the current context within which the communication campaign is to operate. By examining the marketing strategy and market conditions, the nature of the target audiences, brand performance and other external and internal issues, it becomes possible to determine the correct promotional objectives. From this point an overall strategy emerges (3Ps of communication strategy, push, pull and profile). The organisation then has to identify which elements of the promotional mix are to be deployed: an integrated approach is becoming more and more common. Other considerations at this point are whether a push or a pull strategy is appropriate, the nature and constitution of the target market and the characteristics of the product. The *creative* aspects are a vital ingredient for success.

- The promotional strategy must be monitored and controlled to see whether it is working. Possibilities include pre-testing and post testing, coupon redemption rates, and electronic monitoring. Budgeting is usually done on an annual basis, with monthly reviews. Seasonal factors must be taken into account and some organisations have contingency funds for one-off opportunities. There are a variety of methods of budgeting, the most important of which is the objective and task method.

- Media strategy is determined by asking what is the message to be communicated, who is the audience, what is the desired response and how much is there to spend. Market, product and target audience characteristics; budget and client preferences need to be taken into account when planning media campaigns, as do the attributes of each individual media option. A multi-media campaign is likely to achieve a greater level of synergy than one which concentrates on options within one medium.

- Marketing communicators need to be fully aware of the range of qualitative and quantitative research data that is available and of the limitations of research. The process of selecting a new *agency* involves initial search; credentials presentation and shortlist; competitive pitch and final selection. The client will gauge competing agencies against set criteria such as expertise in the client's field of business, previous work handled, resources provided and costs. Personal chemistry between the individuals involved will also play a part.

- Achieving integration requires acceptance of the *need* for it, the establishment of a genuine two way communications, and the development of a useable model. Relationship marketing has many links with integrated marketing communications: both are shaped by the need to get closer to the customer.

- Marketing communication strategies (eg 'inform the consumer') specify the reasons why the communication is taking place in relation to business objectives. Tactics (eg public relations, sponsorship) specify where and how to reach the target groups that can take or influence the decision to purchase.

- A successful brand is a name, symbol, design or some combination of these things which identifies the product of a particular organisation as having a sustainable differential advantage over similar products. A variety of branding strategies are possible, such as family branding, brand extension, and multi-branding. The strength of retailers is now such that own label brands threaten manufacturer's brands.

> - Marketing communications will only be able to sustain a brand if the product itself consistently lives up to the image created. A successful **branding strategy** requires careful initial research in all markets and a long-term commitment to sustaining the brand. Once established brands can be transferred to other products, even if they are quite unrelated to the original product. **Brand valuation** is a means of analysing and measuring the effectiveness of marketing expenditure. It can play a significant part in overall strategy formulation and in the management of the organisation.

18 TUTORIAL QUESTION: AUDITING, SEGMENTATION AND POSITIONING

(a) A marketing audit looks for problems and opportunities. What specific matters might be studied?

(b) What are the stages of segmentation?

(c) Describe six approaches to developing a positioning strategy.

Guidance notes

1. The three principal areas of study in a marketing audit are likely to be the marketing environment, marketing objectives, strategies and plans and marketing activities (organisation, systems, productivity). See how many points you can get under each of these headings.

2. Only an outline answer is wanted for (b) (we give a diagram). If you are not sure about what is involved in any of the stages it is time for more revision.

3. The positioning of a product or service is concerned with how it creates and establishes an image within the minds of the consumer and how it is subsequently evaluated against alternative product offerings.

19 SEGMENTATION, TARGETING AND POSITIONING   *32 mins*

Identify in a short report, the value of segmentation, targeting and positioning in successful marketing communication strategies. Give examples of successful campaigns based on these principles.   **(20 marks)**

20 TOOTHPASTE POSITIONING (6/99)   *32 mins*

As manager for a new brand of toothpaste you have been asked to prepare a brief report about the way in which you intend to position the brand.

In your report you should explain your understanding of positioning, set out the theoretical positioning strategies and then using your brand, illustrate how each strategy might be implemented.   **(20 marks)**

21 PROMOTIONAL MIX (Specimen)   *32 mins*

In your capacity as an entrepreneur who has established a successful regional marketing communications agency you have been asked to make a presentation to an audience of local business people.

Prepare notes for this presentation entitled 'The Strategic Significance of the Promotional Mix'. You aim to cover each of the main tools of the promotional mix and provide brief examples to illustrate each point.   **(20 marks)**

Question bank

22 PROMOTIONAL MIX AND BRANDING (Specimen) *32 mins*

The Promotional Mix developed for a branded consumer product is different to that developed for an industrial or technological product aimed at the business-to-business market.

Using an example from each sector to illustrate your answer, write a report about:

(a) The nature of these differences and the impact they each might have on an organisation's integrated marketing communication activities. (10 marks)

(b) Suggest how these two mixes might evolve in the future. (10 marks)

(20 marks)

23 PLAN LINKS (6/99) *32 mins*

Your manager has asked you to explain how the different parts of a marketing communications plan are linked together. In response to this request:

(a) Prepare a set of notes indicating how the different parts of the plan are interconnected. (10 marks)

(b) Highlight a single element of the plan that you feel is of paramount importance to the success of such plans. Justify your selection. (10 marks)

(20 marks)

24 ANALYSING THE CURRENT SITUATION *32 mins*

The development of an effective marketing communications plan commences with an analysis of the current situation. Explain how the outcomes from this analysis influences the objectives, strategy, message, media and other decisions that follow in the preparation and implementation of these plans. **(20 marks)**

25 MARKETING COMMUNICATIONS OBJECTIVES *32 mins*

Show, with specific examples, how marketing communications objectives are derived from an organisation's mission statement. In particular demonstrate how objectives, strategies and tactics are related in a communications plan. **(20 marks)**

26 MARKETS AND STRATEGIES *32 mins*

Although the principles of marketing communications are the same for both consumer and industrial markets there are significant differences in the details of how promotion is carried out. Describe the characteristics of the two types of markets and the implications for choosing marketing communications strategies for industrial markets.

(20 marks)

27 INTERNAL COMMUNICATIONS *32 mins*

More and more companies are recognising the benefits of internal marketing communications programmes. The more sophisticated communications programmes can blend internal and external messages and meet the needs of both employees and customers. For an organisation of your choice, set out the objectives, activities and benefits of such a programme. **(20 marks)**

Question bank

28 INTERNAL MARKETING COMMUNICATIONS (12/98 & Specimen) *32 mins*

The increasing awareness and emphasis given to internal marketing communications suggest that an organisation's employees are an important market segment in their own right. Write a report explaining why this group is now perceived as important and suggest how such internal communications might be used to improve communications with other externally based stakeholder groups. **(20 marks)**

29 PLANNED COMMUNICATIONS (12/99) *32 mins*

The use of planned communications in marketing channels is an important aspect of most communications strategies.

Write brief notes explaining why it is important to communicate with channel members, and suggest what might be the key influences that shape the design and implementation of such communication activities. **(20 marks)**

30 INTERNAL MARKETING COMMUNICATIONS : TECHNOLOGY (12/99) *32 mins*

The increased recognition and use of internal marketing communications by organisations throughout the world suggests that an organisation's employees can be regarded as an important, if often neglected, target audience.

Prepare a draft memorandum to be sent to your immediate colleagues for comment, explaining why internal marketing communications are important, and suggest how the use of technology might assist management to communicate effectively with this particular audience. **(20 marks)**

31 BRANDS HATCH *32 mins*

A successful brand is one that customers perceive as offering superior value. For any brand of your choice, describe, in a short report, the nature of the brand and demonstrate how marketing communications contributes to building the long term value of the brand.

(20 marks)

32 BRANDING AND MARKETING COMMUNICATIONS *32 mins*

Branding is a common strategy adopted by both manufacturers and retailers in consumer markets. Using examples of brands from a country of your choice, evaluate the effectiveness of branding as a marketing communication strategy. **(20 marks)**

33 INTERNET *32 mins*

Evaluate the ways in which the rapid growth of the Internet is changing the way businesses communicate with their customers, suppliers and within their own organisations.

(20 marks)

34 BUSINESS-TO-BUSINESS BRANDING (12/98 & Specimen) *32 mins*

Many organisations in the business-to-business sector have begun to use branding as a significant part of their marketing communications strategy. Write a report explaining this

development. Use examples to illustrate your points and comment whether this trend is likely to continue. **(20 marks)**

35 TUTORIAL QUESTION: PROMOTIONAL BUDGETS

(a) Describe the methods that may be used to determine the advertising budget and the advantages and disadvantages associated with each one.

(b) List ten steps in applying the objective and task method.

Guidance notes

1   Try to distinguish between methods used widely and those used rarely.
2   Make sure that you identify advantages and disadvantages, too.

36 TUTORIAL QUESTION: INTER AND INTRA-MEDIA DECISIONS

(a) Describe the factors that govern media choice.

(b) (i) What is a media schedule?

  (ii) Distinguish between a burst campaign and a drip campaign.

Guidance notes

1   For (a) we describe the nature of the medium, the positioning of ads within the medium, the way in which people use media, the amount of time spent with the medium, the creative opportunities offered, lead times and quantitative considerations. Expand upon these points.

2   For (b) you might like to practise sketching out a media schedule diagram, too, since your exam may well require you to do this. There are examples later in this Kit.

37 BUDGET PROCESS (6/99) *32 mins*

You are a newly appointed marketing manager for a company that makes hair care products which are sold through supermarkets and major national distributors. You have identified the need to review the process by which the marketing communications budgets are determined each year.

Prepare an internal paper for the marketing and sales departments reviewing the available methods and outline your proposals by which these budgets should be set in the future. **(20 marks)**

38 EVALUATE REPOSITIONING *32 marks*

As a journalist working for a marketing magazine, write an outline for an article which evaluates a campaign that was intended to (re)position an industrial or consumer product of your choice. As part of your answer you should evaluate the situation facing the organisation, explain how the campaign was designed to meet the objectives identified and comment on the apparent effectiveness of the programme. **(20 marks)**

39 EVALUATE EFFECTIVENESS (6/99) *32 mins*

Prepare an outline for a presentation, to be made to members of a local business group, in which you evaluate the effectiveness of a recent marketing communications campaign. You may use any campaign from a country of your choice. **(20 marks)**

40 MEASURING EFFECTIVENESS *32 mins*

Write a brief report setting out the criteria for measuring the effectiveness of marketing communications. Illustrate this report with three examples of campaigns you consider to be particularly effective. **(20 marks)**

41 MARKETING COMMUNICATIONS EXPENDITURE (12/98 & Specimen) *32 mins*

As a marketing manager write a short article for inclusion in a company magazine suggesting how the amount of money spent on marketing communications might be strategically important. Use examples to illustrate your article. **(20 marks)**

42 COMPETITOR'S ADVERTISING SPEND (Specimen) *32 mins*

In some markets it is important to determine a competitor's advertising spend. Prepare a memorandum to be sent to your Marketing Manager suggesting why this activity might be important and review four methods an organisation might use to determine its optimum advertising spend. **(20 marks)**

DO YOU KNOW? - SUCCESSFUL MARKETING COMMUNICATIONS STRATEGIES

- *Check that you know the following basic points before you attempt any questions. If in doubt, you should go back to your BPP Study Text and revise first.*

- It is vitally important that you get into the habit of studying and analysing examples of marketing communications. You should aim to build a varied portfolio of examples that you can use in your examination.

- The following comments may help you to focus your efforts in particular areas.

- *Industrial* marketing communications strategies can be very different from consumer campaigns. There are differences in such areas as purchase motivation, customer needs, product specifications, level of customer service needed and so on. This calls for different approaches in employing the various promotional tools.

- The marketing of *services* is similar to the marketing of products in many ways, but there can be differences due to such factors as professional and legal constraints, the nature of capacity available, and the buying process itself. Personal selling is more important.

- In *non profit marketing* communications there is likely to be less money available, messages are likely to be subjected to greater scrutiny and the objectives of the communication will be quite different from those applying in consumer marketing. The major categories of non-profit communicators are political parties, social causes, the government, religious bodies and professional bodies.

- The main feature of marketing communications for *small businesses* is that resources are limited. This will mean that more is done in-house and at a local level, though all of the usual promotional tools can still be employed.

- In attempting to understand the impact of communications it is important realise that every variable interacts with other variables and cause and effect cannot easily be distinguished. Effective communications are those that increase brand *awareness*, stimulate *trial purchase* and *reinforce* brand loyalty. The amount of communication to which people are now being subjected means that it is becoming increasingly difficult to communicate successfully.

43 CURRENT CAMPAIGN *32 mins*

Briefly describe any one current strategic marketing communication campaign with which you are familiar. Set out the criteria by which you would judge the effectiveness of the campaign. Use these criteria to evaluate the marketing communications strategy adopted in the chosen campaign. **(20 marks)**

44 PUBLIC INTEREST *32 mins*

Governments have increasingly used modern marketing communication methods to achieve their objectives. Choose a government campaign with which you are familiar. Describe the objectives of the campaign, evaluate its effectiveness and outline the ethical issues involved in implementing such a campaign. **(20 marks)**

45 AN ACTUAL STUDENT'S ANSWER *32 mins*

For any charity or government campaign of your choice write an outline report which describes the campaign and specifies its objective and target audiences. Evaluate the effectiveness of the chosen campaign. **(20 marks)**

46 TUTORIAL QUESTION: BRANDING

(a) What are the reasons for branding?
(b) What factors underlie the strength of a brand?
(c) For what products is branding not appropriate? Give five examples.

47 EXAMPLES OF PLC (6/99) *32 mins*

Using examples, prepare a memorandum to be sent to your manager explaining how useful the product life cycle might be when developing promotional strategy.

(20 marks)

48 LOYALTY SCHEMES (12/98 & Specimen) *32 mins*

Examine the growth in customer retention and loyalty based schemes and comment on their effectiveness as a strategic marketing communication instruments. Use any two loyalty schemes of your choice to illustrate your answer. **(20 marks)**

49 CUSTOMER RETENTION (12/99) *32 mins*

Using two examples form the consumer market to illustrate your answer, prepare a short report for your Manager explaining how customer retention schemes might add value to your communications strategy **(20 marks)**

DO YOU KNOW? - CROSS-BORDER MARKETING COMMUNICATIONS

- *Check that you know the following basic points before you attempt any questions. If in doubt, you should go back to your BPP Study Text and revise first.*

- Different viewpoints exist concerning the globalisation of markets. On the one hand, there is the argument that consumers are converging in tastes and that companies have an opportunity to market standardised products worldwide. An alternative view is that consumer markets are fragmenting and that products and services need to be adapted to individual preferences.

- The international marketing communicator needs to decide whether or not it is appropriate to standardise communications across markets.

- Companies operating outside their home markets need to be aware of the implications of cultural differences for all aspects of the marketing mix. Verbal and non verbal communications, aesthetics, dress and appearance, family roles and relationships, beliefs, learning and work habits are dimensions of culture of particular relevance to communications.

- Planning and buying media across borders can be a complex task. Media availability can vary greatly from country to country. Media conventions which apply in a home market may not apply elsewhere.

- Laws and regulations governing marketing communications must obviously be observed Each country will have its own set of restrictions which apply to advertising, packaging, sales promotion and direct marketing.

- Research should be used to support decision making before a campaign is planned. Research can also help evaluate whether objectives have been met at the conclusion of a campaign. However, obtaining accurate, unbiased, up to date information can be difficult. Conducting primary research on an international basis requires the help of experts.

- Clients and their agencies can choose to handle international advertising campaigns in a number of ways. Although a variety of factors will influence the management of any particular campaign, the organisational structure of the client company will play an important role.

- Some agencies have expanded abroad by setting up their own subsidiaries overseas. Others have established alliances with local agencies already in existence.

- There are arguments both for and against using the services of an international advertising agency. The current preference amongst large clients is to centralise advertising with an internationally based agency, rather than choose local agencies on a country by country basis.

- The standardisation versus adaptation debate has implications for agency management. If campaigns are totally standardised across markets, the lead market agency office will take the major role in designing and implementing the global campaign; local agency subsidiaries will have minimal input.

- The process of selecting an international advertising agency involves initial search, credentials presentation and shortlist, competitive pitch and final selection. The client will gauge competing agencies against criteria such as response to the brief, types of communication service provided, expertise in handling local and international campaigns, and similarity of management style and culture to that of the client.

Question bank

50 TUTORIAL QUESTION: DIFFERENCES

(a) What are the arguments for and against standardising communications internationally?

(b) What dimensions of culture are relevant to the marketing communicator?

(c) For each of the following media identify one key consideration regarding its use internationally.

  (i) Press
  (ii) TV
  (iii) Outdoor
  (iv) Cinema
  (v) Radio

Guidance notes

1 We have answered in a word or phrase for (b). Try to expand on this and give some examples if you can.

2 For (c) several points could be made under each heading.

51 TWO COUNTRIES IN THE KITCHEN   32 mins

For any two contrasting countries of your choice, describe how cultural, economic and media differences will affect the development of marketing communications strategy for consumer products. **(20 marks)**

52 WITH OR WITHOUT?   32 mins

Choose a country with which you are familiar. Write a short report to a manufacturer of tea and coffee who is considering entering the beverage market in the country of your choice. Outline relevant cultural and social trends, the likely target end user, the retailing structure and the choice or appropriate media in the country through which to promote the company. **(20 marks)**

53 GLOBAL CAMPAIGN   32 mins

Once clients and their agencies find themselves considering global advertising strategies the initial attractiveness is reduced by complex international issues. In a short report to the managing director of a company considering a global campaign, summarise the advantages of the campaign and the pitfalls they could face. **(20 marks)**

54 ADVANTAGES AND DISADVANTAGES OF INTERNATIONAL AGENCIES
                                                      32 mins

The multinational full service advertising agency has grown in importance. However, the present structures have been attacked as being too large, inefficient and relatively unproductive. Write note on the advantages and disadvantages of such international agencies, and the changes that they face in the next five years. **(20 marks)**

DO YOU KNOW? - MINI-CASES

- The mini-case is now worth 40% of the total marks in the exam, but it is compulsory so you *must* do well here. The best way to do well is to get some practice in advance. Make sure that, at the very least, you have made a good attempt at all of the key questions listed below and also the mini-case in the test Paper at the end of this Kit.
- There is extended advice on how to tackle a mini-case at the front of this kit.
- In several cases the matters described in the mini-case have been overtaken by subsequent events. However the scenarios have been left as originally constructed by the examiner, since to update them would be to distort the question as originally set.

55 MINI-CASE: BRITISH GLASS RECYCLING COMPANY 64 mins

The need to protect our environment is of increasing concern to politicians, industrialists, environmentalists and a growing proportion of the public. The European Union has taken a proactive position and has, among other things, set targets for the recovery and recycling of waste materials, including glass. In the UK the government has set a target that 50% of all glass packaging has to be recycled by the year 2000. This represents 900,000 tonnes of used glass per annum. Similar targets are in place throughout the European Union.

For the packaging industry, recycling offers numerous benefits such as savings on raw materials, energy and waste collection costs. It also cuts back on the use of landfill sites, helps conserve the environment and also creates employment. For those organisations actively involved there are opportunities for positive public relations messages.

The British Glass Recycling Company (BGRC) is a company set up in 1993 as a joint venture between Rockware Glass and United Glass to develop the UK national glass recycling programme. These companies are the two largest glass packaging manufacturers in the UK. BGRC receives waste glass from local authorities and private collectors (for example, retailers, restaurants and clubs), offers them a guaranteed market and a fair price. However, there are problems associated with glass recycling in the UK, which explains to some extent why the national glass recycling rate is only 30%, one of the lowest rates in the EU.

First, there is a 'green cullet' problem. Cullet refers to waste glass of which there are three colour types: amber, clear and green, each of which has slightly different chemical compositions. Demand for glass packaging in the UK is for clear glass. As clear glass cannot be made of cullet which contains coloured glass and as the vast majority of waste glass is green, imported from other European countries in the form of wine and beer packaging, the green cullet problem represents a significant constraint on the UK reaching their recycling target. The UK glass industry also has a policy not to pay for glass that has not been colour separated.

The second issue concerns the public and their attitude towards recycling glass. Generally public support for glass recycling is positive partly as a result of the visual reminders provided by bottle banks (waste glass collection containers) sited around urban areas. These banks are constructed so that members of the public separate waste glass into their colour groups. However, some contamination can still occur, if only due to grease, dirt and bottle caps.

By the mid 1990s there were approximately 19,600 bottle banks in the UK, or 1 for every 2,850 people, one of the poorest ratios in comparison to other European countries. Of these banks, 73% are provided by local authorities, while the others are operated by private organisations who derive good revenue streams from the collection and sale of used glass. Public use of these sites is partly a function of the banks' proximity to residential areas and

Question bank

partly due to the attitude of the public to recycling. However, the siting of bottle banks is problematic because of the noise of breaking glass. The public want more convenient bottle banks but not outside their house or in their road.

Research indicates that 31% of AB women see recycling as a public duty whereas only 20% of men share this view. Interestingly, it is the young and old who have a particular affinity with the recycling concept. It is quite apparent that middle aged men (72% of men aged 25 to 34), are the most ambivalent towards recycling. As it is this segment that are more likely to have a direct influence on children and their attitudes, this might be regarded as a weakness to the long-term development of glass recycling in the UK.

Whilst measures are being taken to encourage the greater use of coloured glass as a principal glass packaging material, efforts to improve the UK recycling rate for used glass need to be encouraged. Greater use of bottle banks needs to be stimulated and more bottle banks need to be provided. In addition, there needs to be greater awareness and conviction that recycling glass is a necessary, important and worthwhile activity.

If BGRC are to improve the rate of recycling in order that they generate a higher proportion of their raw materials from recycled glass, then they need to promote the concept more rigorously and change the attitudes of the public towards the recycling concept. The funds available for a communication programme are limited (under £500,000) so additional financial resources may need to be acquired, perhaps by attracting others to launch a joint campaign.

Required

You are to assume the role of marketing manager at BGRC and are required to prepare an outline strategic marketing communications plan for the three years ending 2001.

(40 marks)

56 MINI-CASE: CAR COMMUNICATIONS (6/99) *64 mins*

You are marketing communications manager for a car manufacturer that is about to launch a new car. The code name for the car is Zen and it is set to replace a car that has been one of the top brands in your country for the past 30 years. The Zen is a mid-market family hatchback and you are considering which overall communications strategy you will recommend to the marketing director.

One of the problems facing all car manufacturers is market congestion and the increased level of choice available to car buyers. Part of this congestion is caused by an increase in the level of car imports. These cars might have a higher specification or perceived image, but the net results is downward pressure on prices. Indeed, price wars are a common occurrence and better avoided if possible.

The launch of a new car is traditionally a very risky and expensive operation. The usual approach is to use a pull strategy with massive consumer orientated advertising, beginning with a launch at a significant motor show, with bright lights, a rotating platform and plenty of journalists to give a strong public relations boost. Direct marketing and sales promotions commence after this to provide for a co-ordinated campaign. Decisions about the level of mass advertising are often influenced by share of voice and share of market statistics.

Ownership trends indicate that many families now own two or sometimes three cars, and in an ideal world every car manufacturer would like each driver to always replace a car with another from the same manufacturer. To assist the development of this level and type of loyalty it is crucial to understand buyer motivations and the location of exactly where car buying decisions are made. Despite huge efforts research has failed to determine all the answers to these questions. However, suspicion is growing that the critical buying decision is made at a car dealership. If this is the case then perhaps more emphasis should be given to a promotional push campaign, focusing on the dealer network. For example, Volkswagen developed the retail concept and formulated a totally new look for its dealers. Vauxhall flew 16,000 dealers from around the world to Morocco for a three day conference to launch the Vauxhall Astra.

It is also becoming clear that corporate branding is a much under used concept in this market. With the lack of market differentiation the increasing influence of corporate ethics can provide competitive advantage. Might there be an opportunity to use corporate branding throughout the organisation's network of employees and dealers? It could provide a competitive advantage by establishing exactly what the company's brand stands for, and for everyone involved to communicate the same message. Marks & Spencer and Virgin have established strong corporate brands and have avoided the expense and complexity of supporting individual product brands. Up until now your company has sold cars, not a brand.

Source: Material adapted from articles in Marketing

As marketing communications manager for the car manufacturer you have been asked by your managing direct to recommend where the focus of the launch communications should be. Write a report to your director which should answer the following two questions.

(a) Decide upon a promotional strategy for your company in support of the launch of the Zen. You should argue the benefits for your strategic approach. (20 marks)

(b) Examine the key strategic factors that need to be considered when determining the level of financial resources to be allocated to your launch campaign. (20 marks)

(40 marks)

In order to answer these questions you are allowed to make reasonable assumptions about the car manufacturer, the competition and the market conditions, as they apply to a country of your choice. You are required to list any assumptions you make.

57 NETLINE TECHNOLOGIES (12/98 & Specimen) *64 mins*

The growth of the mobile phone industry has been dramatic over the past decade. The market size has continued to expand as more people have become familiar and comfortable with the technology. Whilst there are a range of different types of users and customer segments, the majority of product packages offered have been based on price and volume of calls made. This may be as a response to the intense competition for new users and the high level of churn (loss of customers to other networks). In this context attempts to find stronger market positions based on the motivations people have for using mobile phones have started to emerge.

However, one of the problems associated with the use of these phones is the annoyance factor. Public irritation with mobile phone users is often provoked by the inconsiderate and loud use of these telephones in public places such as restaurants, theatres, pubs and travel facilities such as train stations and airport termini. For example, a survey by Synergy Brand Values identified at 44% of people agreed that the use of mobile phones should be prohibited in public places.

As if in answer to this issue, Netline Technologies have invested in the development of a device that can deactivate mobile phones. Developed initially for military purposes, the product is now regarded as having many consumer applications. The device, branded as C-Guard, prevents calls being made or received by jamming the airwaves with radio waves.

The device is activated the moment it senses that there is an incoming call or when a call is about to be made as a phone searches to open a line. This means that it is now possible to ban the use of these telephones in designated places and can also help people to avoid those embarrassing moments when they forget to switch off their telephones, for example, in places of religious worship.

One potential difficulty concerns people who need to be able to receive calls due to the nature of their work. To overcome this, Netline have adapted the system so that it can recognise particular telephone numbers so that, for example doctors can be reached whilst at dinner when all other diners would be prevented from receiving calls.

C-Guard has the potential to allow for the creation of 'Phone-Free' areas in restaurants and trains, rather similar to non-smoking areas. The system, set to retail at roughly $750, also permits theatres, cinemas and other places of public entertainment for their patrons, whilst airports and airlines can automatically disarm potential safety hazards. Scientists and the medical profession in particular can improve the quality of their work without fear of disruption and costly delays caused by interference to their equipment.

Netline Technologies have patented and protected the C-Guard device although it is anticipated that there will only be a short period of time, of less than a year, before imitation devices are brought to the market by competitors. Netline recognise the urgency associated with the need to establish themselves in the market and have now embarked upon marketing the brand in countries and regions where the mobile phone is well established. Their policy has been to appoint regional (often country specific) distributors under a franchise arrangement. Franchise holders are responsible for the purchase of C-Guard system boxes and for the appointment of sub-dealers or retailers, perhaps their own subsidiary companies, to provide local coverage. They are also responsible for the distribution, training, installation, maintenance and marketing of the C-Guard system in their region.

Distinct and consistent branding is an important part of the marketing strategy and associated communications. Franchisees are contractually required to adhere to strict brand identity policies and are only to use promotional materials developed centrally by Netline.

Franchisees see the potential of being first into the market with a simple to install, easy to maintain product that provides clear user benefits. It is also expected that there will be further facilities that can be offered to up-grade a system and that there will be further advanced products based on the technology developed for C-Guard. End users will be encouraged to see the benefits of being associated with the 'C-Guard' protection system. Meanwhile, Netline will encourage members of the public to look for the 'C-Guard' sign and ask for it by name.

Required

As Marketing Communications Controller for Netline Technologies you are required to prepare a short internal report for the attention of the Marketing Director.

This report should:

(a) Identify and evaluate the key strategic issues associated with the marketing communications of C-Guard during the first two years of its launch. (20 marks)

(b) Make appropriate recommendations to address the issues you have identified.

(20 marks)

(40 marks)

You are not required to prepare a marketing communications plan.

58   DUTTON ENGINEERING (12/99)   64 mins

During the 1990s Dutton Engineering's impressive growth was based on a strategy that was focused on the development and maintenance of strong customer relationships. Rather than spend money speculating about the generation of new customers, Dutton's policy has been to invest and build relationships with current customers.

Dutton manufacture steel and aluminium components, and in order to help realise their strategy they removed their middle management and devolved responsibility to teams of production orientated personnel, who focus upon their client's total requirements. Clients talk directly to these 'Production Cells' who are empowered to make decisions and manage all aspects of their client's requirements. There are no appointed cell leaders, managers or even secretaries, as each cell manages itself organically and recruits its own new staff.

The role of senior management has been to manage time and resources through the use of management information systems. They are able to identify areas across and within Production Cells where productivity might be improved, and help ensure that 85% of the man hours in each Production Cell are used to generate revenue. As a result of this approach revenue has doubled to £2.3m, profits are stable at 6.5%, sales per worker are double that of the national average in the sector, yet staff numbers have remained relatively stable. Not surprisingly, Dutton have become the centre of attention for its innovative and seemingly successful approach.

The company's success has been built around 42 client companies, some of whom are very loyal. Part of the company's philosophy has been to 'meet and beat customer's expectations', and the attitude of staff in each Production Cell reflects this perspective. Through high levels of quality production and customer involvement, new orders have been won. However, the growth experienced to date has been based on new orders from existing clients and very little new business has been acquired. Senior management are regarded (by the Production Cells) as responsible for generating new customers, yet they see their role as managing and teaching the 'Dutton Way'.

Little effort appears to have been made to attract new customers and there is no Marketing Department or sales force. These are costs that do not fit the current culture and are regarded as activities that would add little value and merely create high overheads. The company currently outsources transport, cleaning and payroll, so outsourcing a sales operation would be a compatible activity.

There has been little planned use of marketing and/or corporate communications, and the primary emphasis has been on strong word of mouth communications, supported by some limited public relations activities. However, a rudimentary web site, some use of telemarketing, the unplanned use of some out of date sales literature, and attendance at exhibitions, constitutes the main thrust of the communications to date. However, the organisation needs to address the balance of its current customer portfolio and attract new clients if it is to achieve ambitious growth targets - to be achieved in the first few years of the new millennium.

Source: material adapted from Sumner-Smith, D. (1998) 'Selling Without a Sales Force', Sunday Times, 25th October, p15.

As a Marketing Communications Advisor you have been asked to consider the information available and to prepare a report which:

(a)   Identifies the key communications issues facing the company.   (20 marks)

(b)   Makes recommendations for Dutton's Marketing Communications Strategy for the next two years.   (20 marks)

(40 marks)

You have been asked specifically **not** to present a marketing communications plan but to focus on the key strategic issues that Dutton Management need to consider. You should justify your recommendations and state any assumptions made.

Answer bank

Answer bank

1 TUTORIAL QUESTION: DEFINING MARKETING COMMUNICATIONS

(a) Marketing communications is all forms of communications between an organisation and its customers and potential customers. More broadly, it is all forms of communications by an organisation with its environment, including internal communication. More narrowly, it can be defined in terms of constituent elements such as sales promotion, advertising, PR, direct marketing and so on.

(b) The promotional toolkit illustrated in the BPP Study Text includes the following elements.

- Word of mouth
- Sales promotion
- Public relations
- Merchandising
- Direct marketing
- Exhibitions
- Internal marketing
- Corporate image
- Packaging
- Sponsorship
- Advertising
- Personal selling
- Branding

These are the most obvious communication methods, though other parts of the marketing mix, including the product itself, pricing policy and distribution channels will also have significant parts to play.

2 MARKETING COMMUNICATIONS STRATEGY

> *Tutorial note.* This challenging question requires a well structured answer. Students are required to have a thorough knowledge of:
>
> (a) the business and marketing planning processes;
>
> (b) the marketing communications planning process;
>
> (c) how to integrate the two processes;
>
> (d) examples of practical and successful communication strategies derived from such an integrated process.

REPORT

To: Marketing Managers
From: Marketing Communications Manager
Date: December 1996
Ref: Presentation on the subject of marketing communication strategy

1 Audience/objectives

The audience consists of marketing managers. We can assume therefore that they are reasonably well versed in the actual marketing planning process.

Although they will be knowledgeable about the planning process their involvement in the detail will vary from person to person. Some will have a close working knowledge; others will only have limited experience of planning directly themselves.

There will also be degrees of scepticism. Some will be committed planners others will not.

Even more important to our specific talk is the fact that the marketing managers can be assumed to have relatively less detailed knowledge of the marketing communications planning process.

The objectives of the talk can therefore be defined as follows.

Answer bank

(a) To show how marketing communication planning is an integral part of the overall company planning process.

(b) To demonstrate that without this link communications planning would be less effective.

(c) To describe the SOSTAC model as a way of bringing about this integration.

(d) Lastly, to illustrate the talk with practical examples of strategy.

2 The total planning process

It is vital that we as marketing managers understand the corporate planning process and the role of marketing planning within it. Furthermore, because marketing communications accounts for a significant share of the marketing mix it is important also to understand the integration of the marketing communications planning process.

Each level of the organisation has a hierarchy of:

(a) Objectives
(b) Strategy
(c) Tactics.

The tactics of the upper level then become the objectives of the next level down in the organisation. The levels we can consider usually are:

(a) Corporate
(b) Functional (including marketing)
(c) Activity (including marketing communications).

These relationships are shown in more detail in the diagrams below. The first is Simon Majaro's Planning Hierarchy. The second shows the relationship of corporate, marketing and communications planning in more detail. The third shows the operational planning stages of marketing communications.

Clearly each of these diagrams of the real situation will vary from company to company according to size, nature of business, and experience of planning. In some predominantly marketing organisations the link between corporate and marketing objectives will be a very close one.

In larger companies with separate operating divisions another level of planning will be introduced. These operation divisions are often called 'strategic business units'.

The planning hierarchy

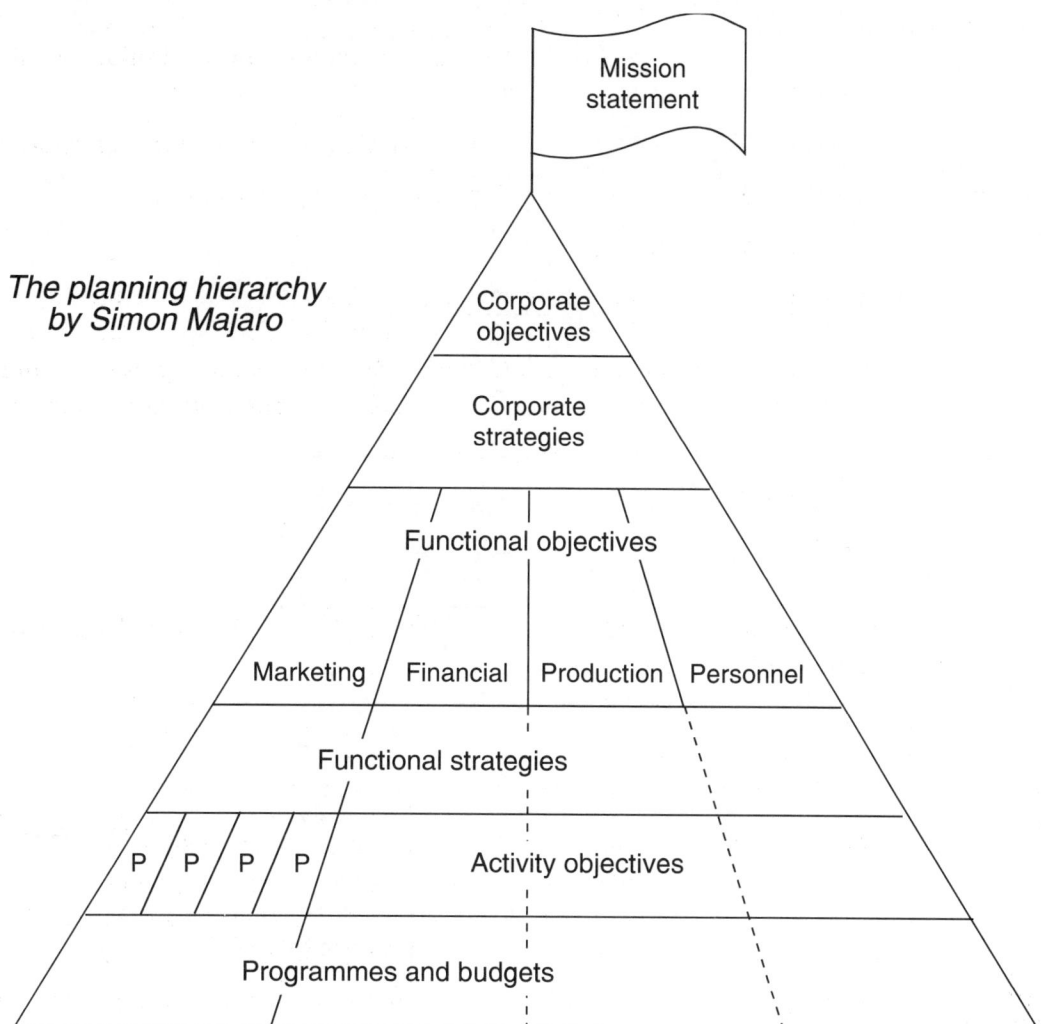

The planning hierarchy by Simon Majaro

Answer bank

The strategic marketing and tactical communications planning process within the overall strategic marketing planning process

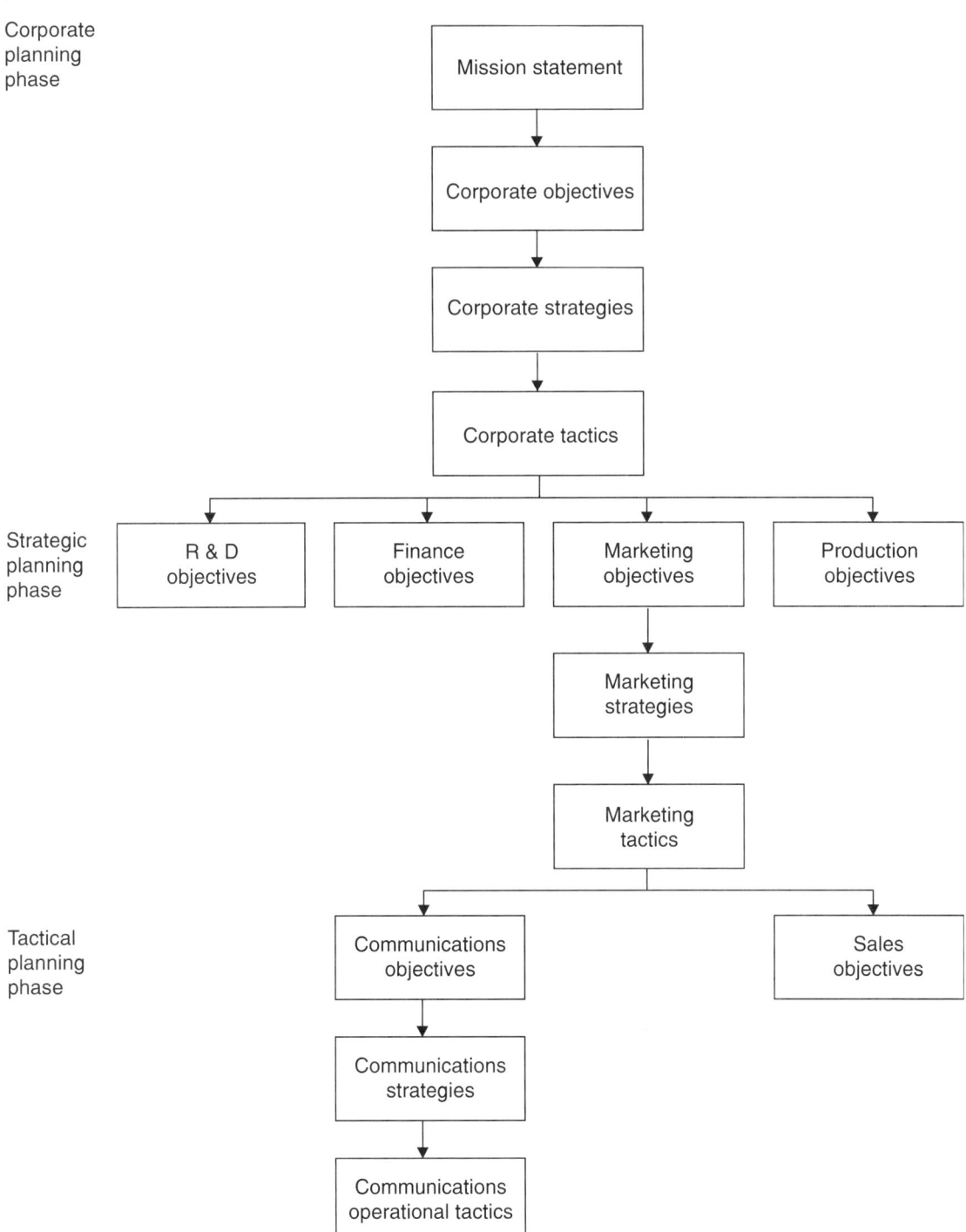

The operational planning stages of marketing communications

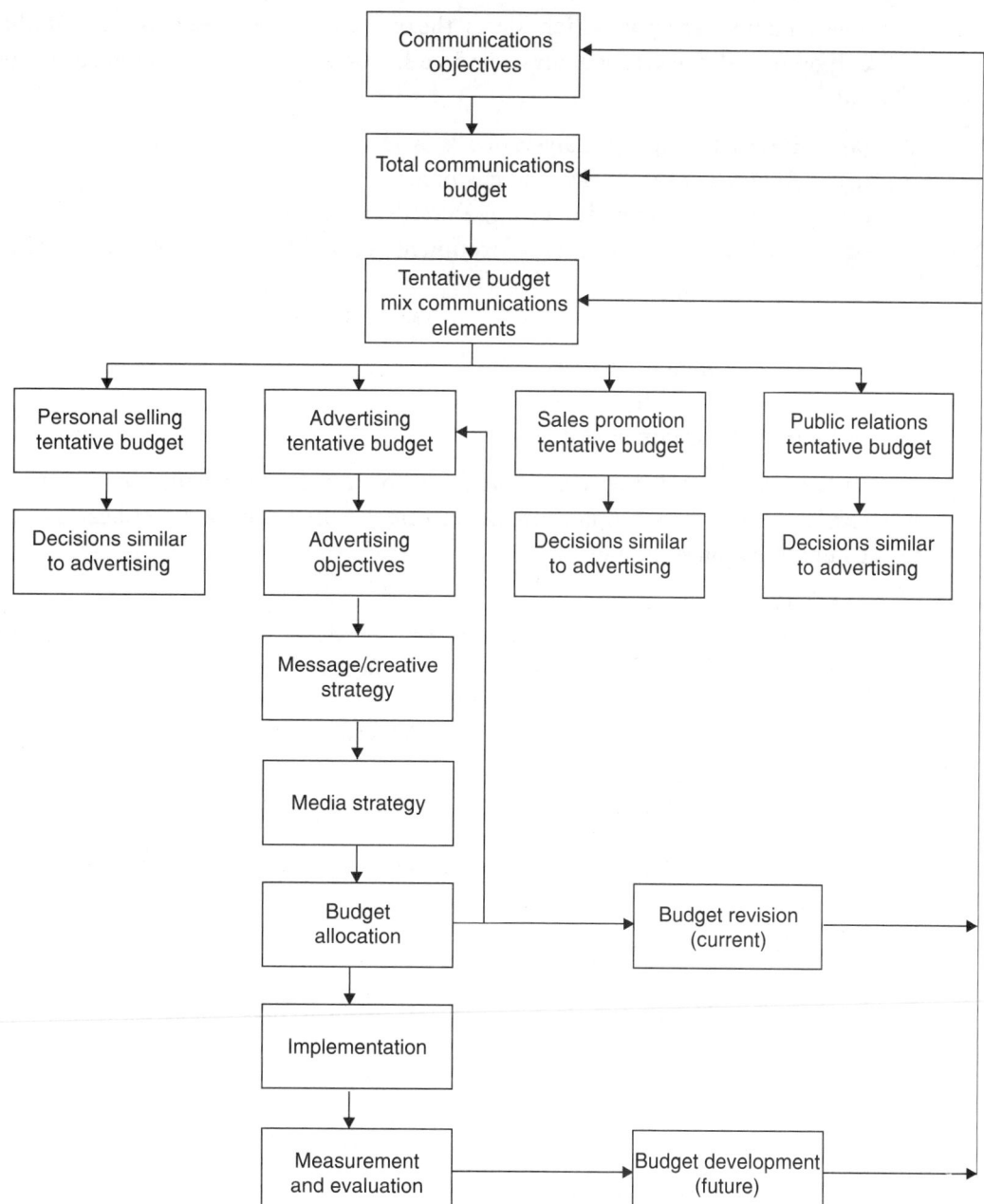

3 The SOSTAC communications planning process

Because marketing communications planning is less well developed and less well understood it is important to demonstrate the vital link to business and marketing planning

It is also important to have a rigorous, memorable and easy to apply marketing communications planning model. Such a model which I would like to recommend to you is that being developed by Smith, Pulford and Berry called the SOSTAC model.

S = Situation analysis
O = Objective setting
S = Strategy development
T = Tactics
A = Action
C = Control

Answer bank

This model is capable of being used in many planning situations but it is being developed specifically for marketing communications planning.

The situation analysis which starts the process can be seen as part of the overall corporate and marketing analysis and audit process. Four areas of analysis are carried out.

(a) Internal company analysis of 4Ps or 7Ps
(b) Analysis of the market and customers
(c) Analysis of competitors using Porter's five forces
(d) Analysis of the external environment evaluating changes in the following areas.

   (i) Sociological
   (ii) Technological
   (iii) Economic (macro)
   (iv) Political/legal
   (v) Environmental

In the case of marketing communications planning in particular, note is made of any strengths, weaknesses, opportunities or threats which have a direct bearing on possible communication solutions

SOSTAC planning model

Stage	Planning elements	Strategic direction
Stage 1	Situation analysis ↓	Where are we now?
Stage 2	Objective setting ↓	Where do we want to go?
Stage 3	Strategy development ↓	How do we get there - broad direction?
Stage 4	Tactics development ↓	How do we get there - individual steps
Stage 5	Action planning ↓	How do we take people with us?
Stage 6	Controls and review	How do we know when we have arrived?

Each of the following elements of the SOSTAC model can then be developed specifically for the communications process as follows.

Objectives

Objectives can be developed under the headings on the Ansoff matrix.

(a) Market penetration
(b) Market development
(c) Product development
(d) Diversification (strategic alliances)

Each of these broad areas will require a different communications objective.

Strategy

Strategy in communication terms is then best developed by reference to particular target audiences. The most useful approach to this is to work through the steps of:

(a) Segmentation
(b) Targeting
(c) Positioning

Positioning is achieved by a judicious choice of the marketing mix including promotions or marketing communications.

Tactics

To help to remember a systematic approach to the tactics of marketing communications we can use 3Ms.

(a) M = methods
(b) M = media
(c) M = messages

Action

To help us develop action plans we consider a different set of 3Ms.

(a) M = manpower (responsibilities)
(b) M = minutes (timescales)
(c) M = money (budgets)

Control

Finally it is necessary to control the effectiveness of the marketing communications process by measuring the achievement of the business, marketing and marketing communications objectives.

4 Examples of strategies

The most powerful examples of marketing communications strategies are those linked directly to the corporate and marketing strategies. A number of such examples are given below.

(a) *Boddington's beer*

Whitbread's marketing objective was to launch the beer nationally in a controlled manner. The communication strategy was to promote the brand as an authentic regional beer brewed in Manchester using the slogan 'The Cream of Manchester'. This reflected the creamy full head obtained from this cask conditioned beer. The media strategy was to use the rear covers of colour magazines to promote the golden colour of the product. Television was not used initially in part because of limited brewing capacity.

(b) *PPP Healthcare*

PPP were facing increasing competition in the health insurance market especially from the commercial insurance companies especially Norwich Union. The PPP management decided to plan for an increase in market share, to distinguish themselves from their rivals and to rebrand themselves. Marketing communications obviously had an important role to play in this. To increase the awareness of the new company name (PPP Healthcare) and to reposition itself as a healthcare company not an insurance company the company chose to use a television and national press campaign stressing the support it provides to customers.

(c) *BMW cars*

BMW cars were exported to the UK mainly as performance cars. BMW (GB) was established in 1979 with the ambitious aim of tripling UK sales by 1990, whilst maintaining high profit-margins. The 'Ultimate Driving Machine' campaign was developed and is still running 17 years later. The marketing communications objectives were:

Answer bank

      (i)   To enrich the image of the vehicle
      (ii) To build positive aspects of the image
      (iii) To raise the brand's image

These objectives have been met over a prolonged period in spite of the sales targets meaning that there would be more of the less exclusive models on the road. An advertising strategy was developed partly through TV but mainly through quality colour magazines.

5 Conclusions

These are examples of successful marketing communications strategies which have produced outstanding business results. This has only been possible because the management of those companies have had clear business and marketing objectives which in turn have provided the drive for clear marketing communications plans.

The marketing communications planning process has therefore to be a close and integrated component of the overall planning process. One way of achieving this is to use the SOSTAC planning framework which is memorable, easy to apply and powerful in its effect.

3 DIFFERENT MIXES

> *Examiner's comment: summary/extracts.* Not an unusual question, but it is framed in such a way that in order to pass, students had to display a rounded knowledge of the topics and have an opinion on how they might develop.
>
> The trick with this question was not to become bogged down with characteristics of the market but to focus on the communication mixes.
>
> Many answers were correctly rooted in buying characteristics, but there was a limited depth of knowledge.

The marketing communication mix consists of a variety of tools and methods. The most common assembly of tools is this.

(a) Advertising
(b) Sales Promotion
(c) Public Relations
(d) Personal Selling
(e) Direct and Interactive Marketing

Within these tools are many sub-tools and methods, but this mix will be used as the basis for the response to this question.

In order to understand the different ways in which these tools have been used in the consumer and business-to-business markets, it is necessary to first understand the *underlying characteristics of these two markets*.

(a) The consumer market is characterised by a *single decision-maker* who takes a relatively *short time* to make a purchase decision.

(b) In contrast the *business-to-business* (bb) buyer has to consider a wide range of criteria, consult a large number of people, and deal with a small volume of products whose overall value can be quite considerable. The types of risk associated with the two purchase situations provide the main point of difference. Consumer markets carry relatively low risk while bb markets carry high personal and organisational risks.

The marketing communications used to reach these two very different markets and to reduce the risks need to differ also. The following diagram helps visualise the differences.

Business-to-business markets   *Figure 1: Principal promotional tools*

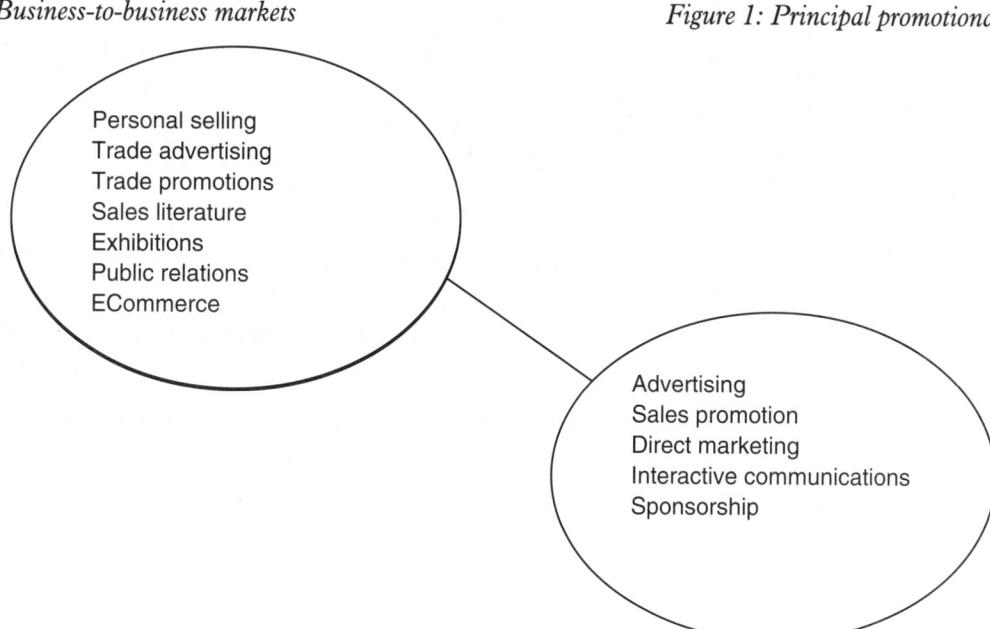

Consumer markets

For many *fast moving consumer goods*, *advertising* is a cost effective way of reaching mass audiences which are geographically widely dispersed. Procter & Gamble and Lever Bros dominate the soap and detergents market and invest heavily in television advertising. The role of advertising is to *create/maintain awareness* and to *remind* users of the brand. *Wella* use broadcast sponsorship (of Friends) and magazine advertising as the main thrust of their promotional activities. Advertising is often used to make consumers aware of sales promotion tools which are used to encourage consumers to trial products. With the increasing levels of media and audience fragmentation however, many manufacturers of consumer products are turning to direct marketing. Heinz ceased all product-based television advertising in 1994 and moved over to a direct marketing strategy. However, it is interesting to note the recent termination of their customer 'At Home' magazine that was part of their direct mail operation and a move back towards a greater use of advertising.

In the *business-to-business market*, the complexity and often protracted nature of the purchase decision process means that personal selling has a much more important role to play in the communication mix. Advertising is often used in trade magazines to generate basic awareness but it is *personal selling* and *exhibitions* that are the focal point of the promotional effort. *Canon* market a range of electronic products for the office and have a range of dealers and distributors who represent them. In order to help organisations make purchase decisions and to help guide buyers through the technical complexity associated with many of the products, personal selling and demonstrations form an important part of the promotional mix. Trade discounts and advertising allowances form an important part of the business-to-business promotional mix for organisations in the marketing channel. Competitions and incentives to sales forces are also popular.

The *Internet* and the use of *Websites* is becoming an important part of the promotional mix for organisations operating in both the consumer and business-to-business sectors. IBM are developing their Website as part of their 'E' commerce strategy whilst most leading companies in the consumer sector are developing sites that are increasingly user friendly and offer transaction facilities.

Answer bank

Public relations is another tool that is of significance to companies in both sectors. Whether used to manage crises or to present products or organisations in a different light, such as the campaign by Monsanto on genetically derived food, all have the common aim of attempting to influence their and others attitudes and opinions.

There are a number of other characteristics associated with the promotional mixes used in both of these markets. These are set out in the following diagram.

	Consumer orientated markets	Business-to-business markets
Message Reception	Informal	Formal
Number of Decision Makers	Single or Few	Many
Balance of the Promotional Mix	Advertising and Sales Promotions dominate	Personal Selling dominates
Specificity and Integration	Broad use of promotional mix with a move towards integrated mixes	Specific use of below-the-line tools but with a high level of integration.
Message Content	Greater use of emotions and imagery.	Greater use of rational, logic and information based messages although there is evidence of a move towards the use of imagery.
Length of Decision Time	Normally short	Longer and more involved
Negative communications	Limited to people close to the purchaser/user	Potentially an array of people in the organisation and beyond.
Target marketing and research	Great use of sophisticated targeting and communication approaches	Limited but increasing use of targeting and segmentation approaches
Budget allocation	Majority of budget allocated to brand management	Majority of budget allocated to sales management
Evaluation and measurement	Great variety of techniques and approaches used	Limited number of techniques and approaches

Differences between Consumer and Business-to-Business Marketing Communications

Source: Fill (1999)

The promotional mixes of organisations in either sector will undoubtedly evolve as technical developments allow greater use of one-to-one or personal communications.

4 TUTORIAL QUESTION: STRATEGY AND OBJECTIVES

(a) (i) *Strategy as a plan:* strategy is a consciously intended course of action, a set of guidelines to deal with a given situation. Strategy is seen, in this case, as 'a unified, comprehensive, and integrated plan designed to ensure that the basic objectives of the enterprise are achieved'.

(ii) *Strategy as a ploy.* A ploy is a manoeuvre intended to attack an opponent or competitor. A marketing company may threaten to enter a rival's market or to discount prices heavily as a way of threatening a rival's plan to enter the company's established market. In another case a company may develop a 'fighting brand' alongside its already established, possibly higher priced mainline brand.

(iii) *Strategy as pattern.* Strategy is seen as a 'consistency in behaviour whether or not intended'.

(iv) *Strategy as position:* a means of locating an organisation in its environment. This may be thought of as a niche in a market place. Another aspect of a position strategy is whether a company chooses to be a leader or a follower in its chosen market.

(v) *Strategy as perspective:* an established way of perceiving the company and its markets. Thus McDonald's employees are trained to emphasise 'quality service, cleanliness and value' whereas Kwiksave employees see themselves as part of a 'no frills' organisation.

(b) See diagram below.

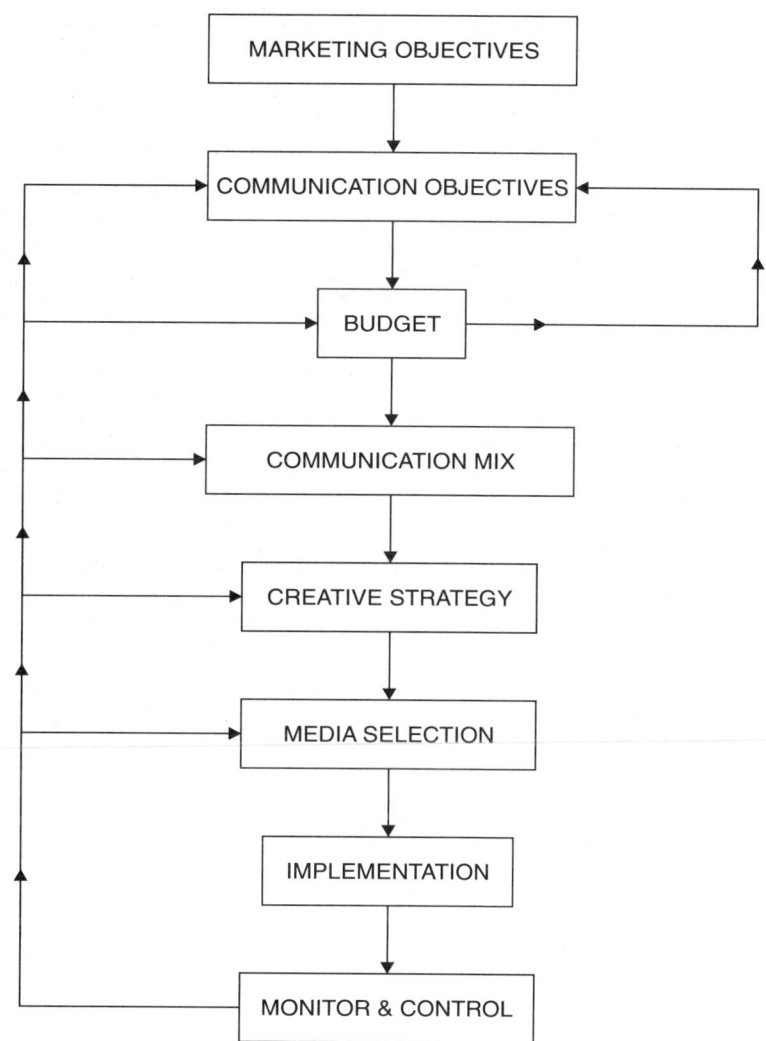

The Communication Strategy Process

(c) Possible objectives are as follows. You may have thought of others.

(i) *Advertising*

(1) To increase sales.
(2) To inform the public of a new product launch.
(3) To announce a sales promotion.
(4) To raise the level of awareness amongst the target audience.
(5) To act as a reminder to purchase the product.
(6) To generate new business leads (integrated with direct marketing).
(7) To maintain brand awareness, position and price premium.

Answer bank

(ii) *Sales promotion*

(1) To reward loyal customers and ultimately keep them.
(2) To act as an incentive to purchase a new product launch.
(3) To acquire other brand users.
(4) To gain shelf space within a retail outlet.
(5) To act as a spur towards short term sales.

(iii) *Public relations*

(1) To build corporate identity.
(2) To create customer confidence.
(3) To build credibility with the City, financiers and suppliers.
(4) To build internal morale within the company.
(5) To establish good press relations.

(iv) *Personal selling*

(1) To increase sales by sales person, product group, region, outlet type.
(2) To increase market penetration of specific customer groups.
(3) To increase average order value.
(4) To improve sales to call ratios.
(5) To target new customer groups.
(6) To improve after-sales care.
(7) To provide market data and identify new product opportunities.

5 ILLUSTRATED INTEGRATED COMMUNICATIONS

> *Examiner's comments, summarised by BPP.* Given the expected nature of the question, students were well prepared and received good marks. The description was well done. Implementation was less well done. More diagrams could have been used. The illustration of a student's own organisation was only done well by the best students.
>
> Besides defining integrated marketing communications as the strategic choice of all marketing communications elements, to meet business objectives good students were able to describe the factors influencing the importance of the subject. A variety of diagrams were available to describe the implementation process. These diagrams could have included Majaro's Hierarchy of Objectives, Strategies and Tactics and Pulford's Seven Levels of Integration besides the more usual ones integrating the marketing mix and the promotional mix.

REPORT

To: ICL Volume Products, Europe
From: Marketing Communications Manager
Date: June 1996
Ref: Implementation of integrated marketing communications

1 Situation analysis

ICL Volume Products is launching a new product PC/TV into a relatively new market and has set ambitious market share objectives. Besides aiming to gain 8% of the European PC market by 1997, ICL is aiming for volume business in the consumer market.

It aims to do this with innovative products like the PC/TV that uses a traditional TV screen integrated with a 486 PC. The new product will be branded Fujitsu/ICL. Also under the same brand there will be a new line of more conventional multimedia PCs for the home. Lastly, ICL has plans to integrate the products with video recorders and also prepare for future digital interactive TV services.

This is an extremely challenging business development plan aimed at the consumer sector. Although ICL is well-known in the business sector this is not the case in the consumer sector. ICL, besides establishing the new brand and launching the new products, aims to become one of the biggest players in the European PC market.

Marketing Communications, therefore, has a major contribution to make to these business plans and it is vital that the communication programme proposed should be fully integrated. This will lead to greater efficiency and effectiveness.

This short paper firstly defines 'Integrated Marketing Communications' then identifies the factors favouring it in the ICL situation. Next we describe seven possible levels of integration before demonstrating the application to the Fujitsu/ICL PC/TV situation.

Throughout, use is made of diagrams and tables to illustrate how an integrated strategy may be implemented.

2 Definition of Integrated Marketing Communications (IMC)

Integrated Marketing Communications has, in the last five years, become a term that is more widely known. However, there is not yet a common understanding of its full scope nor of its exact definition. Integrated marketing Communications involves

- 'The strategic choice of elements of marketing communications which effectively and economically influence transactions between an organisation and its existing and potential customers, clients and consumers.'

- 'The management and control of all marketing communication elements.'

- 'Ensuring that the brand positioning, proposition, personality and messages are delivered synergistically across every element of communication and are derived from a single consistent strategy.'

The total process is illustrated in the diagram below.

Answer bank

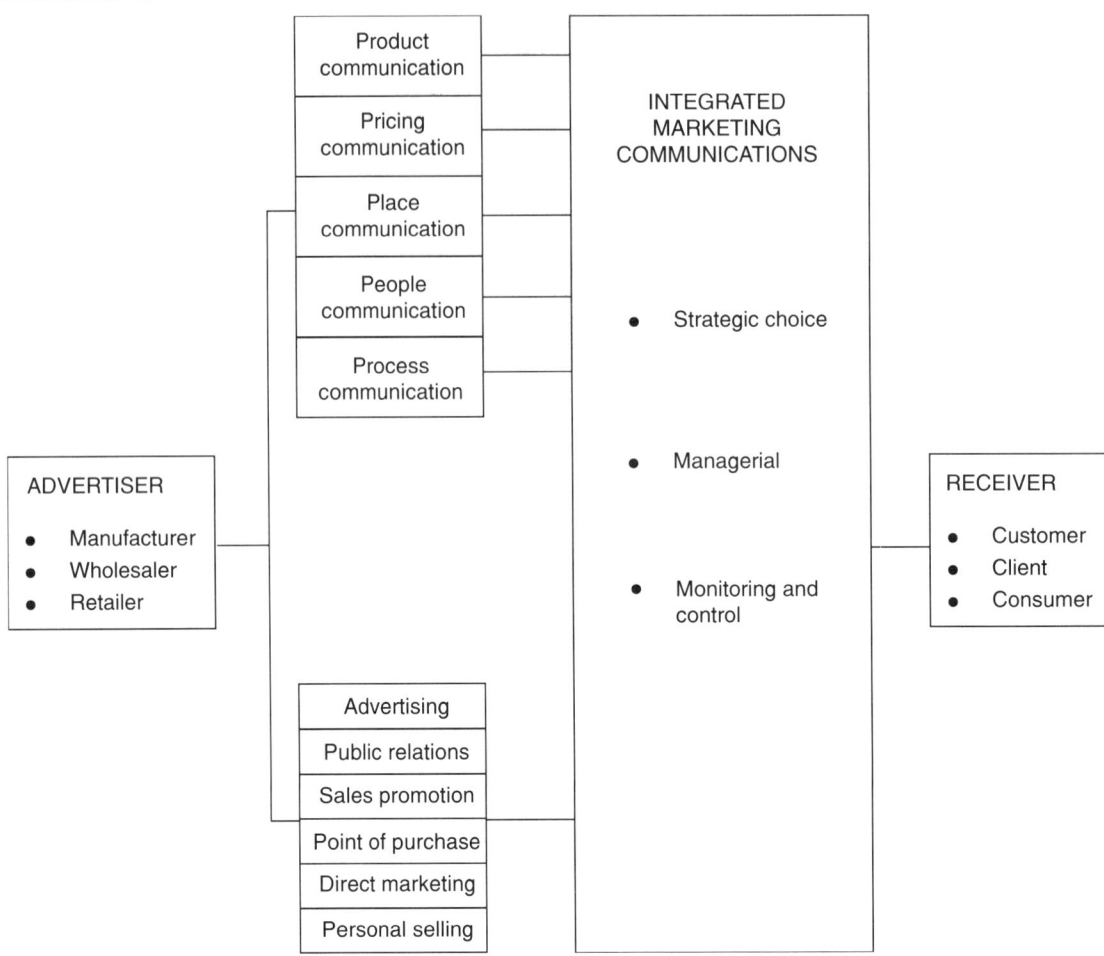

3 **Factors favouring and barriers to IMC:**

There is a growing number of factors favouring a move towards greater integration of the marketing communication process but also a number of barriers preventing this integration.

DRIVING FORCES

1. Pressure on communication budgets.
2. Fragmentation of the media.
3. Growing international communications.
4. Development of the Internet.
5. Increasing power of computers
   - databases
   - electronic storage
6. More sophisticated client managers.
7. Move from mass advertising (which is expensive) to selected media.
8. Advantages of promotional combinations.
9. Increasing understanding of the IMC process.

RESTRAINING FORCES

1. Resistance to change.
2. Old planning systems downgrade promotional decisions to tactical level
3. Traditional organisation structures with responsibility for only one element of communications.
4. The chief executive keeps a tight control and is unconvinced of the benefits of IMC.
5. External agencies organised in limited specialist areas.

10. Proof that IMC works.

4 Seven levels of integration

In order to understand the full meaning of integration it is important to define what is meant by the word integration. Several academic centres are giving thought to the integration issues. The following *seven level approach* is being developed by Alan Pulford of the Department of Retailing and Marketing of the Manchester Metropolitan University.

	LEVEL	DESCRIPTION OF INTEGRATION
1.	Vertical Integration	Linking together of business, marketing and marketing communication objectives.
2.	Horizontal Integration	Between the business function of marketing and manufacturing, human resources and finance.
3.	Marketing Integration	Of all elements of the marketing mix (4Ps, 7Ps, 16Ps).
4.	Communication Integration	Of the total promotional mix (Advertising, PR, Sales Promotion, POP, Direct Marketing, Selling).
5.	Creative Integration	Unifying creative themes across all communications.
6.	Internal/External Integration	Linking together all internal and external resources, ensuring agencies work together.
7.	Financial Integration	Ensuring that economies of scale are obtained and that investment in any promotional element is optimised.

5 Implementation for Fujitsu/ICL PC/TV

It is now possible to demonstrate how the process can be implemented in the case of Fujitsu/ ICL. Three strategic management elements have been added to the seven integration levels to complete the procedure.

Answer bank

ELEMENT	DESCRIPTION OF IMPLEMENTATION
1. Top Management Commitment	Senior Fujitsu/ICL management support must be gained for this major strategic investment in Europe.
2. Marketing Orientation	Fujitsu/ICL must change the orientation of the company from its present business marketing to consumer marketing. This will involve organisational changes and training and development.
3. Communication as a Competitive Advantage	Communication of the new Fujitsu/ICL brand and associated innovative products must be seen as a substantive long-term competitive advantage.
4. Vertical Integration	The business, marketing and marketing communications objectives of Fujitsu/ICL can be integrated.
5. Horizontal Integration	The marketing of the new range of products is only possible after their manufacture, distribution and financing has been carefully co-ordinated.
6. Marketing Integration	The new products, their prices, distribution and promotion must be carefully integrated.
7. Communication Integration	A complete range of promotional methods may be identified and integrated into an activity timetable and budget plan.
8. Creative Integration	The brief to the agency creative department should specify that the identity of the new Fujitsu/ICL brand should be carried through all communications.
9. Internal/External Integration	This entails coordination of the work of external agencies (advertising and PR) and regular meetings with other internal departments to ensure integration.
10. Financial Integration	If creative work is used in a uniform and consistent manner this will aid customer understanding and will save costs.

6 INTEGRATED MARKETING COMMUNICATIONS

Comments by the senior examiner. This question follows my predecessor's campaign for greater understanding and application of integrated marketing communications. The need for this knowledge has not decreased, indeed the need can be said to be even greater now with the increasing fragmentation of the media and the realisation that all elements of the communications mix must work together.

This proved to be a popular question among both UK and international students. Given the expected nature of the question, students were generally well prepared and achieved good marks. There were three components to the question. Firstly, the description was well done. Second, implementation was less well done. More diagrams could have been used. Third, the illustration of a student's own organisation was only done well by the best students. However, those students who failed to provide examples probably failed the question, as the practical or applied aspect of the programme is very important.

Besides defining integrated marketing communications, as the strategic choice of all marketing communications elements to meet business objectives, good students were able to describe the factors influencing the importance of the subject. Among the diagrams that might have been included in an answer are Majaro's Hierarchy of Objectives, Strategies and Tactics, and Pulford's Seven Levels of Integration, besides the more usual ones integrating the marketing mix and the promotional mix.

Answer bank

MEMORANDUM

To: Managing Director
From: CIM Student
Date: 4 June 1997
Ref: Integrated Marketing Communications

The purpose of this memorandum is to present a case for the development, implementation and maintenance of Integrated Marketing Communications (IMC) at Cult International Plastics.

Situation Analysis

Cult International Plastics is launching a new product into a relatively new market and has set ambitious market share and business objectives. In addition to achieving a market share of 10% of the domestic market in 1998, Cult is aiming to become the preferred supplier for leading builders' merchants supplying the building trade and DIY stores supplying the domestic sector.

It aims to do this with a stronger, lighter and more flexible plastic extrusion that can be shaped and cut on site. This will provide greater opportunities for customised products and lower costs.

Marketing communications has a major role to play not only in informing target markets but also in positioning Cult as a leading and innovative supplier to the building sector. It is vital that any proposed communication programme should be fully *integrated*, both in terms of delivering messages and providing efficiency and effectiveness.

This paper sets out the advantages of IMC, some initial ideas about how it could be implemented at Cult and provides examples with a view to establishing its credibility as a leading edge approach to communications management.

Definition of IMC

The development and acceptance of IMC over the past few years, as a term synonymous with good marketing practice, has been wide and rapid. However, it is apparent that there is little uniform agreement about what it means and how it should be implemented.

IMC involves:

> 'The strategic choice of elements of marketing communications, which effectively and economically influence transactions, between an organisation and its existing and potential customers, clients and consumers'

> 'The management and control of all marketing communication elements'

> 'Ensuring that the brand positioning, proposition, personality and messages are delivered synergistically across every element of communication and are derived from a single consistent strategy'.

The diagram on the next page presents a view of IMC.

Answer bank

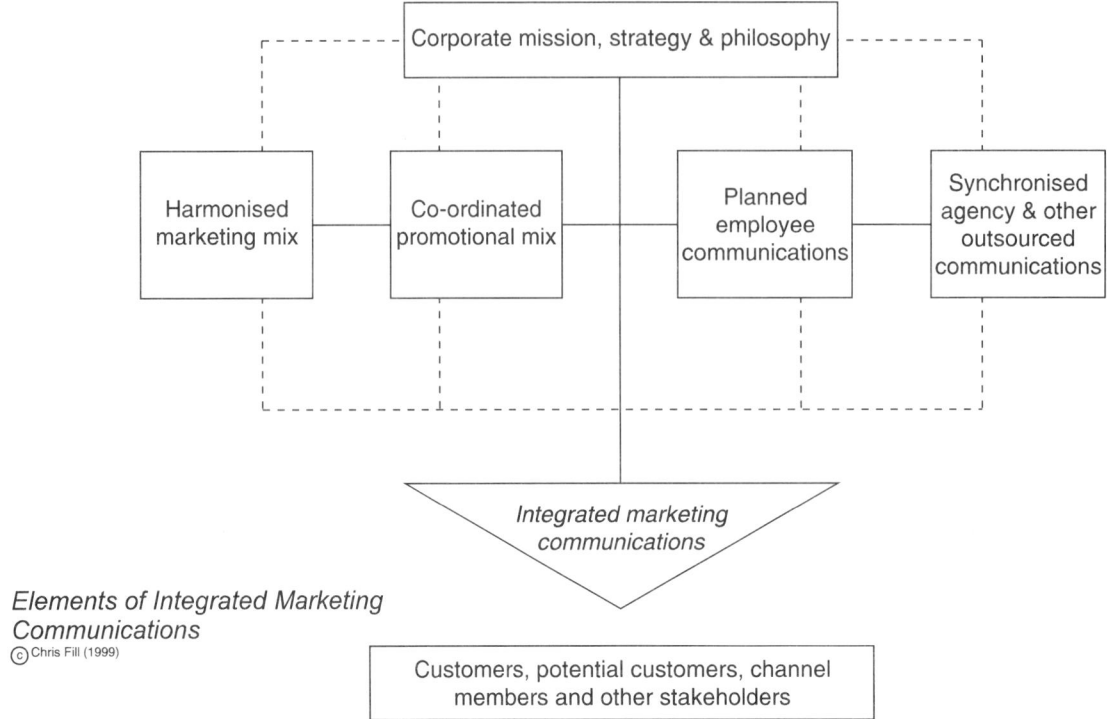

Elements of Integrated Marketing Communications
© Chris Fill (1999)

Benefits of adopting IMC

The benefits of moving towards the adoption of IMC are quite clear in my opinion and even if we are unable to achieve all of them in the medium term the fact that we are able to consider the totality of our communications will give us the opportunity to achieve a competitive advantage.

(a) With increasing inflation in media costs IMC gives us a chance to reduce our communication expenditure and achieve greater effectiveness.

(b) The technological advances that have been made in the past few years means that there are new ways to reach our customers and potential customers. If we do not consider them then we may risk losing some of our customers.

(c) IMC means that there are opportunities to link our communications with our distribution channel partners and provide a more co-ordinated and two-directional flow to our promotional activities.

(d) Internal communication opportunities exist and by linking our internal and external communications we may be able to promote increased understanding of the needs of our employees, customers, channel partners and a range of other important stakeholders.

(e) Our customers are changing their lifestyles and are using a wider range of media to achieve their goals. By utilising IMC we will be in a better position to reach our customers and deliver consistent messages that do not confuse them or drive them to our competitors.

(f) Our growth in international markets places greater emphasis upon the need to control and co-ordinate our marketing and corporate communications. IMC provides that opportunity and this will be important when dealing with customers who are located in many different overseas markets.

(g) The establishment of IMC will enable us to appoint a single advertising agency to handle all of our above-the-line work in different countries and to bring together our other agencies in Public Relations, Direct Marketing and Sales Promotion to develop co-ordinated and consistent campaigns.

Levels of IMC

There are a number of levels associated with IMC and the diagram below sets these out succinctly.

Elements of Integrated Marketing Communications
© Chris Fill (1999)

Action Plan for Cult Plastics International

Should we agree to commence the implementation of IMC, an action plan will be required to ensure that not only do we achieve the benefits set out earlier but that we plan events in such a way that we are able to overcome any resistance to this new approach.

I propose that the following be considered as a possible action agenda.

(a) Launch the IMC concept
(b) Train teams throughout the organisation.
(c) Develop plans to deliver IMC at different levels
(d) Test plans for viability
(e) Implement
(f) Review implementation, adjust and control activities.

The success or failure of IMC will, like other major strategic developments, rest with employees' perception of top management's involvement and endorsement of IMC. I urge you to make your self visible over this matter and to be seen as a firm believer in IMC.

It appears that the development of IMC by other companies has been limited because of the narrow perspective they have taken to the subject and of the need to reorganise the allocation and control of resources. I suggest that as a first step we attempt to coordinate the activities of the promotional mix and the marketing mix with the corporate goals. Integration with some of our external partners should follow at a later date. It is better to achieve a set of restricted goals rather than achieve only partial success with a wide range of goals.

Answer bank

Examples of IMC

To illustrate how IMC has been used by other organisations I include the following examples. It should be remembered that the context in which these campaigns were developed varied widely and there may have been internal and external conditions that framed the way the communications were developed. Our situation is unique: our approach will need to accommodate the different forces acting upon us and so should not attempt to replicate all the actions of these organisations.

(a) *Walkers Crisps* have embarked upon a series of campaigns that have incorporated a consistent communications mix. The objective was to revive and reposition the brand and this has been achieved using television with Gary Lineker as the central spokesperson to appeal to both adults and teenagers.

   (i) Lineker has been a consistent element throughout all the campaigns and is presented and perceived as a cheeky but fun endorser for the brand. Advertisements with a number of related spokespersons such as Paul Gascoigne and the Spice Girls have been mixed with messages with unrelated spokespersons such as everyday people and even a nun. These campaigns have been used in association with sales promotions such as competitions from which a tremendous amount of PR media coverage has been generated.

   (ii) The market has grown by 11% but Walkers have achieved growth of 21%. They have revived their brand, achieved market leadership and profitability and repositioned themselves as the number one snack food brand in the UK through the use of IMC.

(b) *Häagan Dazs* demonstrated the effective use of IMC when they entered the UK market. Ice cream was traditionally a seasonal children's food and the market had experienced little growth or innovation. The business strategy adopted was to create a new market segment, one that is now referred to as the 'super-premium segment'.

   (i) The positioning intention was to present Häagan Dazs as a luxury, fashion-orientated food for adults. To achieve the business goals, the entire marketing mix was coordinated: the product reflected high quality, the high price induced perceived quality, the distribution in the launch was through up-market restaurants in prestige locations and 5-Star hotels, where Häagan Dazs was the only branded ice cream on the menu.

   (ii) The promotional campaign used celebrities from many walks of life as opinion leaders to create a word-of-mouth ripple effect. The quality of the media used and messages themselves reflected the same quality theme. The brand has since become firmly established and, although the arrival of Ben & Jerry's and other up-market brands has increased competition and rivalry, the brand remains distinctive and continues to use an integrated approach to its communications.

Conclusions

To conclude I should like to reaffirm that in future our communications should be based upon an integrated approach drawing together the goals, the strategies, the tools and all those involved in our communications with all stakeholders.

7 MORE INTEGRATION

> *Tutorial note.* The rise and prominence of integrated marketing communications has been well documented and tested in previous papers. One of the difficulties with IMC is the lack of agreement about what it is and how it should be developed in organisations. The evidence indicates that there are very few companies fully utilising the concept, although many are moving forwards. This question requires students to apply the concept within a particular context and provides the opportunity for them to demonstrate their skills at adapting knowledge to specific situations.
>
> *Comments by the senior examiner.* The regular appearance of this question cannot be guaranteed in the future. IMC by its nature is an integrative tool. So, it may be beneficial to use some of the IMC concepts as part of an answer to other questions in the paper.
>
> *Please note that the views expressed in this answer are suggestions made by the new Senior Examiner for illustrative purposes only. They are not necessarily the views of Saatchi and Saatchi and they should not be attributed to them.*

SAATCHI & SAATCHI

Integrated marketing communications: advantages and adoption methods

The purpose of this short paper is two-fold. The first is to set out the advantages of Integrated Marketing Communications (IMC) and the second is to highlight ways in which IMC can be implemented within organisations.

At Saatchi and Saatchi we believe that the future of marketing communications lies within the integrated approach. We believe that by helping you we might be able to work together to establish IMC and make it work for your organisation. I shall be happy to discuss the contents of this paper and any questions you might have as a result of reading it.

Definition of IMC

The development and acceptance of IMC over the past few years, as a term synonymous with good marketing practice, has been wide and rapid. However, it is apparent that there is little uniform agreement about what it means nor how it should be implemented.

IMC involves:

'The strategic choice of elements of marketing communications, which effectively and economically influence transactions, between an organisation and its existing and potential customers, clients and consumers'

'The management and control of all marketing communication elements'

'Ensuring that the brand positioning, proposition, personality and messages are delivered synergistically across every element of communication and are derived from a single consistent strategy'.

The diagram below presents a view of IMC.

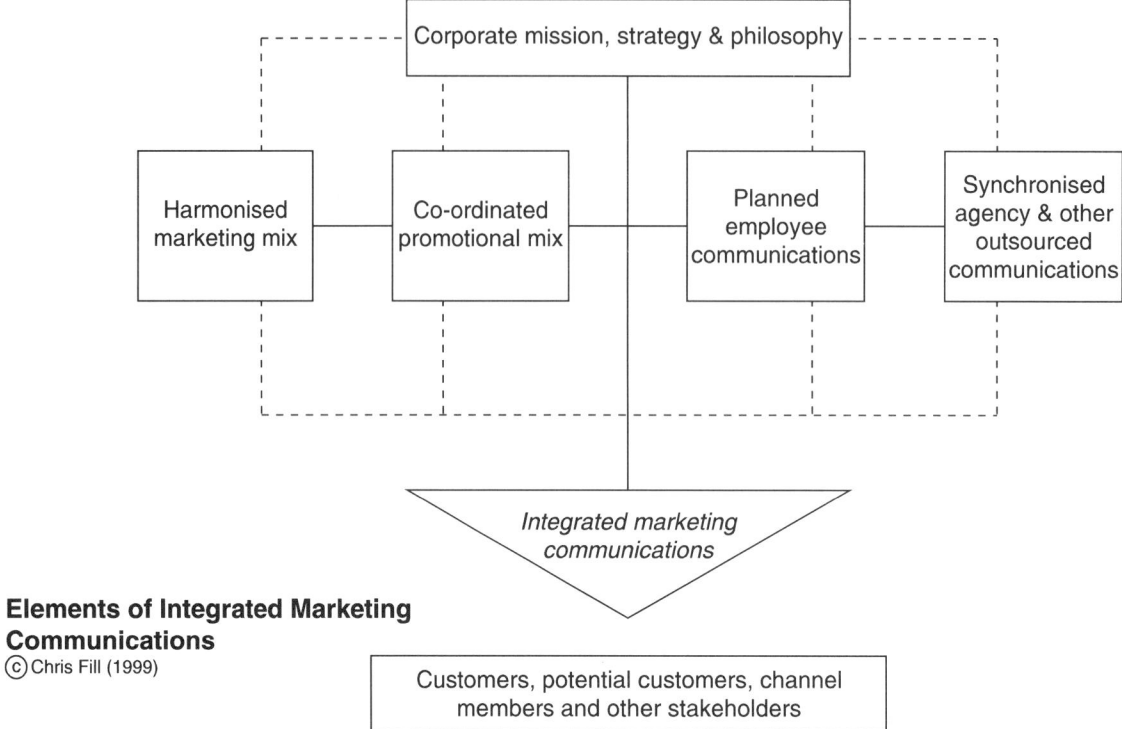

Elements of Integrated Marketing Communications
©Chris Fill (1999)

These views are important and have contributed to our understanding of the subject. At Saatchi & Saatchi, IMC is seen as the co-ordinated dialogue between an organisation's internal and external stakeholders. This suggests a strong strategic perspective and requires organisations to share information with others who are critical when it comes to helping it to meet its corporate goals.

Benefits of adopting IMC

The benefits of moving towards the adoption of IMC are quite clear and even if we are unable to achieve all of them in the medium term the fact that we are able to consider the totality of our communications will give us the opportunity to achieve a competitive advantage.

In order to fully appreciate the diversity of the IMC approach it is useful to consider the drivers which have propelled the development of IMC.

ORGANISATIONAL DRIVERS FOR IMC

* Increasing profits through improved efficiency
* Increasing need for greater levels of accountability
* Rapid move towards cross-border marketing and the need for changing structures and communications
* Co-ordinated brand development and competitive advantage
* Opportunities to utilise management time used more productively
* Provide direction and purpose

MARKET-BASED DRIVERS FOR IMC

* Greater levels of audience communications literacy
* Media cost inflation
* Media and audience fragmentation
* Stakeholders need for increasing amounts and diversity of information
* Greater amounts of message clutter
* Competitor activity and low levels of brand differentiation
* Move towards relationship marketing from transaction based marketing
* Development of networks, collaboration and alliances

COMMUNICATION-BASED DRIVERS FOR IMC

* Technological advances (Internet, databases, segmentation techniques)
* Increased message effectiveness through consistency and reinforcement of core messages
* More effective triggers for brand and message recall
* More consistent and less confusing brand images
* Need to build brand reputations and to provide clear identity cues

Note: this table is derived from a forthcoming book by Chris Fill, the new Senior Examiner, who holds the copyright.

From this it may come as no surprise that the benefits of IMC can be quite spectacular. The main advantages are as follows.

IMC has a strong impact on efficiency and effectiveness. Costs can be reduced and this is reflected in improved levels of profitability.

With increasing media inflation IMC provides organisations with an opportunity to reduce communication expenditure and achieve greater effectiveness.

The technological advances that have been made in the past few years mean that there are new ways to reach potential and existing customers. IMC provides a new way of considering all customers and so reducing the risk of losing some existing customers and gaining new ones.

IMC means that there are opportunities to link marketing (and corporate) communications with members of the marketing channel and to provide a more co-ordinated and two-directional flow to promotional activities.

Improved internal communication opportunities exist and by linking internal and external communications it is possible to promote increased understanding of the needs employees, customers, channel members and a range of other important stakeholders.

Customers are changing their lifestyles and are using a wider range of media to achieve their goals. By utilising IMC organisations are in a better position to reach customers and deliver consistent messages that do not confuse them or drive them to competitors.

Growth in international markets places greater emphasis upon the need to control and co-ordinate marketing communications. IMC provides that opportunity, and this is important when dealing with customers who are located in many different overseas markets.

The establishment of IMC enables organisations to appoint a single advertising agency to handle all of the above-the-line work in different countries and to bring together other agencies in Public Relations, Direct Marketing and Sales Promotion to develop co-ordinated and consistent campaigns.

Answer bank

Methods to accelerate the adoption of IMC

Having decided that IMC offers a number of strategic and operational benefits it is important to find the right way of implementing the concept in the shortest period of time. There is no right way, although some lessons have been learnt from those that have seen the benefits of this way of operating and have implemented it over the past two or three years.

An action plan is important and an agenda should be established at the earliest point in time. This will help ensure not only that the benefits are realised but that any resistance to this new approach is anticipated and overcome quickly.

Evidence suggests that the following should be considered as an action agenda.

ACTION AGENDA

(a) Launch the IMC concept internally among senior managers
(b) Cascade the idea of IMC throughout the organisation
(c) Train teams throughout the organisation.
(d) Develop plans to deliver IMC at different levels
(e) Test plans for viability
(f) Implement
(g) Review implementation, adjust and control activities.

The success or failure of IMC is, to a large extent, like other major strategic developments and rests with the employees' perception of top management's involvement and endorsement of IMC. We strongly advise senior managers and the CEO to make themselves very visible over this matter and to be seen as firm believers in IMC.

It appears that the development of IMC by some companies has been limited because of the narrow perspective they have taken to the subject and of the need to reorganise the allocation and control of resources. As a first step it is suggested that organisations attempt to co-ordinate the activities of the promotional mix and the marketing mix with the corporate goals. Integration with external partners should follow at a later date. It is better to achieve a set of restricted goals than to achieve only partial success with a wide range of goals.

Conclusions

Saatchi & Saatchi believe that the adoption of IMC will be crucial to the growth and development of all organisations. This organisation has begun the process of implementing the approach and we recommend that clients consider the concept further and seek to draw together their goals, their strategies, their tools and all those involved in their marketing communications.

8 IMPLEMENTING INTEGRATED COMMUNICATIONS

> *Tutorial note.* In order to facilitate a smooth transition between examiners I decided to include a question about integrated marketing communications. This question has a slightly different twist to it and is deliberately specific in its orientation. It is unlikely that direct questions about IMC will be included on a regular basis in future. Students will be expected to incorporate relevant and essential points about IMC in answer to a variety of Section A and B questions.
>
> *Examiner's comments.* This was the single most popular question, but badly answered, as the strategic impact was not considered.

Integrated Marketing Communications (IMC) is a term that has emerged in recent years to convey the essence of *harmony and consistency* within the promotional mix. Numerous definitions have been offered to explain the concept but *little agreement* has been reached about what exactly IMC means.

The term refers at one level to a *common message* which is communicated throughout the promotional tools and media used. This is however a somewhat simplistic approach as in order to achieve this thematic consistency, much more has to be accomplished than meets the eye. To achieve a common message requires that all *internal communications are balanced with the external communications*. IMC means that there is harmony and internal consonance with the corporate objectives, strategy and marketing goals. To achieve this requires that all relevant stakeholders share a common vision and agreement about how the organisation and its brands are presented to the outside world and how the values of the organisation are to be represented. Agencies involved with the marketing communications activities must share the ideals that the organisation it is working with.

If this wider perspective of IMC is accepted then it should be clear that IMC has a *strategic impact* and that IMC is in itself a strategic approach to marketing communications. By assuming this view of IMC it is possible to consider the range of cues organisations present to their various audiences and in doing so begin to appreciate the complexity and difficulties involved in establishing some level of integration.

The advantages of IMC are numerous the most important of which appear to focus upon cost efficiency and clear, consistent communications.

Advantages of integrating marketing communications

(a) A *strong corporate image* which provides credibility and trust for stakeholders is vitally important in many competitive markets.

(b) *Products are presented to customers in a consistent*, clear and unambiguous manner. The message can be delivered through a variety of media but at all times the message is the same one. Therefore branding can be enhanced through clear IMC.

(c) What follows from clear, consistent communications is the possibility of competitive advantage in the markets in which the organisation operates.

(d) By linking *internal and external communications* a strong identity can be presented to customers and other stakeholders.

(e) The *cost effectiveness* of the marketing communications budget can be improved by reducing the level of duplication on the media spend and by centralising media buying into a single agency.

(f) IMC requires that *internal communications* are harmonised and work to meet corporate objectives. The major HR benefit of this approach is that employee motivation can be improved considerably as levels of understanding and communication improve.

In essence, the development of IMC constitutes a change of culture and a reorientation to a customer based culture. For some organisations the degree of change will be small but for others the change might be revolutionary.

For the successful implementation of IMC, everyone in the organisation and many of those who provide outsourced facilities (such as the agencies) should work together. The role of the Chief Executive is paramount in this process, as it is the skills of the leader that determine whether a management initiative fails or succeeds. Top management support is required to provide direction, focus and pace of change.

There are no right or wrong ways to implement IMC, but some approaches are better than others. What is important is that the development of IMC and the actions of the Chief Executive will to a large extent be determined by the context within which they are

Answer bank

working. For example, the management of change and the development of a new culture is a considerably more challenging task in a multinational organisation than it is in a small company that employs just twenty people. Resources and the speed of change in the market will also be important factors. Having said that there a few elements that all Chief Executives might wish to consider.

(a) Training is important not just for employees but also for senior managers.

(b) Reappraisal of the number and types of agencies the organisation is involved with.

(c) Reconsideration of the structure and level of structural integration that exists in the organisation.

(d) Delegation of the practical operational issues associated with IMC is necessary but responsibility rests with at all times with the Chief Executive.

(e) Undertake a communication audit to determine the size of the gap between the actual communication facilities, media and message content with that is seen as desirable. Devise and agree a plan to rectify and reduce the size of the communication gap.

(f) An IMC budget should be created to help monitor the costs associated with the move to and establishment of IMC. Whilst these costs will be outweighed by the savings that will come on stream it is good practice to demonstrate the benefits and to introduce the process if it is not already established in the organisation.

The Chief Executive has an important role to play in the implementation of IMC but the overriding factor is the CIS's role as change agent, the person who is charged with communicating why the change is necessary, telling how it will be done and keeping people going whilst the change process is in action. There a number of formal and inform activities that must be completed but through networking and being seen to care, it is much more likely that IMC will be successfully implemented.

9 TUTORIAL QUESTION: TECHNOLOGY

(a) When combined within the marketing and selling functions, telemarketing plays an important role in the following areas.

  (i) *Building, maintaining, cleaning and updating databases.* The telephone allows for accurate data-gathering by compiling relevant information on customers and prospects, and selecting appropriate target groups for specific product offerings.

  (ii) *Market evaluation and test marketing.* Almost any feature of a market can be measured and tested by telephone. Feedback is immediate so response can be targeted quickly to exploit market knowledge.

  (iii) *Dealer support.* Leads can be passed on to the nearest dealer who is provided with full details.

  (iv) *Traffic generation.* The telephone, combined with postal invitations, is the most cost effective way of screening leads and encouraging attendance at promotional events.

  (v) *Direct sales and account servicing.* The telephone can be used at all stages of the relationship with the prospects and customers. This includes lead generation, establishing buying potential for appropriate follow-up and defining the decision-making process.

  (vi) *Customer care and loyalty building.* Every telephone contact opportunity can demonstrate to customers that they are valued.

(vii) *Crisis management*. If for example there is a consumer scare, immediate action is essential to minimise commercial damage. A dedicated hotline number can be advertised to provide information and advice.

(b) The emergence of the *information superhighway* will potentially have a huge impact upon the marketing of products and services together with associated communication techniques.

The ability to shop from home and choose items directly with the use of scanners can be integrated with direct advertising. Infomercials (which combine information with a commercial) which the consumer has chosen from a databank will be relayed directly to the home down cable links. These may take the form of recipes, DIY hints, car repairs and so on. Consumers will also be able to purchase the necessary ingredients or parts simultaneously, simply by pointing a mouse on a computer screen at the desired goods and clicking its buttons

It is estimated by Verdict Research that home shopping will become a £300m market in the UK within the next few years. US operator QVC (Quality, Value and Convenience) launched television shopping in 1993 in the UK through satellite, which is available to cable and Sky subscribers.

The speed of adoption will depend upon how readily the public accept and use the new technology and to what extent they will be deterred from actively browsing around the shops. This will vary from country to country and community to community.

The superhighway will also enable viewers to interact directly with the television programmes they watch. It may be the case that certain channels with specialist broadcasts (for example a channel devoted to golfing, cookery or motor sport) will be characterised solely by advertisements from within those areas of interest. Viewers will then be able to conduct a dialogue with the screen to find out more information about the particular programme, product or service which is being covered.

Advertising opportunities will abound as advertisers choose individual channels to suit the special interest and viewer profile.

However, as the packaged goods manufacturers responsible for big name brands are aware, the need to communicate your product to the widest possible audience is the key to maintaining a brand's position. It may be possible in the future to *reward* the viewer for watching your commercial. Machines placed on top of televisions could print out money-off coupons for specific products which the viewer has just watched. These would be redeemable against that product over a specified time period.

Taking this a step further, it could be possible to tailor advertisements to individual requirements, as information on individual viewing habits is monitored through interactive television.

10 OBJECTIVES

> *Examiner's comments*
>
> Most candidates knew the role objectives play in a marketing communications plan. However, a number of candidates saw the word 'integrated' and went on to write on integrated marketing communications without relating it to the question.
>
> A number of students did badly on the second part of the question. Note that this area is likely to come up again. Students who can show that they have understood the concept of linkages in the marketing communication planning process will do well in this subject.

Answer bank

Introduction to Objectives

1 The use of objectives in any management related activity is essential. Within marketing communications the derivation and use of objectives can be critical for a number of reasons. They can provide the following:

- Direction
- Consistency in decision making
- The time period for the activity to be completed
- A means by which the values and scope of the activity are communicated to all participants
- A means of evaluation

2 These general roles highlight the scope and importance of objectives. An organisation however, can have a number of different goals, many of which can be seen as hierarchically aligned.

3 An integrated marketing communications (IMC) plan requires that all the goals of an organisation be incorporated or at least reflected in the lower level communications. For example, the mission of an organisation provides a framework for the organisation's objectives which in turn should be represented in the business and marketing objectives. The goals for a marketing communications plan (or campaign) should be similarly aligned.

Different Types of Promotional Goals

4 The goals for a marketing communications plan can be referred to as the promotional goals. They consist of three main elements: Sales, Communications and Corporate related issues.

5 The Sales goals refer to the market share, sales value and ROI figures that commercial organisations generate on a regular basis and to which all managers can easily refer. These figures can be drawn down easily from the marketing plan. Unfortunately, these do not account for the communication task facing each Marketing Communication or Brand Manager. They fail to incorporate a customer perspective and give little or no direction to the creative team assigned to the advertising aspect.

6 In response to the short comings of the Sales goals it is necessary to incorporate a set of Communication related goals. These refer to tasks concerning awareness levels, the provision of information (developing knowledge/understanding) and changing perceptions and attitudes towards a brand.

7 Finally, it is my belief that if we are to generate IMCs then it is absolutely imperative that these product related goals are counterbalanced by goals relating to how the organisation itself is perceived by the other stakeholders. This refers to corporate identity and image issues and the nature of the task facing an organisation depends on the gap between what stakeholders think about the organisation and how the organisation would like to be perceived.

Linkages with Other Parts of the Marketing Communication Planning Process

8 The Promotional Goals are developed through the Contextual Analysis, either through market research, the marketing plan or through analysis and understanding. As an integrated plan it is important to understand that these goals impact on nearly all the other parts of the planning process.

- They constrain the number of promotional strategies to be considered and selected.
- They impact on the type of message to be formulated and delivered to the target audience(s). This in turn affects the development of the brand.
- The choice of media to be used to convey the message will also be influenced by what is to be achieved and how quickly. For example, if the plan requires the development of prompted awareness then a reach media strategy is more likely to be appropriate than a frequency strategy.
- The amount of resources that can and are allocated to the plan will reflect, in part, the nature of the task that needs to be accomplished.
- The goals will also impact on the schedule and timing of the implementation of the marketing communication activities. Good integration requires that there be consistency and harmonisation across the promotional mix.
- The promotional objectives will be used to evaluate how successful the plan/campaign has been.

9 There is no doubt that the use of carefully specified (SMART) objectives is a crucial part of the development of an Integrated Marketing Communications plan.

11 TUTORIAL QUESTION: CONSUMER BUYING BEHAVIOUR

(a) The general stages in the buying process have been identified by Kotler as follows.

(i) Need recognition
(ii) Information search
(iii) Evaluation of alternatives
(iv) Purchase decision
(v) Post purchase evaluation

(i) The process begins when the buyer *recognises a need* or problem. This can be triggered by internal stimuli, such as hunger or thirst, or external stimuli, such as social esteem. If the need rises to a *threshold level* it will become a *drive*, and, from previous experience the buyer will know how to satisfy this drive through the purchase of a particular type of product.

The task for the marketer is to identify the circumstances and/or stimuli that trigger a particular need and use this knowledge to develop marketing strategies that trigger consumer interest.

(ii) Once aroused the customer will *search for more information* about the products that will satisfy the need. The information search stage can be divided into two levels. The first is *'heightened attention'*, where the customer simply becomes more receptive to information about the particular product category. The second stage is *'active information search'*. The extent of active search will depend on the strength of the drive, the amount of information initially available, the ease of obtaining additional information and the satisfaction obtained from the search.

The task for the marketer is to decide which are the major information sources that the customer will use and to analyse their relative importance. According to Kotler consumer information sources fall into four groups.

(1) *Personal sources*: family, friends, neighbours, work colleagues
(2) *Commercial sources*: advertising, salespeople, packaging, displays
(3) *Public sources*: mass media, consumer rating organisations

(4) *Experiential sources*: handling, examining, using the product

Through this information-gathering process the consumer will learn about competing brands and their relative pros and cons. This will enable the consumer to narrow down the range of alternatives to those brands that will best meet his or her particular needs - what has been called the 'choice set'. The marketer's task is to get his brand into the customer's *choice set*.

(iii) Most current models of *evaluation* are cognitively oriented - in other words they take the view that the customer forms judgements largely on a *conscious and rational basis*. Kotler states that, as the consumer is trying to satisfy some need with the buying process, he will be looking for certain benefits from the product chosen and each product will be seen as a 'bundle of attributes' with varying capabilities of delivering the benefits sought and hence satisfying the need. The composition and the relative importance of the components of this bundle of attributes will differ between customers, and therefore the marketer should determine what importance the customer attaches to each attribute.

In order to ensure that the brand has the best chance of being chosen by the consumer, the marketer has a range of options for action.

(1) *Modifying the brand*. Redesigning the product so that it offers more of the attributes that the buyer desires. Kotler calls this 'real repositioning'.

(2) *Altering beliefs about the brand*. Kotler recommends that this course of action be pursued if the consumer underestimates the qualities of the brand, and calls it 'psychological repositioning' ('Not just for breakfast').

(3) *Altering beliefs about competitors' brands*. This course of action would be appropriate if the consumer mistakenly believes that a competitor's brand has more quality than it actually has, and can be referred to as 'competitive repositioning'.

(4) *Altering the importance weights of attributes*. The marketer would try to persuade consumers to attach more importance to the product attribute in which the brand excels.

(5) *Calling attention to neglected attributes*, particularly if the brand excels in these attributes. ('Have you forgotten how good they taste?').

(6) *Shifting the buyer's ideals*. The marketer would try to persuade consumers to change their ideal levels for one or more attributes.

(iv) The *decision processes* involved in a major purchase such as a car are very different from the decision processes involved in the purchase of chocolate confectionery. Assael presents a typology of consumer decision making based on the *extent of decision making* and the *degree of involvement* in the purchase.

Assael's typology comprises four types of decision-making.

(1) *Complex decision-making* occurs when *involvement is high* and the consumer *searches and considers alternatives*, such as in the purchase of major items like cars, brown goods, white goods etc.

Complex decision making will not occur every time and if the brand choice is repetitive the consumer learns from experience and purchases a brand known from previous experience with little or no decision making (*brand loyalty*).

(2) *Low involvement decision making*

- Customers sometimes go through a decision making process even if not highly involved in the purchase because they have little experience of the product area (*limited decision making*). In this case the customer will go through the process of information search and the evaluation of alternatives, albeit to a lesser extent than for complex decision making.

- Limited decision making may also occur when the *customer seeks variety;* for example, customers may be likely to switch between low involvement brands in a quest for interest in the product area. Such *variety-seeking behaviour* is likely to occur when the customer perceives minimal risk and has little commitment to a particular brand. The brand switch is unlikely to be preplanned and may occur at the place of purchase: for example, while he is actually going round the supermarket the customer may decide to try a new type of biscuit.

(3) '*Inertia*', comprises low involvement with the product and no decision making. Inertia implies that the customer is buying the same brand, not out of any brand loyalty, but because it is not worth the time or trouble to search for an alternative.

(v) *Post purchase* of the brand the consumer will experience some level of satisfaction or dissatisfaction, depending on the closeness between the consumer's product expectations and the product's perceived performance. These feelings will influence whether the consumer buys the brand again and also whether the consumer talks favourably or unfavourably about the brand to others.

(b) Rice identifies five characteristics associated with the success of new products.

(i) *Relative advantage:* the extent to which the consumer perceives the product to have an advantage over the product it supersedes, implying that, the greater the perceived advantage, the greater the probability of adoption.

(ii) *Compatibility:* the degree to which the product is consistent with existing values and past experiences of the potential customers, the assumption being that the less a product is compatible with consumer values, the longer it will take to be adopted.

(iii) *Complexity:* the degree to which a new product is perceived to be complex and difficult to use. The more difficult it is perceived to be, the harder it will be for the product to be accepted.

(iv) *Trialability.* It is believed that new products are more likely to be adopted when customers can try them out on an experimental basis.

(v) *Observability:* a measure of the degree to which adoption of the product, or the results of using the product, is visible to friends, neighbours and colleagues. This seems to affect the diffusion process by allowing potential customers to see the benefits of the product, and thus increase (or even create) a 'want' for themselves. This process can be given added impetus if the product is seen to be used by celebrities or other role models. This factor obviously lends itself more to some products than others.

12 TUTORIAL QUESTION: ORGANISATIONAL BUYING BEHAVIOUR

(a) Dibb *et al* identify four types of organisational markets - producers, resellers, governments and institutions.

Answer bank

(i) *Producer markets* comprise those organisations that purchase products for the purpose of making a profit by using them to produce other products or by using them in their own operations. This may include buyers of raw materials and of semi-finished and finished items used to produce other products.

(ii) *Reseller markets* consist of intermediaries such as retailers and wholesalers who buy the finished goods in order to resell them to make a profit. Other than minor alterations, resellers do not change the physical characteristics of the products they handle.

(iii) *Government markets* comprise those national and local governments who buy a variety of goods and services to support their internal operations and to provide the public services that are within their remit, normally making their purchases through bids or negotiated contracts.

(iv) *Institutional markets* comprise those organisations that seek to achieve charitable, educational, community or other non-business goals.

(b) *Cell 1: the purchasing agent*. This represents the buyer, located in the quadrant which is within the organisation and within the purchasing department. Various factors will influence the buyer, including social factors, price and cost factors, supply continuity and risk avoidance.

(i) *Social factors* include the relationships, friendships and antipathies that exist between buyer and suppliers and the extent to which these impinge on purchasing decisions. Whilst in an ideal world such social factors should not influence decision making, they are, in reality, an important factor in the equation.

(ii) *Price and cost factors* are obviously important and can include such things as the economic state of the buying organisation, the level of competition among suppliers, any cost/benefit analyses that might have been conducted, the purchasing budget and the personality and background of the purchasing agent (for example, an agent with an accountancy background may be more cost conscious).

(iii) *Supply continuity* is a function of the number of suppliers that are available and the importance of the purchased item to the organisation.

(iv) *Risk avoidance* is a common motivation for organisational buyers. Buyers can typically cope with risk in a number of ways.

    (1) Exchanging technical and other information with their customers and prospects.

    (2) Dealing only with those suppliers with which the company has previously had favourable experiences.

    (3) Applying strict (risk reducing) rules.

    (4) Dealing only with suppliers who have a long-established and favourable reputation.

    (5) Introducing penalty clauses, for example for late delivery.

    (6) Multiple sourcing to reduce the degree of dependence on a single supplier.

Cell 2: the buying centre. This cell equates to the Decision Making Unit, where the focus is within the firm but between departments. Some of the influencing factors in this cell include organisation structure and policy, power, status and conflict procedures, and gatekeeping.

(i) With regard to organisational structure and policy, the place of the purchasing department within the organisation is very important as it will determine such matters as the level of influence and the reporting relationships. Policy and history will determine the extent to which the buyer can take autonomous action.

(ii) Power, status and conflict procedures relate to the degree to which the buyer or purchasing department wishes to change or maintain the status quo. For example, decentralisation and divisionalisation of the organisation may motivate outside departments to initiate their own buying decisions.

(iii) Gatekeeping controls the flow of information in the organisation and the person who acts as the gatekeeper can exert considerable influence.

Cell 3: professionalism. This cell examines the influence of professional standards and practice in other organisations, the main factors being specialist journals, conferences and trade shows, word of mouth communication and supply-purchase reciprocity.

(i) Specialist journals, conferences and trade shows are likely to be the source of much professional knowledge and provide a good vehicle for the updating of such knowledge. In addition, professional organisations usually attempt to set standards for professional conduct.

(ii) Word of mouth communication, or the professional 'grapevine' can act as a potent force within the profession.

(iii) Supply-purchase reciprocity refers to arrangements whereby two organisations reach an agreement to supply each other.

Cell 4: the organisational environment. This cell is concerned with factors outside of both the purchasing department and the organisation, including economic, commercial and competitive forces, the political, social and legal environment, technological change, co-operative buying (through, for example, the formation of consortia), and the nature of the supplier. It is often assumed that large organisations make inflexible suppliers as their size enables them to adopt a 'take it or leave it' attitude. However, they probably offer a more reliable and less risky service.

Answer bank

13 TWO PRACTICAL MODELS

> *Examiner's comments, summarised by BPP.* Unfortunately, very few students were able to illustrate their answers with meaningful applications. This reflects previous answers to similar questions. It appears that whilst models are well used in *marketing* strategy thinking, this is not the case with *communications* strategy.

What are models?

A model is a simplified interpretation of a system or process which can be used to assist understanding, develop calculations and scenarios and predict the occurrence of events. In subjects such as communication and buyer behaviour there are a number of complex variables that need to be understood in order to anticipate likely outcomes to events. For example, these events may be advertising messages, word-of-mouth communications, attitudes and brand or purchase experiences.

There are a number of different types of model as defined by the Market Research Society.

- Micro or Macro
- Data-Based or Theory Based
- Descriptive or Predictive
- Behavioural or Statistical
- Qualitative or Quantitative
- Static or Dynamic

Strengths and Weaknesses of Models

Marketing communications models have a number of strengths and weaknesses which impact on marketing managers.

Advantages

(a) They provide a succinct range of parameters which managers can use to aid their planning, strategy and tactics. Research topics can be prompted as a result of the use of suitable models and frameworks.

(b) Models help ensure that managers ask the right questions and that the totality of an issue is covered.

(c) Models can help the planning and implementation process by ensuring that a logical sequence of activities is adopted.

(d) The use of models to assist understanding of complex activities is important when different variables can be the cause for concern or under performance.

(e) Models are of particular use when they can be used to predict events (such as behaviour), as a response to a stimulus (such as a sales promotion or DRTV campaign).

Weaknesses

Just as models have a number of strengths they also contain a number of drawbacks.

(a) One danger is that they can encourage managers to adopt a prescriptive approach such that they ignore the context in which the event is currently situated.

(b) The use of models may discourage lateral thinking and team work, with the consequence that opportunities are overlooked or ignored.

(c) Some models may be inaccurate or such a simplification that they do not really represent the system or process they were originally designed to interpret. For example, the linear models of communication fail to consider the context in which communication occurs, the interaction and behaviour of the people involved or the influence of the intervening variables in the process.

Example One

The attitude construct, *Cognitive - Affective - Conative*, is a very simple model which suggests that communications aimed at changing behaviour need to first be rooted in the provision of knowledge and information, then stimulate a feeling or degree of preference and then motivate an individual to act or behave in a particular way.

Cognitive	Affective	Conative
Learn $\longrightarrow$	Feel $\longrightarrow$	Do

Many advertising campaigns and subset models have been built around this construct. The AIDA model and the Hierarchy of Effects models such as those of Lavidge and Steiner, have been developed around this sequential progression.

When new products or brand variants are launched the first task is to make the target audience aware of the availability of the offering and to provide them with sufficient information.

The next task for these brands, and those that are already established in the market, is to stimulate interest and/or remind potential or current buyers of the brand so that they form particular (positive) feelings towards it.

This can be seen in terms of marketing communication messages that suggest that people (like you) prefer this brand over another, or that this brand matches your requirements, or that the rewards obtained from using this brand will match the individual's expectations. The Oxo series of advertisements seek to identify with the target audience by portraying a typical family in action, so that the viewer sympathises with the family predicament and associates the context with Oxo as the only gravy-cube brand worth buying.

Behaviour, or the conative construct, is manifest in messages that instruct a particular course of action such as requesting a brochure, buying a product or requesting a trial.

This model is useful in that different promotional tools can be seen to be of particular use at particular stages. Advertising and direct marketing to develop awareness, public relations and advertising to generate preference and feelings, with personal selling, direct marketing, sales promotion and point of purchase activities aimed at provoking action.

Example 2

The second model to be considered is the linear model of communication developed originally by Wilbur Schramm.

The communication process

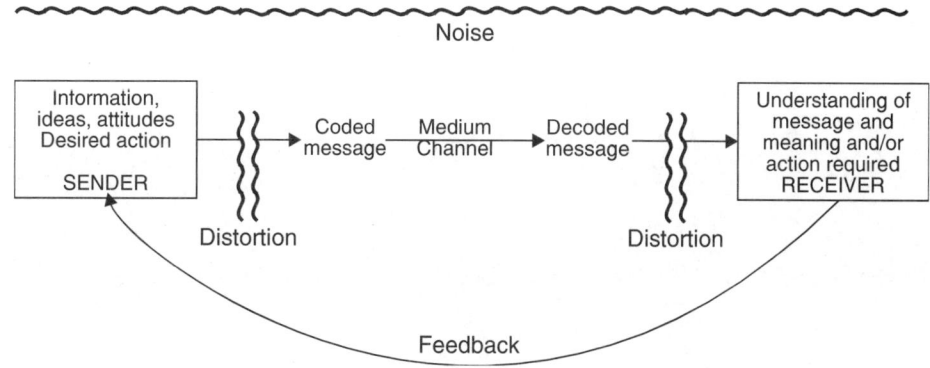

Answer bank

This is an early descriptive model that explains how communication was thought to work. A source devised a message that was transmitted through a channel of communication that is then noticed, decoded and interpreted. Feedback to the source may occur and noise in the communication system may prevent reception or distort interpretation.

This model is useful in that it can encourage managers to identify correctly the problem that exists and then devise and construct messages that they feel their target audiences will be able and willing to understand and act upon as necessary. This model impacts upon the source credibility, message design, media planning and market research (feedback) to understand whether the correct message has reached, and been interpreted correctly by, the target.

Whilst this model is a useful tool it suggests that communications operate in a vacuum (despite the noise element) and does not take into account the behaviour and interaction of the people involved.

Conclusion

Models play a particularly useful role in marketing communications through their ability to simplify the different processes and to educate individuals not only about how the process works but also what actions need to be undertaken at each stage in the development of marketing communication activities.

However, they are not good predictive tools and are certainly not a replacement for management judgement.

14   LIFE CYCLE

> *Tutorial note.* The use of models to assist understanding of marketing communications models is a well-established concept. The overall relevance of the PLC as an aid to marketing management has been long been questioned but as an educational tool it is useful. Apart from aspects of deployment across the different stages the strategic implications of the PLC and its impact on the marketing communication mix is important.

The Product Life-Cycle and marketing communications

The Product Life-Cycle model was originally developed to explain how sales of a particular type of product vary throughout the time of it is commercial availability. This period of time, or lifecycle as it is termed, can be traced as a sales curve which approximates to a normal distribution curve, although the demand is steeper at the beginning than at the end. This is shown in the diagram below, which also reveals that the life span can be divided into 4 main periods: introduction, growth, maturity and decline.

Answer bank

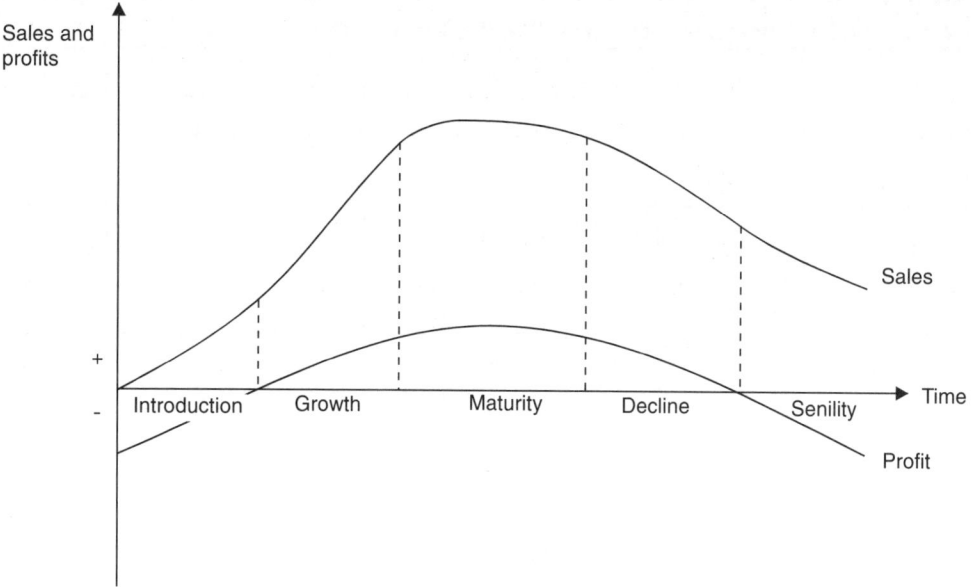

At each stage in this cycle different marketing strategies should be used to reflect the different levels of risk, customer experience and competitive conditions. This paper will concentrate on the different marketing communications methods that need to be deployed at these different stages although reference will also be made to other marketing issues.

To assist this process the Pepsi brand will be superimposed on the cycle to demonstrate the different promotional methods. Before progressing it is worth mentioning that the PLC is only of significant use at the industry level, as it is only at this point that the traditional curve can be theoretically supported. At the individual product or brand level the normal distribution curve is hard to identify: indeed with shorter periods of new product development the curve can be truncated quite sharply as shown in the next diagram.

Product Lifestyle Variants

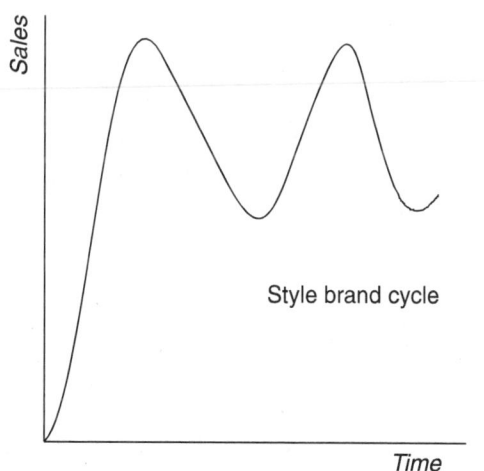
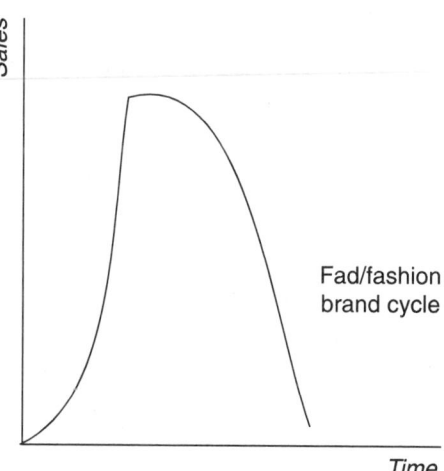

Answer bank

Marketing Mix Characteristics across the Product Life-Cycle				
	Introduction	Growth	Maturity	Decline
Product	Basic product	Basic product	Augmented product to differentiate	Brand extension or eliminate from range
Distribution	Exclusive/selective	Selective	Intensive	Selective
Pricing	Penetration/ skimming	Maintenance	Price competition	Maintain or lower
Promotion	Heavy investment to create awareness and differentiation	Reduce weight of promotional visibility	Heavy use of promotion activity to create trial in non user segment and to maintain regular users	Gradually withdraw promotions and use selectively to reach loyal users.

Introductory stage

When Pepsi was first introduced to the UK market it was necessary to communicate with two main target markets: consumers and the trade.

However, personal selling is of major importance to sell into the trade and to create the distribution outlets and product availability. Sales promotion in the form of sales literature will be important secondary support materials.

Communications to reach the consumer market should be designed to generate awareness and interest in the brand. Public Relations is useful to arouse interest and to build brand values. With some consumer products it has proved useful to start a whispering campaign among innovators and opinion leaders. In addition, Public Relations is useful to reach opinion formers such as the media who may write stories and articles about the brand, which are seen, read or heard by the target market.

Pepsi used a heavy weight advertising campaign to reach their mass audience. This proved successful because customers do not require a lot of information about this type of product and appear to be influenced by the values and position the brand adopts in comparison to their own lifestyle and their current preferred soft drink. Television and poster work will normally figure prominently in the media schedule at this stage of the lifecycle. Spokesperson and celebrity endorsement are important aspects of the message.

Growth stage

During this stage of development public relations need to be maintained but the mass advertising campaign is normally relaxed, as early adopters and the early majority form the main user groups. Advertising is used to differentiate the brand and to convey brand values: in Pepsi's case this was done by stressing the difference in taste (The Pepsi Challenge).

For brands such as Pepsi, sponsorship activities are important and these need to be agreed at this stage and supported accordingly.

For the trade market personal selling switches from a prospecting emphasis to one which seeks to service the increasing number of distributors and to reward those that took up the brand at an early stage.

Answer bank

Consumer Market	Introduction	Growth	Maturity	Decline
Advertising	X	x	x	x
Sales Promotion		x	x	
Personal selling (field marketing)	X	x	x	
Direct Marketing		x	x	
Public Relations	X	x	x	x

Consumer market	Introduction	Growth	Maturity	Decline
Advertising	X		x	
Sales Promotion		x	x	X
Personal selling (field marketing)	X	x	x	
Direct Marketing		x	x	X
Public Relations	X	x	x	x

Mature stage

As the product enters the mature stage so competition in the market place becomes increasingly difficult. There is a danger that as the market becomes saturated and there are no new buyers, competition becomes price-based, with sales promotions becoming more important. Price wars often emerge but if the brand values have been correctly identified and communicated then brands are advised to avoid price competition as a much as possible.

Sales promotions have another role to play and that is to attract lapsed or non-users of the brand. Discounts, two-for-one deals, taste test sessions/sampling and brand events are useful. Sales promotions can also be used to reward current loyal users, and direct marketing activities, linked into sales promotions, will help to prolong the life of the brand.

Advertising remains important for consumer brands and FMCGs in particular. Repositioning of the brand may take place, just as Pepsi used Project Blue to differentiate the brand. Many major celebrities (eg Andre Agassi and Cindy Crawford) were used to attract attention to the brand, and advertising and public relations - important for a low-involvement product such as a soft drink - were used to convey new brand values.

In-store promotions become increasingly important to support the trade and to assist consumer decision making. Personal selling needs to concentrate on maintaining distribution and obtaining maximum shelf frontage. Trade allowances and joint advertising deals may be useful, if not critical to the success of the brand at this stage.

Because of the competitive conditions, strong sponsorships activities and associations with key celebrities set up previously will now start to prove useful. Originally Pepsi used Michael Jackson and Madonna to support the brand. Currently they link with girl power values associated with the Spice Girls, tying in well with the new generation position.

Decline

As sales start to fall away and the decline stage is entered so promotional support needs to be gradually withdrawn. A move away from mass market promotions to a more selected target market approach is advisable as the number of non-users or laggards attracted to the brand is going to be very small. Trade support will be difficult as shelf space will be given to new fresher brands.

Brands are often subject to renewal at the outset of the decline stage and are re-launched in a new, more modern format. If this strategy is followed then advertising and public relations will again be important.

Answer bank

Conclusion

This broad brush look at the promotional activities tied into the lifecycle is not complete without mentioning integration. All the promotional activities, at all stages in the cycle must be integrated in such away that both internal and external communications are co-ordinated and provide consumers and members of the marketing channels with consistent harmonised messages, that add value and convey the essence of the brand.

15 CHANGING ATTITUDES

> *Examiner's comment.* This question was definitely the least favourite and attempted by very few. Unfortunately those that did attempt this question did not do very well. The answer presented below is a composite of three student answers with a bit of my own input in order that you can see what was expected.
>
> I was surprised by how little students knew about attitudes and attitude formation. In some way attitudes lie at the heart of marketing communications. The desire to inform, persuade, remind/reassure and differentiate is about changing or sustaining attitudes. Those students who had revised by using the previous mini-case about Recycling Glass might have picked up on the need to change the attitudes of men 18 to 34 who had a negative attitude to recycling. Many advertising campaigns (eg NSPCC Full Stop, Virgin Atlantic, GAP, Standard Life and even Budweiser are all about attitude formation and development).

Introduction

Attitudes are the enduring elements of a consumer's psychological make-up, derived from through perception, motivation and learning. Attitudes influence how, what and when buyers' purchase goods and services. Attitudes tend to be consistent within an individual and can be considered as predispositions to behave in a particular way. What this means for marketers is if it is known that a target audience has a negative attitude towards a brand then it is important to try to change the attitude into a positive attitude or intention to buy the brand.

Attitudes are thought to consist of three elements. These are the cognitive (knowledge) affective (feelings) and conative (action) elements as observed in simple sequential models such as AIDA and DAGMAR. More commonly this is referred to as learn-feel-do.

Attributes

Products and brands consist of a variety of attributes. These attributes will be physical (tangible) aspects of a product and some will relate to the imagery (intangible) elements of a product. They will be strong or weak according to individual perception, experience and motivation. Attitudes are developed towards products and particular attributes have significant value for an individual at any one point in time. Competition between major brands is often based upon the perceived strength of particular attributes. For example, the ability for a washing powder to wash clothes whiter (Daz) or for an engine to be more environmentally friendly (Mitsubishi) or for a brand of clothing to be more appealing to a particular target market (GAP).

Attitudes need not only be related to attributes as they can be can be formed as a result of direct experience of a product, particularly when there is low involvement, or through an interpretation of the information received about product, particularly when there is high involvement.

Changing attitudes

There are a variety of ways in which attitudes can be changed.

1   Change beliefs about a product's particular attributes

2 Change beliefs about competitors' attributes
3 Change beliefs about what attributes are important in a sector

Attitudes can be changed using the promotional tools. However, what is more important is what is actually said in the message that is delivered.

1 *Change beliefs about a product's particular attributes*

New, improved or trial offer is known to be of appeal to users and non-users and hence is a powerful means of inducing behaviour and hence changing attitudes. For example, if research found that peoples attitude toward a brand of soup was negative it would be important to find out what it was that made people negative about the brand (taste, varieties, packaging, price, imagery and associations?), correct it and then communicate the change to the target audience.

Through use of the promotional tools and using appropriate messages it is possible to change peoples perception, beliefs and eventually attitudes towards a product. For example, the Economist was for a long time regarded as a somewhat worthy yet heavy publication and only of interest to economists and other learned readers. Using an appeal directed at aspirers and channelled through posters and TV, business people who wanted to demonstrate this well informed profile were encouraged to become regular readers.

2 *Change beliefs about competitors' attributes*

This is designed to achieve a shift in the perceived ranking of a competitive or substitutional products. This is achieved through the use of 'comparative advertising' and public relations. A topical issue is the competitive dispute between British Airways and Virgin Atlantic over the adoption of the Union Flag on their aircraft. BA announced their decision to reverse the decision about the design on their tailfins the day before Virgin unveiled their new livery incorporating the Union Flag.

3 *Change beliefs about what attributes are important in a sector*

It is also possible to introduce new attributes previously unused by any competitor or to switch emphasis to a new attribute. For example, most shampoo products stress health and beauty but Wash and Go introduced a practical attribute by incorporating a combined functional aspect of shampoo and conditioner so saving buyer's time.

This involves realigning the perception of particular attributes. For example Volvo had always been presented itself as being first and foremost the safest car. This appealed to a target segment for whom safety was a high ranking attribute. However, as more cars improved its safety attributes and Volvo were unable to use this as significant point of competitive advantage it began to focus on style and performance and so present attributes that were more readily accepted by other audiences and buyers.

Conclusion

Attitudes are derived from our belief system and are relatively stable in character. In that sense they are difficult to change but marketers need to be able to change attitudes as competitive conditions vary and technology develops. Attitudes can be formed as a result of buyer's perceptions of the strength and priority of a brand's attributes. Attitude formation is integral to positioning and is therefore of strategic importance to those managing the marketing communications process.

16 PERCEIVED RISK

> **Examiner's comments.** Candidates who knew about perceived risk and could then go on to explain how marketing communications reduced it did well. Few students knew a number of ways that risk could be reduced. This is an area that students should work on.

Introduction

Perception relates to how individuals *interpret* the stimuli they receive and how they *organise* the stimuli in order to make sense and understand the world. Of course, people sense and perceive stimuli in many different ways depending upon a number of criteria. For example, each person's experiences, culture, education, income and social and psychological make-up frame their perceptive abilities.

Perceived risk stems from perception and is associated with the risk an individual experiences when purchasing products and services. Six main types of risk have been identified as follows.

Perceived risks

> Performance
> Physical
> Financial
> Social
> Ego
> Time

The degree to which these *risks* impact on individuals varies through time, across product categories and by particular circumstances. Invariably, one or two of these risks dominate a single purchase decision with the other risks subsumed and/or under control. One of the tasks of marketing communications is to help reduce these dominant risks or lower them in such a way that they become manageable and do not threaten or deter a potential purchase.

For example, finance is very often a dominant risk with many expensive purchases, associated with high involvement purchase decisions. To overcome this type of risk, promotional messages might emphasise value for money, announce a Winter Sale, confer status, or suggest high quality or association with an aspirational group or lifestyle. Volkswagen are currently running a successful campaign that stresses the low (and less than expected) cost of the Polo.

Product performance risks can be countered with guarantees, money back, size, extended warrantees and associations with tradition, experience and in some cases craftsmanship. Tyre manufacturers have for a long time emphasised the construction of their tyres and their ability to stop a car on a 'euro'. Safety therefore, became a position adopted by many in the market, for example, Goodyear, which was endorsed by a police officer, and more currently Continental, braking on the flat roof of a building.

Fashion and clothing items often employ *social and ego risks* as the dominant factors. These are addressed by images and messages that either deflect attention to other attributes such as the material, the cut of the item, price, or attempt to appeal to an individual's perceived self image. A further approach is to suggest rewards such as admiring glances from significant others or association with an admired celebrity for example a sporting hero or pop star.

Branding is an important means by which perceived risk can be reduced across a number of areas. Used extensively in the consumer sector, branding enables customers to understand and recognise a product/organisation's values quickly and communicates an entire bundle of intangible benefits and satisfactions that appeal to prospective buyers. Consistency in communication is therefore important in order that these values be easily observed and maintained to facilitate easier shopping/buying experiences.

Source credibility is also an important means by which perceived risk can be minimised or managed. Enabling buyers to not only *recognise* a brand or source of a message is one thing but in order that they *believe* in the source there must be an element of *trust* and perceived *expertise* associated with the source of the message. Therefore, whether the message is transmitted through sales personnel, sales promotion devices, direct marketing or through advertising and public relations instruments it is the credibility attributed to the source that is of major importance.

Perceived risk is not only a factor in the consumer market but is present in the business-to-business sector as well. The use of more factual information and rational benefit appeals predominates, reflecting reduced emotional content and social and ego risks. Performance, financial and time risks tend to be more prevalent. These are addressed through warrantees, delivery promises and quality guarantees.

XYZ sell *cables and wires* to the telecommunication sector. Buyers undertake exhaustive research in order to specify the correct cable configuration and their decision making units apply rigorous criteria to ensure that product performance risk is minimised. XYZ use the cable specification information to communicate quality and to explicitly communicate professionalism and cable technology leadership. To do this, personal selling and sales literature combined with demonstrations and third party references constitute the main thrust of the marketing communication activities. Whilst parts of the consumer sector have recently started to lay greater emphasis on *customer retention* activities, the business-to-business sector has for a long time tried to build lasting *relationships* through courtesy, prompt attention and the reduction of performance risk through product quality.

The development of technology has assisted both sectors - consumers partly through the Internet and also through management of large amounts of information. The business-to-business sector has fostered the development of relationships through E-commerce, which also serves to reduce time risks.

Conclusion

There is no doubt that perceived risk is an active an important element in the decision making process of both individuals and organisations. Marketing communications can be used to reduce these risks and to stress other benefits associated with product purchase.

17 CLIENT NEEDS

> **Examiner's comments.** This was not a popular question. The answers produced were not detailed enough to score well. Agency's structures and their client relations are an important area in this syllabus.

Introduction

Advertising agencies have been subjected to a number of significant external pressures in the last ten to fifteen years. Their response to these pressures has been mixed and in many cases cautious, perhaps mindful of the need to monitor and avoid fashion swings and management fads.

Reasons for possible incompatibility

The reasons why some of these organisations have failed to keep pace with their clients' needs are as follows.

Answer bank

1. Hierarchical structures
2. Market complexity
3. Reliance on the commission payment scheme
4. Failure to implement integrated marketing communications
5. The plethora of new media and subsequent fragmentation
6. Audience fragmentation
7. The variable quality of overseas support
8. Poor positioning
9. Agency complacency

Many of these points are interrelated and the causality factor often hard to determine. Time does not permit a full examination of all these issues, so I shall select a few and consider some of the points in more detail.

The *structure* adopted by many advertising agencies is *hierarchical* and in many ways ill-suited to flexibility and the necessary speed of reaction required by many clients. These structures have strong historical roots, and in that sense are hard to change. International operations demand consideration and preferably experience of *cross cultural issues*, networking and, in many cases, *delegation* to country agencies, some of whom may require more support and guidance than others. Hierarchies require authority and control in order that they function appropriately. Such conditions may not always exist overseas, may be incompatible with client structures and may hinder the decision making process.

Developing international and global brands is a *complex activity* which requires special skills, from both a client and agency perspective. These may be hard to secure. When looked at in terms of the level of investment associated with international brand support, the issue becomes increasingly more complex and difficult.

Management consultancies have taken a lot of strategic work away from many advertising agencies. This has had a knock-on effect in terms of international brand support. Poor positioning therefore has been a contributory factor to this problem of incompatibility.

The plethora of *new media and subsequent fragmentation* of both audiences and media have proved problematic. Some traditional full service agencies have developed central media buying units in order to provide added value for clients but the issue of media planning and scheduling has become more complex. When an international dimension is superimposed, so the degree of complexity increases.

Complacency and a lack of drive to change is a contributory factor in many cases. A predilection to preserve the status quo regarding their relationships with clients suggests that some agencies lack strategic vision and may also not be fully aware of their *clients' goals*. The fault may, perhaps, lie with clients not communicating their marketing communication strategies effectively. Matters are certainly not helped by the willingness of many clients to change agencies mid term, or as a result of merger and acquisition activity.

How might agencies adjust?

There are therefore, many potential gaps between the expectation of clients and their respective agencies. One of the choices agencies need to make is whether to anticipate client needs internationally or whether to remain orientated to the domestic arena and make ad hoc arrangements to support any client who develops an overseas requirement.

How integrated does the agency need to be? Full integration for all agencies is obviously not practical, feasible or strategically viable. However, in terms of meeting client needs, restructuring and adaptation to the new environment with a view to establishing differing levels of integration, and in this case international support, may be useful. Gronstedt and Thorson (1996) suggest five different agency structures, ranging from the Consortium of agencies at one level through the Dominant Agency, the Corporation, the Matrix and the Integrated Organisation at the other level. These represent different means by which agencies might structure themselves in order that they might develop across international markets and meet the needs of their clients. It is interesting to note that at each end of this spectrum of integrated structures, the levels of integration and staff expertise are inversely related. The consortium allows for high levels of expertise but little integration whilst the integrated agency offers high levels of integration, obviously, but low levels of expertise. Agencies need to establish the right balance to suit their client needs.

At the heart of this problem about incompatibility there seem to lay three main issues. These are about Structure, Strategy and Relationships. Agencies and clients need direction and knowledge in order that they can manage these three variables and in doing so reduce or at least minimise any gap in expectations and support.

18 TUTORIAL QUESTION: AUDITING, SEGMENTATION AND POSITIONING

(a) A marketing audit might look for problems and unexpected opportunities in the following areas.

   (i) The *marketing environment*

      (1) What are the organisation's major markets, and what is the segmentation of these markets; what are the future prospects of each market segment?

      (2) Who are the customers, what is known about customer needs, intentions and behaviour?

      (3) Who are the competitors, and what is their standing in the market?

      (4) Have there been any significant developments in the broader environment (eg economic, or political changes, population or social changes etc)?

   (ii) *Marketing objectives, strategies and plans*

      (1) What are the organisation's marketing objectives and how do they relate to overall objectives? Are they reasonable?

      (2) Are enough (or too many) resources being committed to marketing to enable the objectives to be achieved; is the division of costs between products, areas etc satisfactory?

      (3) Is the share of expenditure between direct selling, advertising, distribution etc an optimal one?

      (4) What are the procedures for formulating marketing plans and management control of these plans; are they satisfactory?

      (5) Is the marketing organisation (and its personnel) operating efficiently?

   (iii) *Marketing activities: organisation, systems and productivity*

      (1) A review of sales price levels should be made (eg supply and demand, customer attitudes, the use of temporary price reductions etc).

      (2) A review of the state of each individual product (ie its market 'health') and of the product mix as a whole should be made.

      (3) A critical analysis of the distribution system should be made, with a view to finding improvements.

      (4) The size and organisation of the personal sales force should be studied, with a view to deciding whether efficiency should be improved (and how this could be done).

      (5) In the light of all of the above, a review of the effectiveness of *marketing communications* activities should be carried out.

Answer bank

(b) *Stages of segmentation*

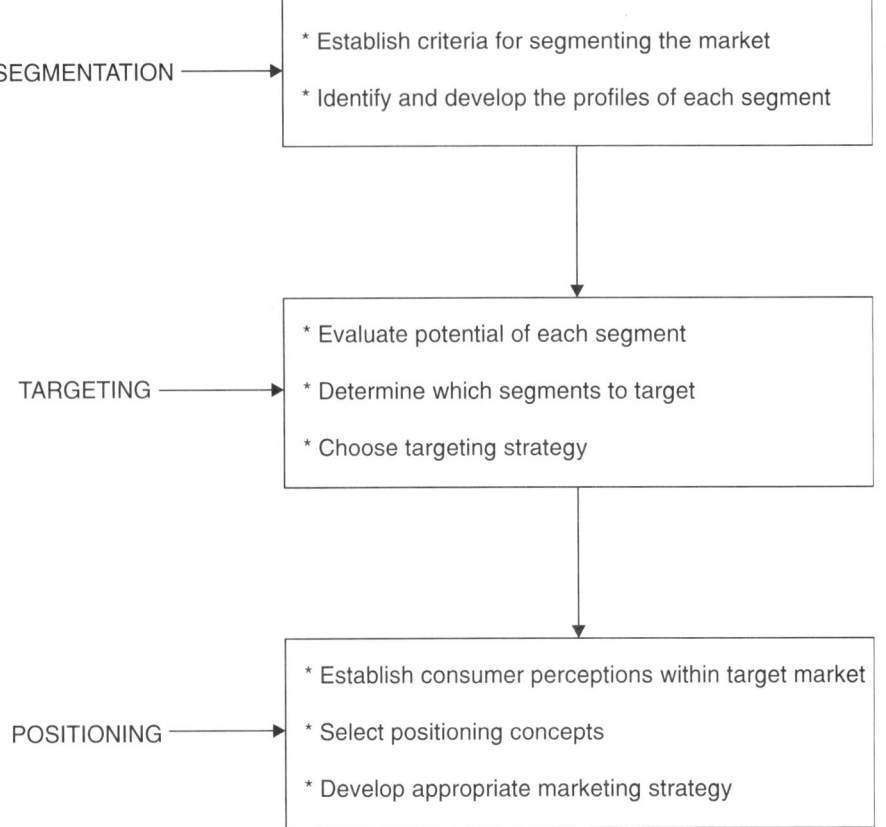

(c) There are a number of approaches to developing a positioning strategy. These include positioning by:

(i) Attribute
(ii) Price and quality
(iii) Use or application
(iv) Product user
(v) Product class
(vi) Competitor

Positioning by *attribute* involves positioning the product by clearly identifying it with a distinct set of attributes which distinguish the product within the market. BMW, the German car manufacturer, whilst positioned within the luxury end of the car market, make constant reference to the engine performance and design as part of their positioning statement. Likewise, Volvo the Swedish car manufacturer have for many years positioned themselves on safety features incorporated into the design of the car. Although most manufacturers have now adopted these techniques, a recent RAC survey (1994) found that 28% of the UK car buying public placed Volvo at the top of the league for safety.

Price and quality are becoming increasingly important as companies attempt to offer more features, better value and improved quality at competitive prices. J. Sainsbury the retail food multiple, promote themselves by stating that 'Good food costs less at Sainsbury's'.

In the third case, the company attempts to position their product or service by deliberately associating it with a specific *use or application*. Kellogg's, the cereal manufacturer, in striving to defend their market position and increase sales, have positioned their main product Corn Flakes as any time of day food, and not just to be eaten at breakfast.

Positioning by virtue of *product user* associates the product with a particular class of user. SmithKline Beecham have positioned 'Lucozade Sport' with the sporting fraternity, and have strengthened this through endorsement advertising using major sporting personalities. Leyland paints, a division of Kalon plc, advertise their paint products as 'The paints the professionals use'.

It is possible to position a company brand within a *product class* or an associated product class. Kraft foods, who produce 'Golden Crown', have positioned their product with respect to the associated product class, butter. Heinz, who produce a range of 'Weight Watcher' foods, position these against normal but more calorific foods.

A *competitor's position* within a market may be used as a frame of reference in order to create a distinct positioning statement. Avis car rental use the slogan 'We're number 2, so we try harder'. Here the market leader is being used as a reference point to create a competitive statement. The key determinant for the marketer is whether claims made within a promotional campaign which use blatant comparisons can be substantiated through better quality, service, value, cost and so on.

19 SEGMENTATION, TARGETING AND POSITIONING

> *Examiner's comments, summarised by BPP.* Segmentation, targeting and positioning are important concepts throughout the diploma syllabi and not just for marketing communications strategy. For this reason the question proved to be popular and was tackled in a reasonably competent manner as far as the segmentation element is concerned. Less well done was the effective choice of targets and too few students were able accurately to describe how to position an image in the minds of consumers. Two further key points. Firstly, this question called for a short report and an outline business report format should have been used. Secondly, examples of successful campaigns were required but not widely given.

REPORT

To: Managing Director
From: Marketing Communications Manager
Date: 11th June 1996
Ref: Segmentation, targeting and positioning in successful marketing communications strategies

1 Value of segmentation, targeting, positioning

The key to developing successful marketing communications strategies is to be able to carry out the process of segmentation, targeting and positioning. A knowledge of this process is, therefore, of value to any marketing communications manager. The process can be illustrated as follows.

Answer bank

MARKET SEGMENTATION	
1	Identif
2	Dev

⬇

MARKET TARGETING	
3	Devel
4	

⬇

MARKET POSITIONING	
5	Develo
6	Develop r
7	Develop pr

It can be seen from this process that we are concerned with the value of dividing up a mass market into identifiable segments in order to identify and influence the individual needs of consumers. Using segmentation these needs can be more easily identified and communication methods and messages can be developed which are effective and efficient. That is, the communication budget, which is inevitably limited, can be used economically and not wasted on segments of the market which are of less interest to our organisation.

2 **Bases of segmentation**

The first part of this process is that of segmenting the market. Here it is important to determine the bases for segmentation. In broad terms, markets can be segmented by means of the factors shown in the table below.

DEMOGRAPHIC	Age, Sex, Occupation
GEOGRAPHIC	Differing neighbourhoods and differing countries
GEODEMOGRAPHIC	Combining the most appropriate demographic/geographic factors
PSYCHOGRAPHIC	Personality, lifestyle

These factors apply to consumer market segments but in industrial markets more complex segmentation may be essential. This is not least the case because there are more complex decision-making processes with many people involved in the final buying decision.

The diagram on the next page shows how major bases for segmentation can be combined together in a way which can be described as 'nesting'. This entails starting with broadly observable or macro factors and progressing to more specific and subtle micro factors.

Answer bank

3 Targeting strategies

The next stage is to target specific segments using criteria which will enable us to choose the most fruitful segments.

Major bases for segmentation (nesting)

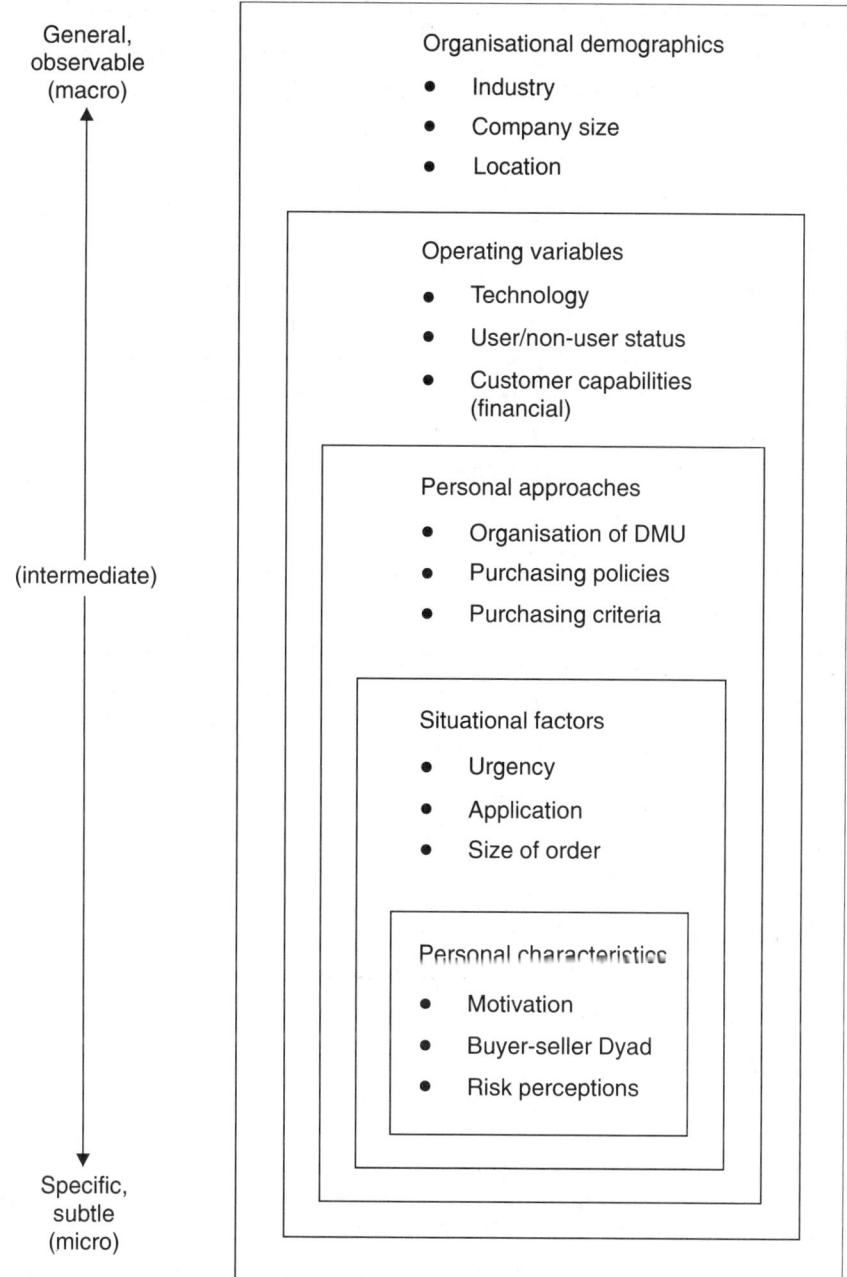

Requirements for effective segmentation

Answer bank

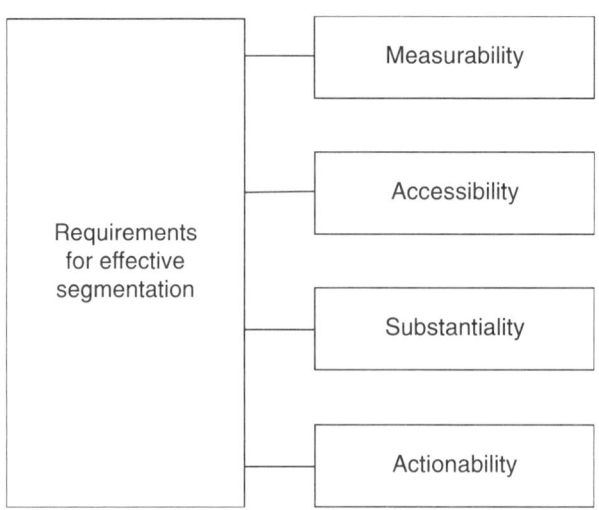

This diagram illustrates the point that the chosen segments must be easy to identify and measure. They must be capable of being reached with promotions programmes. They must be large enough to provide a stream of profits and, lastly, we must have the organisational capacity to reach the segment.

There are then three broad market coverage strategies that can be followed.

Market coverage strategies

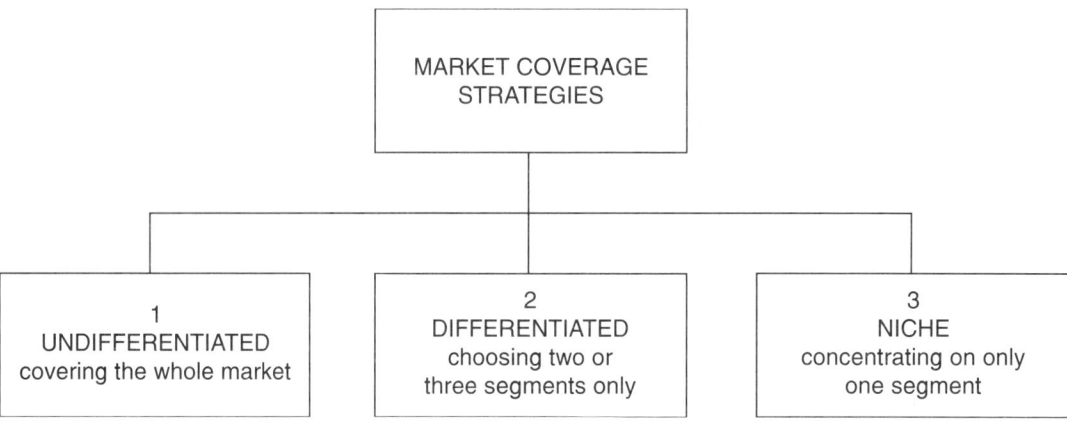

4 Positioning strategies

Positioning strategy follows on logically from targeting strategy. Positioning is the vital step of communicating the organisation's chosen marketing mix to the target customer. This communication should be executed so that the product or service occupies a particular position in the mind of the consumer. Successful positioning can be achieved by adopting a customer perspective and by understanding how customers really do perceive particular attributes. The process of sustaining a successful positioning is the concern of brand managers.

A brand can be defined as a name, symbol, design or combination of these, which identifies and positions the product or service as having a sustainable differential advantage.

Positioning then is the act of communicating information about an organisation's offer and image so that the target market understands the organisation and its image relative to its competitors. Positioning has developed in importance because of increasing competition and the increasing sophistication of consumers. With the speed of communication and advancing technology customers are able to perceive the similarities of physical form and function of competitive products. Therefore, it is important to position organisations as brands in the minds of customers.

All products and organisations have a position. It can be accidentally actioned or deliberately chosen. Positioning should be the natural conclusion to the sequence of activities including segmentation and targeting.

Positioning Approaches

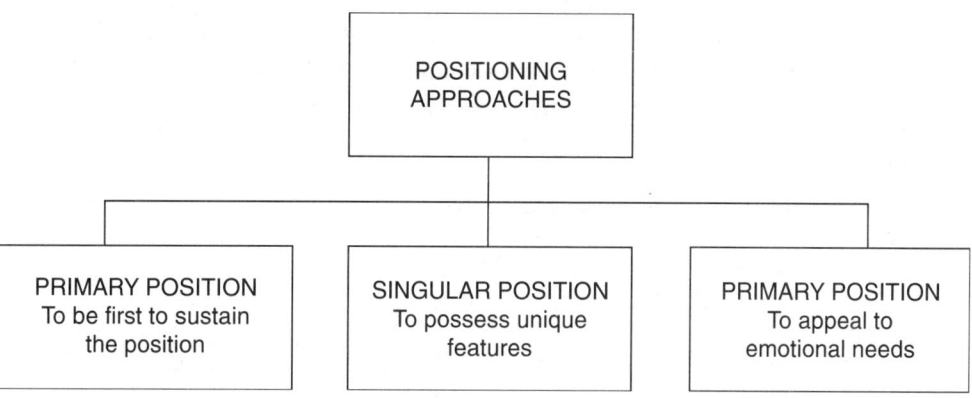

Positioning Strategies

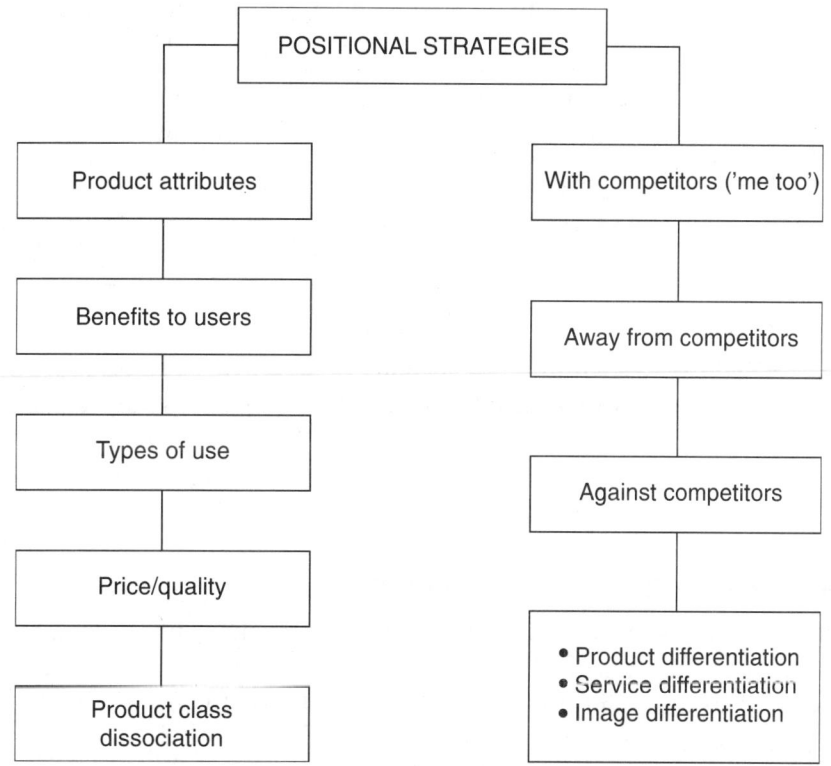

5 Successful campaign - Boddingtons Beer

Boddingtons was a traditional regional brewer whose products were restricted to the North West of England until 1989 when they were bought by Whitbreads. There followed a highly successful national campaign devised by Bartle, Bogle and Hegarty which was a winner of a Gold Award in the 1994 IPA Advertising Effectiveness Awards.

Answer bank

1 *Initial image*

Boddingtons bitter beer was a cask conditioned beer with a strong regional heritage and a loyal local following. Its distribution was limited mainly to the North West, ie largely to the Granada regional TV area.

2 *Corporate objective*

Whitbreads set themselves the following objectives.

'To grow Boddingtons Bitter into a national brand'
'At the same time to protect the volume of the brand in the North West'
'To launch canned Boddingtons nationally'

3 *Targeting*

There were two main targets.

- Heartland drinkers in the North West
- New drinkers in the rest of the country

Initially, the most discerning and most difficult to impress bitter drinkers were targeted.

4 *Positioning*

There was a need to position Boddingtons in the minds of discerning bitter drinkers before moving to a wider audience. Gaining credentials could not be rushed. Positioning concentrated on the brand's 'truths'.

- Product truths of being a creamy, clear, golden coloured, refreshing drink
- Image truth of Mancunian character, solid, straight talking

The positioning statement chosen was:

> 'BODDINGTONS THE CREAM OF MANCHESTER'

5 *Implementation*

A tightly targeted press campaign was mounted with the single minded use of the outside back covers of magazines. Television was only added after two years and originally only on Channel 4. Overall the brand has grown 300% in volume and is now the UK's fourth largest bitter brand with brand leadership in the canned bitter segment.

6 Successful campaign - British Airways

British Airways has been successfully repositioned by a long-term marketing communications strategy planned and executed by its advertising agency, Saatchi and Saatchi. The campaign was a winner of a Gold award in the 1994 IPA Advertising Effectiveness Awards.

1 *Initial image:*

In 1982 British Airways was running at a loss and was seen as the least attractive investment of all privatisation targets.

Staff were demoralised and demotivated. This led to a lack of efficiency and progress.

Consumers viewed British Airways as a shambling bureaucracy, as Anglo-centric, not international.

2   *Corporate mission:*

The airline set itself the mission:

'to become the best and most successful international airline in the world'.

3   *Targeting:*

British Airways aimed to attract more customers but particularly it aimed to attract customers willing to pay a higher price.

4   *Positioning:*

British Airways aimed to position itself as offering value/desirability by:

- making a virtue out of size
- giving it a sense of prestige and status
- showing it understood and cared for customers

The positioning statement chosen was:

> 'THE WORLD'S FAVOURITE AIRLINE'

5   *Implementation*

A totally integrated campaign was planned and consistently carried out over a ten year period. This includes 'master-brand' television advertising to present the global face of British Airways and claim the high ground. Sub-brand advertising (Club World, Club Europe) communicated more specific benefits for individual customers.

20 TOOTHPASTE POSITIONING

> *Examiner's comments.* Positioning is an important strategic element of a communication programme. More questions about positioning should be expected. This answer represents a preferred style, theory/knowledge then application.

To: Managing Director, Gamble and Lever Co
From: CIM Student, Brand Manager: Smile
Date: 8 June 1999
Subject: Positioning of a new brand's toothpaste

1   *Introduction*

Gamble and Lever have decided to launch a new toothpaste into the UK market. Part of the brand strategy is to establish a position in the market so that customers understand clearly what Smile is, particularly against competitive brands.

2   *Positioning*

Positioning is about designing products and presenting them to customers in such a way that they are meaningful and are perceived to be competitively distinct in customers' minds. Positioning is about how a customer perceives one product relative to another.

Positioning is not about the physical, tangible aspects of a product, it is about what a customer thinks about the tangible and intangible elements of a product regardless of whether they are correct. To successfully position a brand it is important to understand the market place, the competitive products and the customer perceptions and needs.

Answer bank

In particular, it is important to understand the current positions occupied by competitors. Perceptual maps are a useful means of determining the way customers perceive players and the attributes that are regarded as important.

The perceptual map can be developed into a preference map in which brands are mapped and the customers' ideal brand is located and positioned on the grid. It is then possible to determine gaps in the market where a new brand could be positioned and strategies developed in order to present the brand such that it closely resembles the Ideal brand.

3   *Positioning strategies*

In order to present products and services in a meaningful way it is important to adopt a clear approach and then develop a strategy. There are three approaches that might be considered.

- Market-related - being first to claim a particular position a market, such as Heineken being first to claim the refreshment benefit.

- Customer-related - the adoption of a unique buying reason such as Fairy Liquid's claim to clean 50% more dishes or British Airways claim to be the World's Favourite Airline.

- Appeal-related - providing a distinct personality such as Pepperami's 'bit of an animal'.

From a strategic point of view there are a number of strategies available. The more popular are:

- Product features - the safety of a Volvo, the vitamins in Weetabix.

- Price/quality - high price/high quality relationship as demonstrated by Aspreys.

- Use - After Eight mints are to be consumed only at a particular time

- User - Flora - for all the family, Sunny Delight for Kids, L'Oreal because your worth it

- Competitor - Diner's Card and American Express tried to substantiate claims that one was better than another.

- Benefit - Buy a TV licence and avoid paying a £400 fine.

The question therefore is that if positioning is so important which strategy is going to best serve Smile toothpaste? By applying each of the strategies to Smile it may be possible to determine which might be the most suitable.

Product features -	Smile the mint flavoured toothpaste for fresh breath or Smile contains an anti-bacterial ingredient
Price/quality -	Gold-Star Smile
User -	Smile for Kids
Competitor -	a lot cleaner and more refreshing
Benefit -	Smile means fewer fillings and treatment.

Once a positioning goal has been agreed it will be important to ensure that all brand cues support the position. For example when Häagan Dazs launched in the UK the high quality position was reinforced through the packaging, the price, the outlets, the advertising (creative and media) and the even the typescript and tone of voice that was adopted. This integrated approach is absolutely necessary if the positioning strategy is to be conveyed consistently and reinforced at all points where a customer interacts with the brand.

There may be occasions when Smile will need to be repositioned. For example, it may be that social values about oral hygiene have developed or new brands or technology make the current position redundant. Whatever the reason, brand management must ensure that they review a brands position on a regular basis.

Conclusion

If Gamble and Lever have selected a segment of the market, targeted accurately and chosen a suitable positioning strategy then this will considerably improve the chances of the brand's success. Integrated marketing communications will be needed to establish and maintain the position in order that customers can build beliefs about a brand and continue to understand and hopefully keep using it.

21 PROMOTIONAL MIX

'The Strategic Significance of the Promotional Mix'

by

CIM Student

December 1998

Slide 1 - Introduction and Welcome

Good evening ladies and gentlemen, my name is Sam Smithers from Grubb, Allen and Pollen. May I take this opportunity to thank you for inviting me to talk to you about marketing communications and in particular the strategic impact of the various elements of the promotional mix.

Slide 2 - Agenda

As you can see, my plan for this session is to first consider the elements of the promotional mix before examining the strategic significance and benefits of an integrated approach to marketing communications practice.

The promotional plan
Strategic significance
Integration
Benefits and difficulties
Conclusions
Question time

I shall be using a few examples to illustrate my points and, of course, I welcome questions at any time, although there will be some time at the end to discuss points of interest. I shall aim to finish at 2045hrs.

Slide 3 - The Promotional Mix

Marketing communications is just a part of the total marketing plan or marketing mix. Indeed the two elements are often confused but in order for clarity the marketing mix is composed of a number of different elements such as price, product, distribution, people and promotional activities. It is these elements in combination that provide the overall marketing plan.

One of these elements, promotion, provides a powerful means by which a marketing mix is presented to its target audience. The successful communication of the marketing mix is paramount if target markets are to understand the offer being made to them.

Answer bank

In order to affect this communication there are a number of promotional tools that are used or 'mixed' together. These are:

advertising, sales promotion, public relations,
personal selling and direct marketing.

These are the tools of the promotional mix.

By mixing the tools together in different ways to meet the needs of the marketing plan, it is possible to achieve one of a number of goals. These are to:

Create awareness
To persuade
To remind/reassure
To differentiate

The first of these is to make an audience aware of an offering, existence or benefits. Before anyone can form an opinion or attitude, it is necessary to be informed of a product's existence.

Alternatively, awareness levels may be adequate so the task may be to persuade an audience to try a product or resist defecting to a competitive product offering.

A third requirement may be to remind and/or reassure an audience of a product or of the experiences associated with a previous purchase.

Finally, communications can be used to differentiate a product offering, to set it aside from the competition.

Slide 4 - Strategic Significance

The word strategy is often used to mean different things to different people. To me, strategy is not about planning or the development of plans. Plans are the articulation of strategy, a means of bringing together the various means by which a strategy is implemented and goals achieved.

Promotional strategy is about the overall direction and focus of communications. There are three main options: a pull strategy, a push strategy and a profile strategy.

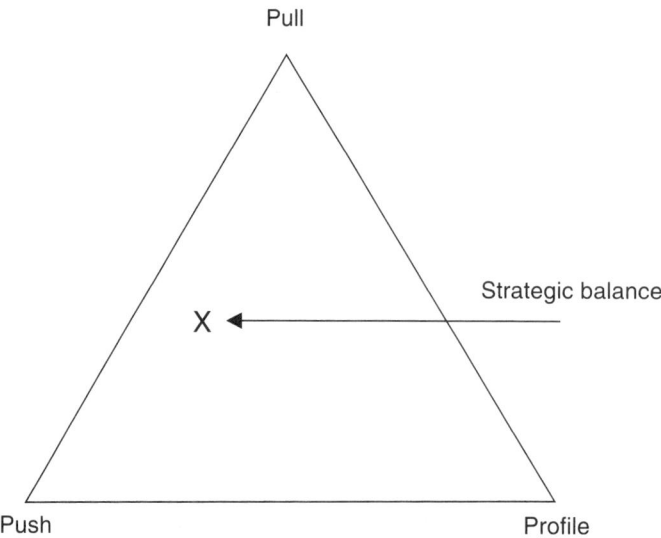

A pull strategy is concerned with communications directed at end users or customers. A push strategy concerns those channel partnerships formed to deliver products and services to end users, commonly referred to as the trade or distributors. A profile strategy concerns the way an organisation is presented to a range of stakeholder audiences and is essentially about corporate image and reputation management.

These three strategies are not used independently of each other, indeed it is important to appreciate that these 3Ps need to work together, and management need to make a judgement about the appropriate balance. As we can see from the diagram, the strategic triangle requires the three approaches to be combined, integrated in such a way that the overall goals will be achieved.

Please remember that this balance need not be static, but must be expected to shift as the context within which each communication campaign changes and evolves, as the environment inside and outside an organisation reshapes itself.

Slide 5 - Integration

Much time and consideration has been given by academics and practitioners to the concept of integrated marketing communications (IMC). Whilst time does not allow me to go into full detail about IMC tonight, may I just say that if IMC is to be achieved then understanding and setting the strategic balance of an organisation's communications is very important.

For successful implementation of each of the 3Ps it is necessary to utilise a different promotional mix. The tools have different properties and enable different goals to be achieved. For example, when launching a new consumer product such as Sunny Delight, it is first necessary to create distribution (push) through the major grocery multiples. This involves personal selling and direct marketing. Once distribution is secured awareness needs to be established in the target audience. This strategy (pull) requires the use of mass communications (in this example) which involves the use of television, poster and print advertising. This can be supported with public relations activities designed to create credible third party comment, and endorsement, about the brand.

Procter and Gamble do not use a profile strategy to any greater degree partly because of their multi-brand policy. However, other companies, such as the AA or British Airways focus a great deal of their communications on raising and sustaining their corporate brands. The corporate brand can act as an umbrella under which product brands can be infused with the corporate ideal and values, saving investment and human resources.

Slide 6 - Benefits and Difficulties

The promotional mix should be integrated if the same consistent message is to be conveyed to each of the various audiences a brand and its parent organisation interacts. By adopting a strategic approach promotional activities can be targeted, streamlined, made efficient and effective.

If the goal is to differentiate through positioning then by using the different tools of the promotional mix and by delivering clear messages positioning can be used as a form of sustainable competitive advantage and thus be difficult for a competitor to replicate.

Communications used by Procter and Gamble enabled Sunny Delight to be positioned as a distinct new refreshing drink for kids. The communications also informed people where to find it in supermarkets (chiller cabinets) and where it should be stored at home (in refrigerators).

A strategic approach can be difficult to establish, particularly when management have little experience of using communications in this way. The structure and form of many communications agencies do not actively encourage a strategic approach to the use of the promotional mix although I am pleased to observe that there does appear to be movement towards a recognition of IMC and the benefits it can bring clients and agencies.

Answer bank

Slide 7 - Conclusions

The promotional mix consists of different tools which are each capable of undertaking different tasks. By setting a communication strategy and then by using the right mix of tools in the right way, it is possible to create awareness, persuade, remind/reassure and differentiate a product brand or a corporate brand.

Slide 8 - Question Time

Thank you for listening to me tonight, have you any questions?

22 PROMOTIONAL MIX AND BRANDING

(a) The nature of these differences and the impact they each might have on an organisation's integrated marketing communication activities.

To: The CIM Senior Examiner

From: A CIM Student

Date: December 1998

Ref: Promotional Mixes

1.0 Introduction

1.1 This brief report seeks to outline some of the differences between the promotional mixes used in consumer and business-to-business markets.

The promotional mixes developed for these two types of audiences have to be different for a number of reasons. Because of time restrictions I have used three here but there are many others.

2.0 Differences

2.1 Number of decision maker: In consumer markets the number of decision makers is limited to a single or perhaps a couple of people. In business markets (btob) there may be many members of the DMU. Therefore, the promotional mix needs to convey a simple consistent message in consumer markets but in btob markets different messages need to be conveyed to a variety of different people in the DMU. This will put pressure on IMCs to ensure that the variety of messages is correct, that they are being conveyed effectively and that the communication budget is appropriate.

2.2 Message content: Messages in consumer markets are (generally) based more on emotion and imagery rather than rational product benefits used in the btob market. This impacts on the media selected and the way messages are presented.

2.3 Balance of the mix: In view of the above it is not unsurprising that the advertising and sales promotions tend to dominate the mix in consumer markets. In btob personal selling has greater share. Recently however, it can be seen that there is a move from above to below the line work in consumer markets. This is because markets and media are more fragmented and that there are more possibly effective and efficient means of reaching consumers than through the use of mass media. The impact on IMC is huge as it means that customers are coming into contact with the brand in a variety of ways which puts pressure on clients to be consistent with the messages they communicate.

Direct marketing has had a tremendous impact on both markets with particular emphasis on the btob market. Direct marketing, in its various guises, enables organisations to communicate more effectively, frequently and more cost efficiently with their business end users and so reduces the cost of the sales force and enables them to focus the efforts of the specialist sales force more effectively.

Answer bank

For a long time the btob markets have practised the use of integrative approaches to communication. Only recently have those operating in consumer markets started to pay concerted attention to developing IMC.

(b)

3.0 Consumer markets

3.1 The mix used to reach consumer markets will continue to evolve away from a reliance on the use of mass media. With rapid technological developments, and in particular, Internet and digital related technologies, clients operating in consumer markets will look to change the pattern of the communications by incorporating a greater proportion of eCommerce related communications (and distribution patterns). Direct marketing will establish a correspondingly important part of the mix. For example, Amazon books have invested in eCommerce as their total communication and distribution platform and established a large share of the retail book market. Other companies have decided to balance their high street retail presence with Web Site approaches. Chains such as Arcadia and Dixons (Freeserve) have adopted this approach very profitably.

3.2 Business to Business Markets

In the btob markets direct marketing and eCommerce are set to become an even more important part of the promotional mix. The drive for more efficient communications and to be able to account for communication budgets and investments means that the UK can be expected to follow the huge growth in eCommerce established in North America.

3.3 The emphasis on personal selling will not disappear but there will be greater use of direct marketing and eCommerce to complement the promotional activities. For example, IBM have developed their strategy around eBusiness and have been enormously successful as a result. If this is compared with the performance of Compaq Computers who have continued to operate through value added resellers, and all things being equal, technologically related communications appear to be well placed.

4.0 Conclusion

4.1 It seems as if the development of the promotional mixes in both markets will be influenced by technology. The death of mass media communications in the consumer market has long been predicted by a few commentators but in my opinion this is unlikely. New methods will be used to supplement, not replace current methods. New brands in both markets will arise to take advantage of the Internet whilst established brands and products will seek to incorporate and integrate a greater proportion of eCommerce activities as part of a portfolio of communication methods.

4.2 More personalised and integrated communications and associated messages will be adopted by consumer markets. In business to business markets a greater use of emotion and imagery can be expected along with the development of brands (such as Intel) and a more flexible promotional mix where the field sales force does not play such a dominant role.

Answer bank

23 PLAN LINKS

> *Examiner's comment.* This question required a clear answer, which element is the most important. It was not important that students select a particular element, just that they selected one and justified their selection.
>
> Many students chose to select 'integration' which although important is not an element of the plan as previously established.

To: Ms Alice Davis: Manager
From: CIM Student: Marketing Manager
Ref: How parts of a marketing communications plan are linked together.

Further to your request to know more about the linkages within marketing communication plans I have set out what the parts of a marketing communication plan are, and then indicated some of the main linkages. In the second part I argue that we should particular importance to the context analysis as the most important part of the plan.

(a) A marketing communication plan is a sub plan of the marketing plan which in turn feeds the business plan. In other words, these plans are all related to each other and in order to improve the chances of business success these plans must be integrated.

Marketing communications planning framework

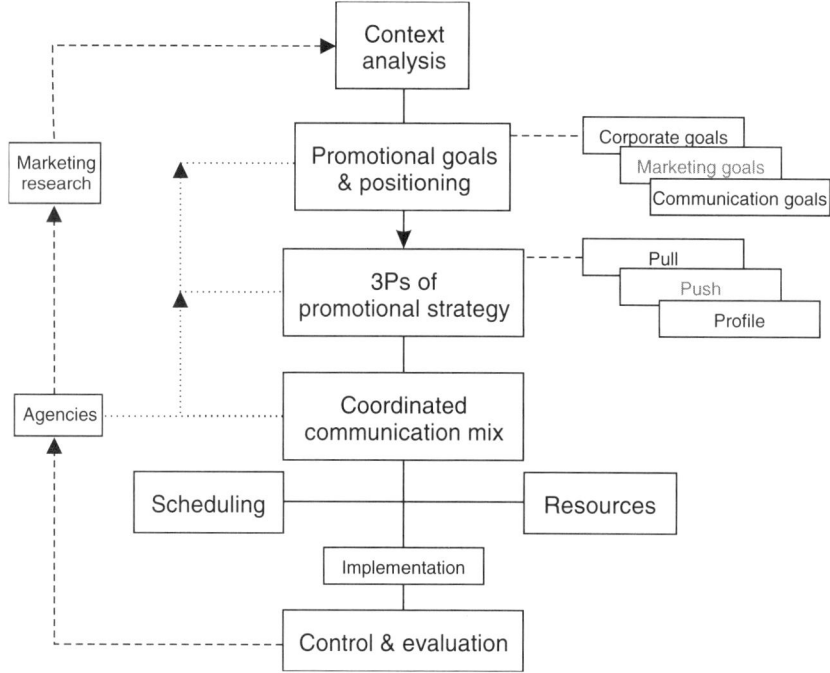

The elements of a marketing communication plan are set out in the following diagram. Whilst the plan may appear to be linear in format, in actual practice many of the elements are actioned in parallel rather than sequentially. In some case parts of these plans are formulated in the minds of those responsible whereas in many large organisations these plans are a formalised articulation of an agreed course of action. Marketing communications can consume large financial and time resources so it is absolutely important that the plans are correct and satisfy the objectives set out.

We know that individually these elements are rather meaningless, it is only by binding them together as a system of inter-related parts do we know that the elements work together and the plans actually work.

At the hub of these plans is a Context Analysis. I shall explain the working in more detail later, but by understanding the situation in which the communication campaign needs to work, for example is it a new or established product, what is the nature of the

Answer bank

target audience, is the market growing or declining etc, is it possible to design a plan that will work. The original communication theory stated that in order to be successful it was important for the source of a message to be able to understand and define the problem accurately in order that they formulate a message using symbols and expressions that could be decoded and understood by the target audience. Well, this principle is still important here, we must understand the problem and then feed the other elements of the plan.

Linkages

In the following table I set out some of the main linkages.

Table 1

Objectives	From the marketing plan, from the customer, stakeholder and competitor analysis
Strategic balance	From an understanding of the brand, the needs of the target audiences and relevant stakeholders
Brand positioning	From perceptions, motivations, attitudes or own brand and those of competitors
Message content/style	Involvement, risk, DMU analysis, processing styles and positioning intentions
Promotional tools and media	Target audience media habits, involvement, preferences and resource analysis.

The marketing plan provides the marketing and corporate objectives. The marketing plan also indicates the positioning intentions.

By understanding the target audience the communication objectives can be derived, positioning confirmed and the overall approach for the creative brief and media plan determined.

By understanding the needs of the different stakeholders it is possible to determine the right balance for the strategic direction. Developments in the external environment can influence the goals, the positioning and the message and media formats. Even the level of financial resources can be affected by swings in economic or political conditions.

The goals themselves determine the positioning, the strategy and the promotional mix plus the budget. It could also be argued that the schedule of activities is also influenced by the goals and the timescale within which the promotional goals are to be accomplished. Additionally, the promotional mix determines the financial resources to be allocated and the shape and pattern of the overall campaign.

The control and evaluation stage is important to ensure that the campaign itself stays on course and in that sense helps bind the plan together. The role of the various agencies engaged in the campaign can also be influential and help ensure all aspects are considered on a pre and post campaign basis.

(b) The most important element of the plan is the contextual analysis. In order to analyse situations in a systematic way it is helpful to consider five main areas: business context, customer context, stakeholder context, external context, organisational context.

Review of the *business context* serves to integrate the marketing plan, understand the market and competitor conditions and develop the segmentation analysis in order that a viable positioning strategy might develop.

Understanding the *customer context* is vital. What are the buying characteristics of the target market, when, how and why do they buy? This information can be used to feed

Answer bank

the promotional goals, the positioning intentions, the balance of the strategy and the promotional mix and resource requirements.

The *stakeholder context* is important as it extends our view of marketing communications to suppliers and distributors in the marketing channel. It also opens up the wider non-buying audiences and suggests we should consider the corporate image held of our organisation.

Changes in the external environment may influence the tone of the message. For example Levis sensed a social move to be 'friendly' amongst the younger generation. As a result the Sta Pres campaign featured a puppet character referred to as Flat Eric, companion for the human central character.

Finally, the organisation itself can have a huge influence on a campaign. The Procter and Gamble traditional hierarchical 'safe' approach has led to product features being the mainstay of their advertising. Unilever however have a more structure which is reflected in their more emotional advertising messages. The organisation will determine the general amount of financial resources to be allocated and will also influence to what degree employees are to be integrated within the marketing communication activities. Internal marketing communications can be a considerable influence as it is at the staff/customer interface that brand values can really be communicated.

Conclusion

All aspects of the marketing communication plan are interlinked. Through interlinking integration can develop which can lead to more effective marketing communications. The most important element to consider is the Context Analysis which if not accurate, can affect the success of the rest of the plan.

24 ANALYSING THE CURRENT SITUATION

> *Examiner's comment.* The origins of this question lay with the perpetually poor situation analysis that students present as part of their communication plan in Section A over the past few years. It seems that SWOT, PEST and over frameworks are regarded as appropriate. They are not, simply because in most cases they are devoid of any communication content.

Any plans needs grounding in a thorough understanding and analysis of the current situation. The role of this exercise is therefore to prepare the ground for an integrated communications activity.

The most common term used to refer to this exercise is *situation analysis*. A more recent term is *context analysis* as it attempts to relate to the communication related aspects associated with the plan. One of the problems experienced by many practitioners and students is the difficulties associated with keeping the analysis focused on communication issues. Agencies have a briefing system that enables the focus to remain on each main task: *Agency Brief*, *Creative Brief* and *Media Brief*. These are an inherent part of the overall system even though there are slight variations in the way individual agencies administer them. However, in order that agencies and other members of the client organisation own and share the communication plan, a structured approach which is rooted in the underlying and particular context facing the client is important.

Answer bank

Components of the Context Analysis

1 **Business context**

   Corporate and marketing strategy and plans
   Brand/organisation analysis
   Competitor analysis

2 **Customer context**

   Segment characteristics
   Levels of awareness, perception and attitudes towards the brand/organisation
   Level of involvement, types of perceived risk
   DMU characteristics and issues

3 **Stakeholder context**

   Who are the key stakeholders and why are they important?
   What are their communication needs?

4 **Organisational Context**

   Financial constraints
   Organisation identity,
   Culture, values and beliefs
   Marketing expertise
   Agency suitability

5 **Environmental context**

   Social, Political, Economic and Technological constraints and opportunities

(a) *Business context.* It is necessary to specify the business goals, marketing objectives and strategy (including segmentation analysis) and the competitive conditions which the product/service is either currently or very likely to experience. Much of this information has already been prepared (or should have) as part of the Marketing Plan. Therefore all that is necessary is to extract the relevant parts from the Marketing plan and insert into the Promotional plan.

(b) *Customer context.* It is necessary in order to probe deeper into the motivations, attitudes, perceptions and overall knowledge of the target group. In addition it also necessary to consider the trade buyers in the marketing channel and fully appreciate their communication needs and motivations.

(c) *Stakeholder context.* It is here that the wider array of influencers is brought into the analysis. Investors may need particular information. A particular group of suppliers must be informed of changes in the corporate strategy that may impact on the level, type or speed of business that they currently provide.

(d) *Organisational context.* The workforce can have an important and significant impact on the success of the organisation. A review of the current communication policies and facilities, training and level of customer orientation can be invaluable. To judge the importance of this element, reference need only be made to Marks & Spencer, TNT Overnight or the efforts of British Airways to provide the very highest levels of customer service. Also, it is important at this stage to consider the financial constraints that are likely to impact on the implementation of the promotional plan. A large budget may mean that television advertising is possible; a small budget will rule this form of media out of the question.

(e) *Environmental context.* Consideration must be given to the wider social, political/legal, technological and economic factors that impact not just on the organisation but on the

Answer bank

whole market or context in which the plan is being prepared. Kellogg's have embarked upon a new pull strategy that reflects not only the founder's original philosophy but also a new awareness people have for their own health and welfare. 'Serving the Nation's Health' is a campaign that draws on different aspects of health, for example, weight, mental health and diet and is a core part of the overall communication strategy.

The question however, requires a view of how these contextual elements influence the subsequent parts of the marketing communications plan. The answer can be seen partly in table 1.

Table 1: Linkages within the Marketing Communication Planning Framework

Objectives	Derived from: • the marketing plan (including the competitor analysis) in the business context • the business context • the customer context • the stakeholder context • the internal context
Strategic balance (3Ps)	From an understanding of the brand, the needs of the target audiences (including employees and other stakeholders) and the marketing goals.
Brand/Product positioning	From the perception, attitudes and motivations of users and non-users
Message content and style	From an understanding of the level of involvement, perceived risk, DMU analysis, information processing styles and positioning intentions
Promotional tools and media	From an analysis of the target audience and their media habits, involvements and preferences, media compatibility, competitor analysis and resource review

The *linkages* between the various parts of the context analysis and the other parts of the plan provide the integrity and substance to an effective plan. For example, the marketing plan drawn into the Business Context provides the Marketing Objectives whilst the Marketing Communication Objectives are taken from the Customer and Stakeholder Contexts. The question about whether to increase levels of awareness, change attitudes or alter the way a brand is perceived (positioned) can only be derived by understanding the current customer and business contexts. A new brand will require *awareness* to be driven first, whereas if a gap is uncovered between what customers perceive about a product and what it can actually do then *knowledge and education* becomes a prime communication consideration.

The balance of the overall communications strategy, between push, pull and profile, is determined not only by management judgement but information extracted from the contextual analysis and the business, customer and stakeholder contexts in particular.

The *messages* that are to be conveyed need to be rooted in an understanding of the *goals*, the *segment characteristics* and the *motivations* and current attitudes of the customers. Choosing the right media is made easier if the levels of involvement, risk and reading/viewing habits are understood. For example, understanding the newspapers and television habits that the target audience have will influence the media buying and the overall media profile.

The budget and financial resources are obviously derived from an appreciation of the initial analysis within the *organisation contextual* review. Having previously determined that a certain level of resources will be made available allows for the development of suitable plan and minimises the need to redesign a programme simply because money is not available.

The final issue is the need to develop synergies and to develop an integrated marketing communication plan. Consideration of the internal communication needs to ensure that all aspects of the plan are co-ordinated, harmonised and understood by everyone concerned adds further emphasis to the need to undertake a thorough context analysis.

25 MARKETING COMMUNICATIONS OBJECTIVES

> *Tutorial note.* Note that the senior examiner uses a sort of report style even though the question does not explicitly ask you to do so. This helps to give the answer a structure. The use of diagrams and bullet points is also encouraged.
>
> *Examiner's comments, summarised by BPP.* Students were expected to answer this question in two ways. Firstly by accurately demonstrating the relationship between objectives, strategies and tactics in terms of a communications plan. Secondly by showing, with specific examples, how to apply the process to their own organisation or an organisation of their choice. Many students were able to carry out the former task but few students carried the process through with carefully chosen examples. This was clearly a question where the use of diagrams and bullet points would give the examiner a good feel for students' knowledge.

REPORT

To: Managing Director
From: Marketing Manager
Date: June 1995
Ref: Developing marketing communications objectives from the organisation's mission

1 Introduction

A key to successful, marketing communication strategy is a complete integrated programme. It is necessary for every element of the programme to contribute in a consistent and synergistic manner. This has the benefits of:

(a) Being highly effective
(b) Being cost efficient
(c) Reinforcing messages to consumers

In this report we show how a hierarchy of objectives may be developed from an organisation's mission statement. The relationship of objectives, strategies and tactics is also discussed.

To demonstrate these principles in practice examples are taken from the launch of a new lager, Carling Premier Lager, by the Carling Brewing Company. Carling is part of Bass plc one of the largest brewery companies in Britain.

> *Tutorial note.* Students will, of course, choose examples from organisations with which they are familiar.

2 Development of objectives

An organisation's mission statement is a description of long-term vision and values. Mission statements have become increasingly common because they provide clear guidance to managers and employees on the future direction of the organisation.

Answer bank

In particular the mission statement can be used to develop a hierarchy of objectives which link the long-term vision and values with specific objectives at each level of the organisation.

The linkage between the mission and *marketing communication* objectives in particular can be seen from the following diagram.

3 Example of Carling Premier Lager

Carling Brewing Company is a subsidiary of Bass plc which is a large leisure and brewing company. Carling is best known for its major product, Carling Black Label, which is Britain's best-selling lager brand. It achieves sales of over 2.5 million barrels per year, nearly 70% more than its nearest rival.

Carling Black Label sales are estimated at £900 million per year, supported by a marketing investment of over £20 million. Carling has undertaken a high profile sponsorship of the Football Association's Premier League. Carling has had a consistent high impact advertising campaign using the theme 'I bet he drinks Carling Black Label'.

In 1995 Carling launched a premium lager called Carling Premier to compete in the growing premium lager sector. The market for standard lager is declining at the rate of about 5% per annum whereas premium lagers are growing at a rate of 5%.

Having given this description it is now possible to show how the marketing communications objectives for Carling Premier Lager can be developed from the business mission of Bass plc.

Bass plc mission

We shall assume that the Bass mission is as follows.

To be the leading provider of leisure and hospitality products and services and to achieve benefits for all Bass stakeholders including:

(a) Shareholders
(b) Customers
(c) Employees
(d) Suppliers
(e) The communities which Bass serves

Carling's business objectives

We shall assume that Carling's business objectives are as follows.

(a) To be the UK's leading lager provider
(b) To earn targeted profits for Bass plc.
(c) To develop new products to meet consumers' needs.

These objectives can be seen to relate to the mission of the Bass Group. Whereas Bass is concerned with the complete leisure field, Carling is concerned with one business sector, lager.

It should be noted that in reality these business objectives will be carefully quantified and will then be used within the company's management control system.

Marketing objectives

Having monitored the decline in standard lager sales and the growth in premium lager sales Carling saw an opportunity for a new Carling premium lager to exploit the brand values and high recognition of Carling. Carling therefore set three marketing objectives.

(a) To enter the growing premium lager sector with an innovative and original product.

(b) To bring new premium values to the lager market. (Carling Premier combines cool refreshment with unique smoothness).

(c) To help the Carling brand access key new drinkers, outlets and occasions.

Marketing communication objectives

We are now in a position to state the key communication objectives which have derived directly from the mission of the parent company Bass plc.

(a) To position Carling Premier as a completely new type of 'smooth chill', premium draught lager with a unique look feel and flavour.

    (i) Less gassy, smoother and easy to drink
    (ii) Never loses its creamy head
    (iii) Served at a special low temperature

(b) To target key customers with certain characteristics.

    (i) Aged 18-34, predominantly male, BC_1C_2 social class
    (ii) Individuals who are cool and stand out in a crowd
    (iii) People who already drink premium lagers and ales

(c) To target key outlets and occasions.

    (i) Special occasions, group drinking
    (ii) City bars
    (iii) Young venues
    (iv) Up-market destinations

(d) To support the product with a heavyweight TV campaign, a major PR launch, and wide coverage in the trade press.

(e) To support every act with a comprehensive package lasting for eight weeks.

4 Relationship of objectives, strategies and tactics

The following diagram illustrates how objectives, strategies and tactics can be linked together.

Answer bank

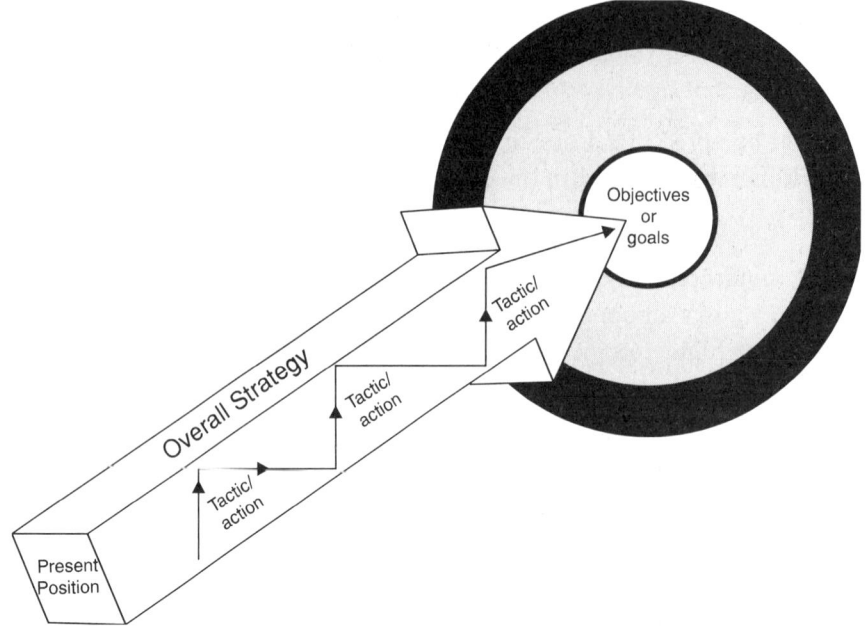

(a) An objective is an end point or goal to be reached and is usually quantified. The following acronym more accurately defines the characteristics of objectives (SMART).

Specific

Measurable

Achievable

Relevant

Timed and targeted

(b) A strategy describes the broad direction of an organisation's actions. It represents a pattern of actions which cumulatively take us in the direction of the objective.

(c) Tactics are the individual short-term actions that are taken. They are represented in the diagram above as a series of short steps.

5 Examples from Carling Premier Lager

The marketing communication *objectives* of Carling Premier have been defined above.

The *strategy* can be seen to include a number of key elements.

(a) The use of the Carling brand name
(b) The development of awareness of an innovative new product
(c) The use of product characteristics of 'smooth' and 'chill'
(d) The use of a heavyweight campaign with both above the line and below the line components

The *tactics* are the more detailed choices of:

(a) Particular media
(b) The timing of the campaign
(c) The decision not to link the product directly to the football sponsorship
(d) The development of point of purchase material

26 MARKETS AND STRATEGIES

> *Examiner's comments, summarised by BPP.* This was a reasonably popular question that was well tackled especially by international students. Good students were able to describe well the differences in characteristics between consumer and industrial markets. Such students presented these characteristics well in the form of grids of factors. Particularly good students were than able to go on and demonstrate the implications for choosing marketing communications strategies for industrial markets. Some six elements of strategy would have gained high marks particularly if backed up by practical examples.

REPORT

To: Managing Director
From: Marketing Communications Manager
Date: 11th June 1996
Ref: Marketing communication strategies for industrial markets

1 Introduction

The principles of marketing have been developed in considerable detail over the last three decades and are now well practised in the field of consumer marketing. The acceptance of marketing principles, however, has been faster among consumer goods producers than in those concerned with industrial marketing, sometimes called business to business marketing.

The amounts of money spent on consumer marketing communications are considerable and perhaps they account for a larger proportion of the marketing budget. This is one of the reasons why marketing communications practice has developed less in industrial marketing situations.

Although the principles of marketing communications are the same for both consumer and industrial marketing there are significant differences in how the marketing is carried out. This report describes the characteristics of the two types of markets and the implications for choosing marketing communication strategies for industrial markets.

2 Characteristics of consumer and industrial markets

In order to be able to plan marketing communications strategies for industrial markets it is important to understand the characteristics of such markets. Also, if we are to use our knowledge and expertise gathered from the more advanced field of consumer marketing we need to be able to compare the characteristics of the two types of market.

The table below summarises and contrasts the characteristics between industrial and consumer marketing.

Answer bank

Major differences between industrial and consumer marketing

	Area	Industrial marketing	Consumer marketing
1	Purchase motivation	Multiple buying influences Support company operations	Individual or family need
2	Nature of demand	Derived or joint demand	Primary demand
3	Emphasis of seller	Economic needs	Immediate satisfaction
4	Customer needs	Each customer has different needs	Groups with similar needs
5	Nature of buyer	Group decision	Purchase by individual or family unit
6	Time effects	Long term relationships	Short term relationships
7	Product details	Technically sophisticated	Lower technical content
8	Promotion decisions	Emphasis on personal selling	Emphasis on mass media advertising
9	Price decisions	Price determined before Terms are important	Price substantially fixed Discounts important
10	Place decisions	Limited number of large buyers. Short channels	Large number of small buyers. Complex channels
11	Customer service	Critical to success	Less important
12	Legal factors	Contractual arrangements	Contracts only on major purchases
13	Environmental factors	Impact sales both directly and indirectly through derived demand	Impact demand directly

3 Business decision-making process

Perhaps the most significant differences are the nature of the buying motivation and the linked nature of the buying decision process. In industrial buying there are many motivations. These stem partly from the technical use of the product but also from financial, security of supply and, to a lesser degree, emotional reasons. The decision-making unit can be equally multi-faceted.

Decision makers and buying motivation

Decision makers		Buying motivation
1	Operations Manager	Uses the product in the organisation's processes - wants efficiency and effectiveness.
2	Technical Manager	Often has to test and approve the product - wants reliability.
3	The Managing Director	May approve major expenditure or change of supplier.
4	The Purchasing Manager	Approves conditions of purchase. Monitors supplier performance.
5	Legal Manager	Draws up or approves legal contracts with supplier.
Decision makers		*Buying motivation*
6	Finance Manager	Approves expenditure and controls debt payment.
7	Health and Safety Manager	May have a role to play with hazardous supplies.

Answer bank

It will be immediately obvious that marketing communications strategy for industrial marketing must reflect this considerably more complex decision-making process.

4 Implications for marketing communications strategy

4.1 *Strategic importance*

Business or industrial marketing can be regarded as involving more strategic decisions in its implementation. Consumer products, by definition, are mass market products often purchased in a routine and habitual manner. This is unlikely to be the case in industrial marketing. Business customers have differing needs and in some cases these needs may be conflicting within the organisation. Identifying business needs is complicated by having to deal with different decision-makers within the company.

4.2 *Impact of time*

The length of time involved for the purchase evaluation and for the life of the product is much greater in industrial markets. Consumers often make buying decisions on the spur of the moment. Industrial buying decisions may take over one year. This then alters both the type of marketing communications and the relationships between the buying and selling organisations.

4.3 *The buying organisation*

Business buyers have several different methods of organising purchasing, and this can affect communication strategy. Some firms purchase on a highly centralised basis. This allows for maximum price advantage and negotiation strength because of economies of scale. Other organisations allow decentralised purchases which leads to local needs being better met. In these cases, two different forms of selling organisation are needed and the communication strategy will be different.

4.4 *Variety of products and services:*

The variety of products in business markets is extremely large. Business products vary from product inputs to items for resale. They can be broken down into three main types.

- Capital equipment (major purchases of fixed assets)
- Production inputs (becoming part of the buyer's process)
- Business supplies/services (ongoing use by the buyer)

Again, each type of purchase will need a different communications strategy.

5 The industrial communications mix

Relative importance of promotional elements.

Answer bank

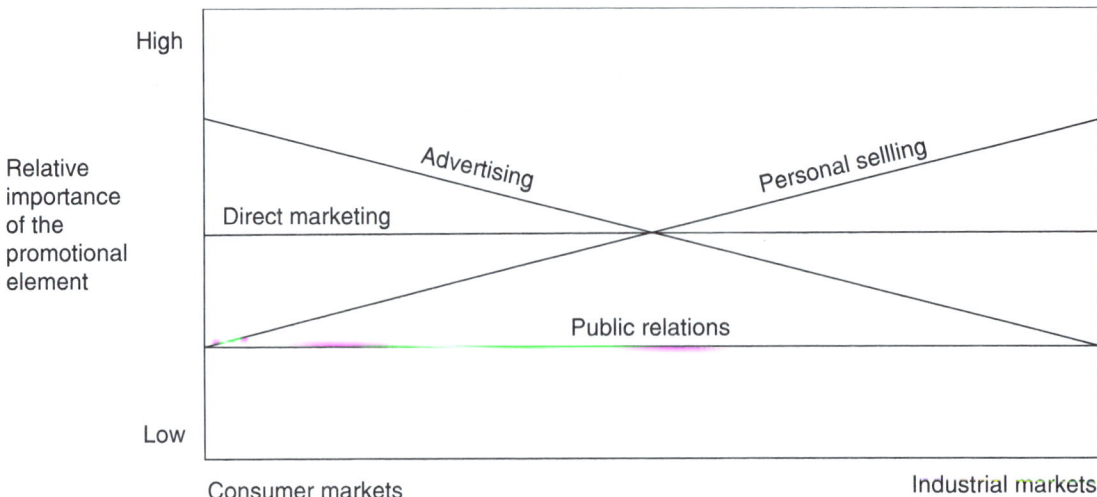

The above chart shows the relative importance of differing elements of the promotional mix between consumer and industrial markets. These differences are reflected in developing marketing communication strategies for industrial markets.

The clearest difference is the importance of personal selling in industrial markets because of the complexity of the decision-making process, the differing industrial needs and the higher value of individual purchases. Advertising, though still important in industrial marketing, is less so than for consumer marketing.

The diagram also shows that both public relations and direct marketing have important continuing roles in both consumer and industrial marketing.

6 Methods of industrial marketing communications

It is clear that the methods to communicate with industrial markets will be of a much greater variety than for consumer markets. This in turn means that industrial marketing decisions can be really challenging and the need for effective integrated marketing communications is important. The range of promotional methods is described below.

1 *Personal selling*

    This is a major component of industrial marketing because of the need to deal with technical and other issues on a face-to-face basis.

2 *Internal selling*

    Increasingly it is recognised that a salesperson has an internal role to play in representing his customer needs to the company.

3 *Advertising*

    A wide variety of publications exist which can be used to target industrial market sectors including:

    - Trade journals
    - Business press
    - Directories

    Advertising is used to create awareness, provide information, generate leads, assist channel members and sometimes to sell off the page.

4   *Telemarketing*

Telemarketing has been proved to be a very cost effective method of order processing, customer service, sales support and account management.

5   *Direct mailing*

Direct mail, another form of direct marketing, has been used by industrial marketers for a long time but its use has substantially increased. It can be used to provide information and generate enquiries. It can be tailored to individual customer needs.

6   *Public relations*

Sometimes in industrial markets this is referred to as publicity. It often focuses on getting editorial coverage in appropriate magazines but has a wider role of building customer relations.

7   *Sales promotion*

Sales promotion is an important area of communication in industrial markets. There is a wide range of methods that are of well established use in industrial campaigns, including the following.

- Literature
- Videos
- Events
- Trade shows
- Exhibitions
- Discounting
- Business gifts

Technical literature is clearly important in specifying the product. Complicated equipment can be captured on video and applications shown. Trade shows and exhibitions continue to grow in importance. Discounting and special price promotions are used extensively in industrial markets. Business gifts continue to have their value if not used excessively.

7   Conclusions

It can be seen that the process of developing effective marketing communication strategies for industrial markets is a complex but rewarding one. The principles of industrial marketing communications are the same as for consumer marketing but the strategies are different. The table below summarises some of the strategic implications.

Principles of industrial marketing communications strategy

Major principles	Strategic implications
Purpose of industrial promotion	Builds up the company's image in the mind of the purchaser.
Communication objectives	Must be geared to specific business objectives.
Communication methods	Different balance than for consumer markets. Personal selling more important.
Choice of media	Important to determine the best media to reach the complex decision-making process.
Measuring effectiveness	Essential to measure the contribution of communications in achieving business objectives.

Answer bank

Finally, it should be stressed that the concept of Integrated Marketing Communications is equally, if not more, important in industrial marketing. This is because there is likely to be a more complex promotional mix and definitely a more complex audience. Consistent delivery of images on a limited budget is therefore important.

27 INTERNAL COMMUNICATIONS

> *Tutorial note.* The increasing recognition that internal marketing can play an important role in an organisation's overall performance means that more attention is being directed to internal marketing communications. The success of an internal programme can be measured partly by the perception of other stakeholders but to be really successful it is necessary to provide consistency between an organisation's external and internal communications.

Introduction

Increasingly organisations are recognising the importance of good communication. For a long time *externally-orientated* communications were seen as important but in recent years the benefits arising from good *internal* communications have also been recognised by a growing number of organisations.

This paper considers some of the main aspects of internal communications and seeks to clarify their objectives, activities and benefits. To assist this process the Wellpart Company, a manufacturer of engine components for the car market, is used to demonstrate some of the key issues.

Internal marketing communications

In order to realise the potential within the workforce it is necessary to communicate with them and treat them as an important part of the communication linkage with customers and other stakeholders. For example, Marks & Spencer invest heavily in their employees through a variety of means. One of the benefits is that the stronger the bond between the employees and the organisation's stated objectives and values, the stronger appears to be their motivation, involvement and willingness to adapt to changing circumstances. As another example, an important part of the Japanese business culture, such as that practised at Panasonic, is the cultivation of shared values and organisational identity.

Objectives

For many companies competition is becoming increasingly fierce and margins tighter. In order to add value and differentiate themselves organisations seek to stretch their assets and derive greater returns. As with most organisations, one of Wellpart's principal assets is their people and it is now an accepted part of their Human Resource Strategy to utilise human assets more effectively. Employees, therefore, represent a major fund of expertise and a means for establishing competitive advantage through channels such as customer service and reputation.

For Wellpart the main objectives of such a programme are as follows.

(a) *Improve the organisation's competitive position.*

By developing good internal communications greater co-ordination and understanding between divisions can lead to faster reactions to changes in the market.

Answer bank

(b) *Generate performance efficiencies*

Through improved communications it is possible to undertake operations more efficiently by reducing costs and improving profitability.

(c) *Develop strategic advantage through management of the corporate reputation*

Wellpart have a programme to develop a customer focused culture within the organisation. By providing high levels of customer service, in tandem with product quality improvements, the goal of a strong positive reputation is more likely to be achieved.

Activities

There are a variety of activities that can be used to meet the objectives associated with internal marketing communications programmes. Wellpart have used a mixture of formal and informal methods from which internal identity appears to have grown.

Formal	*Informal*
Internal education and training	Sales literature
Newsletters/Wellpart house magazine	Reward days
New product launches	Staff functions
Conference days	Social trips
Open management style	Intranet / e-mail
Regular information provision	Notice boards

Internal marketing communication allows for the delivery and identification of key strategic messages. These are normally the mission, objectives and any important strategic developments. In addition, it is important to provide information and updates about how well the organisation has progressed towards the achievement of the corporate goals.

Benefits

The reasons for investing in better communications with the workforce are many and varied but it appears that for Wellpart, by improving the quantity and quality of internal communication the organisation's performance has improved since the programme was introduced. Just by providing information about company objectives and progress towards the goals, a greater sense of company involvement has emerged.

(a) *Improving the organisation's competitive position*

Due to increasing competitive rivalry and pressure on margins it is important for Wellpart to develop their strategic and competitive market position. Through improved communication externally with customers and members of the marketing channel and by developing the internal communication it has been possible to bring new products to the market far more quickly. A further advantage is that by being first into new sectors Wellpart has been able to achieve better market shares and improved margins.

A further benefit has been the improvement in the brand equity valued by members of the marketing channel as well as end-user customers. Customers receiving external communications can have messages reinforced when they contact Wellpart. Staff providing clear concise and accurate information can improve source credibility and thereby enhance trust and commitment.

(b) *Generating performance efficiencies*

There are a number of performance-related benefits. Improved co-ordination leads to increased efficiency levels which reduces duplication and improves profits.

Answer bank

Improvements in education and training, and new opportunities to enter into regular dialogue with colleagues and managers in distant locations, help to develop motivation and group identity. Internal communications allow for the rapid transfer of information and this enables faster response times and fosters group cohesion. Staff turnover can be reduced and a workforce with more varied skills can provide for greater flexibility, which is important when operating in dynamic markets.

(c) *Developing strategic advantage through management of the corporate reputation*

Perhaps the main goal of the internal marketing communications programme is to develop new relationships between employees and customers and other stakeholders. By providing better communication and higher levels of customer satisfaction the quality of exchange-based relationships is improved. This can become a source of advantage, as many customers prefer to deal with people who believe in the company and share its values.

Conclusion

The development of internal marketing communications programmes has provided Wellpart with a broad variety of benefits. However, their potential has only been realised when they have been co-ordinated with the external communication programme. Indeed the argument for separating corporate and marketing communications is severely reduced when the benefits of blending and even integrating are observed.

28 INTERNAL MARKETING COMMUNICATIONS

> **Examiner's comments.** This was a popular question and many answers were of a high standard. To do well the student had to link internal and external aspects. Corporate communication and corporate identity are increasingly important elements of the syllabus.

Introduction

The notion that employees constitute an important market segment is relatively recent but has been gaining increasing acceptance by both organisations and academics. Employees are seen as important because they have particular needs and wants some of which are satisfied by work which they exchange for pay and intrinsic benefits such as belonging, self esteem and self identity.

It is only through employees that management are really able to achieve their corporate goals. Therefore, the direction and philosophy of an organisation, whether it be in the private or public sector, is an integral part of an organisation's strategy and its communications with externally based stakeholders.

The benefits of internal marketing communications

- Staff motivation
- Staff retention
- Resource utilisation
- Developing competitive advantage
- Moving towards integrated marketing communications

Staff motivation

Involvement and participation within the organisation and its strategic and operational activities improves motivation and organisational identity improves. By encouraging employees to identify with the mission and values of an organisation, any gap between an organisation's external identity and its internal identity is narrowed.

Staff retention

In a period when staff skills are at a premium and difficult to replace it makes good sense to preserve the current work force. Good communications are therefore important to retaining qualified and valued member of the workforce. This in turn can breed experience and contribute to the development of better products and services and improved, credible external communications. B&Q, a DIY warehouse in the UK, feature their own staff in their television advertising. This helps develop employee identification as they are perceived to be valued, and externally it provides a point of differentiation from the other DIY stores in the sector and a form of trust as these staff know what they are selling.

Resource utilisation

Good communications can help identify areas where there is duplication of effort and, where possible, improve the level of resource utilisation.

Competitive advantage

The service element of the product offering is important so there must be increased attention given to training and skills. Associated with this is the competitive shift as more and more product offerings become less distinctive in their own right. Differentiation through the service component has provided companies such as KwikFit, TNT Express and British Airways with competitive advantage.

Links with external communications

The development and increased focus on integrated marketing communications means that internal marketing communications cannot be ignored.

Many external stakeholders communicate on a regular basis with the employees of an organisation. Customers are obviously a very important group and need to be treated in the right manner in order to build levels of customer satisfaction. Suppliers and distributors, shareholders, financial service providers and members of the local community also communicate. All receive messages from the organisation, interpret them in particular ways and through the images formed develop, maintain or alter the reputation of the focus organisation.

Employees are essentially *opinion formers* and through 'word of mouth' communications and behaviour they help shape the views external stakeholders have of them as an organisation as a whole. In this sense therefore, internal marketing communications are an integral part of the move toward integrated marketing communications and therefore cannot be ignored or left alone. The way an organisation is perceived by *employees* may differ to the way the organisation is perceived by *external stakeholders*. The extent of any such *gap* is said to be reflected in the strength of the organisation's overall identity. It follows that management should assist their employees to understand what is *central* to the business, what is *distinctive* about the business and what is *enduring*.

29 PLANNED COMMUNICATIONS

> Examiner's comments
>
> Students did not know what a marketing channel was and marks suffered accordingly. This area will become more important in the next few years.
>
> Students should ensure that they understand communications and relationships between intermediaries: the push approach.

Answer bank

Organisations need to work with other organisations if they are to achieve their own goals. Manufacturers need to work with wholesalers and agents and distributors, retailers and value added resellers if they are to be able to present their products and services to their potential end user customers.

Manufacturers also need to work closely with their suppliers, those upstream from their current position in the marketing channel. All these organisations may be independent of each other but they all need each other to complete activities that they themselves do not have the skills or resources to accomplish. Therefore, the members of a marketing channel are said to be interdependent.

As organisations need to work together it follows that communications between the members of the channel are also of vital importance. Communications are necessary in order to help differentiate their products and services in the minds of the member, to persuade them to take stock, to provide information to enable them to understand the technicalities of the product and to inform their customers and finally communications are necessary to remind and reassure the partner organisation.

Contemporary thought suggests that the development of trust and commitment is absolutely imperative if a cooperative relationship is to be shaped such that any two organisations in the network are able to understand each other and work to support one another as necessary.

In addition to the points noted above there is a need for organisations to help motivate and to direct the activities of other partner organisations. These communications with channel intermediaries are referred to as push related communications. They are known as push because the information is being pushed through the channel down towards the end users.

The question refers to the identification of the key influences that shape the design of communication activities in the marketing channel. The problem with this is that what is key in one situation may not be key in another. Key influences will vary according to markets and certain trading and competitive conditions. However, some factors may be common across channels.

1. The Type of Intermediary
2. The Balance of Power in the Channel
3. Type of Product/Service
4. Buyer Characteristics
5. The Competition
6. The Structure Exchanges in the Channel
7. Resources
8. The PEST Factors
9. Current Strategy
10. Strength of Corporate Identity.

This list cannot be regarded as complete although these are the common factors that should be considered. The four main elements are expanded below.

The Type of Intermediary

The distinction here is between whether the intermediary is a retailer, wholesaler of distributor. The role and function of the intermediary will influence the type of information they need and the frequency and style in which the communication needs to be provided.

The Structure Exchanges in the Channel

This refers to whether the members of the channel regard transactions between each other as necessary just to get the job done or whether there is a long term view and a relationship that is important to both parties.

The Competition

The communication campaigns of a competitor can have a strong impact on the communications between channel members. For example, should a competitor offer a discount then there is pressure upon others in the channel, especially from distributors, to also reduce prices in order to maintain a competitive position. The launch of new products and services by competitors can also influence promotional campaigns. New positioning strategies might be developed, information about which needs to be passed through to all members.

Resources

The current type and form of communication may have become embedded in the channel and expected by other members. Whilst this is not a key influence, what lies behind it might be. For example, current operating methods and strategy may be indicative of the prevailing business strategy, organisational culture and the amount of marketing communication resources that are made available.

Personal selling is an important part of the promotional mix in inter-organisational communications. Changes due to new technology may result in a reduction in the size of the sales force and in the calling patterns and frequencies of the revised sales force. Advertising support for joint campaigns may be increased or reduced as budgets change as will the level of training and across company project team support, where appropriate.

As a final comment, the willingness of channel partners to share information with others in the channel indicates the degree to which members trust and support each other and suggests what level of commitment between members of the marketing channel there may be.

30 INTERNAL MARKETING COMMUNICATIONS: TECHNOLOGY

> Examiner's comments
>
> Some candidates produced good answers, realising that this question was closely related to the mini-case in the exam.
>
> Candidates failed to underline the importance of technology, especially for multi-national companies whose employees can be continents apart. Many answers lacked substance. Various technological advances, including email, were mentioned but not put into the context of effective communication.

Memorandum

Comments welcomed by 21 December 1999

Importance of Internal Marketing Communications

The drive to develop integrated marketing communications and the increased interest in corporate branding and associated communications has focused attention on the role of employees as an internal stakeholder. The potential impact they have on an organisation's external stakeholders and on organisational performance appears to have been underestimated for a long time.

Answer bank

One of the benefits of developing integrated communications is that if achieved it is likely that all stakeholders will perceive a consistent and harmonious set of identity cues and form more uniform images.

The role of internal marketing communications can be seen from three perspectives.

1 The **DRIP** factors whereby:

   D Employees need to understand how the organisation is *differentiated* to the others in the sector and how different they are as a workforce.

   R Employees need to be *reminded* how good they are and what the overall targets are that they are all striving to achieve. They also need to be *reassured* that they are valued and that they are supported and appreciated.

   I It is important that this audience is kept *informed* of company developments and that they understand how, when and why the company is acting in the way it is.

   P Sometimes they need to be *persuaded* to undertake certain tasks or actions.

2 There are also **transactional** impacts where good internal communications can help coordinate the actions of staff and project teams, improve the use of resources and direct developments within the organisation.

3 Finally, internal marketing communications is an important mechanism through which **affiliation** with the organisation can be encouraged. For example, it provides identification with the company, can motivate employees and promote and coordinate activities with those external to the organisation.

Impact of Technology

It appears that internal marketing communications is important and can lead to improvements for the company and for us as individuals. The recent advances in technology have enabled many organisations to reduce the amount of paper and time spent on internal communications and made the process far more efficient.

The use of the Internet has not only changed the way many organisations communicate with their customers, especially in the business-to-business sector, but has also enabled communications with discrete audiences. Intranets and web pages only accessible by staff provide a fast and effective way of delivering information, reminding staff of their role and the company's position and providing a means of enhanced identification. Some organisations provide their mission and corporate objectives, staff handbook, address book details, internal catalogues, notice boards, chat rooms and other company information which is accessible by everyone internally.

Email provides for global communication which is both quick, inexpensive and accurate in the sense that there is little chance of message corruption en route. Electronic files containing spreadsheets and reports can be transmitted at electronic speeds and enable savings to be made in terms of labour and printing costs.

Training materials can be standardised and this can help ensure that all staff are trained in the same way and assist in the delivery of uniform messages. British Airways use video conferencing on a regular basis for management communication and they also used the same technology for the simultaneous launch of their now infamous "new" corporate identity in 1997.

The final benefit to be mentioned is that product information and updates can be communicated more efficiently and effectively through intranets either to employees or members of the market channel (internal members).

Conclusion

The rapid development of technology has enabled management to communicate more effectively and efficiently with their employees. It has also allowed employees an opportunity to communicate more effectively with other employees and management. If two way communication is valued by management then increased use of technology will be an important and necessary requirement.

31 BRANDS HATCH

> *Examiner's comments, summarised by BPP.* This question proved difficult to answer well. Most students were able to talk about the nature of a brand but few demonstrated their knowledge about how marketing communications can help build a brand over the long term. Very few students were able to analyse the nature of this long term value.

REPORT

To: The Marketing Manager
From: Marketing Assistant
Date: June 1997
Ref: The nature of brands and marketing communications

Nature of Branding

A *brand* is a combination of a name, logo, service, packaging, symbol or design which identifies a product as having a sustainable differential advantage. A successful brand is one that creates and sustains a strong positive impression in the mind of the buyer.

The brand provides a quick way *for buyers to recognise products* that provide satisfaction because the brand conveys *information* about content, taste, performance, quality and durability. Decision making is made easier and is at the expense of brands that do not offer comparable value.

Branding provides *opportunities for manufacturers* to offer new products and services through brand extensions. Branding also allows for premium pricing. For instance, Andrex and Velvet toilet tissue have competed for many years on a range of attributes but both brands have been able to sustain price premiums of up to 30% simply because the brands offer superior sustainable value, as perceived by consumers.

Branding also offers *advertising and personal selling* opportunities to communicate quickly and succinctly with buyers. Branding provides a short-hand form of communication that benefits all those involved with the process: clients, distributors, customers, suppliers and agencies.

There are many types and forms of brands but essentially the following can be identified: multi-product brands such as Heinz, Kellogg and Cadbury; multi-brand products (Ariel, Persil and KitKat). In addition it possible to identify own-label brands such as Sainsbury's Novon and Tesco's chocolate chip biscuits.

There are also variations dependent upon the relationship between the parent company name and the product. In some, such as Ford, the model of the car is incorporated within the name so that the Ford Escort 1.6L constitutes a combination form of the brand. Other brands, such as Kwikfit, provide the main platform by which the product offering and the company is identified.

Answer bank

Contribution of marketing communications

Marketing communications, and advertising in particular, play a very important part in the *development and maintenance of brands*. Marketing communications enables the totality of the brand formulation, as assembled in the marketing mix, to be communicated to the target audience.

Awareness of a brand (or a product modification) needs to be established first and then buyers need to be knowledgeable of the particular aspects of the brand that differentiate it from competitor brands. Buyers need to be able to see how it might resolve a problem or be useful to them.

For example, Philadelphia Cheese had a 47% market share in the late 1980s but was under attack from own-label supermarket products and other luxury cheeses such as Boursin, from the 'cheese board' sector.

Advertising was used to *reposition Philadelphia* as a high quality, premium but less esoteric brand. To do this two girls were used, one a product novice the other a product expert, and one educated the other about Philadelphia cheese. The treatments use a direct, pragmatic and slightly tongue-in-cheek approach which clearly appeals to the target ABC1 audience. A number of different executions have been made, to the extent that the popularity of the 'Philly Girls' is an endorsement of their identification with the brand and the values that the brand purports.

The advertisements have generated a range of other co-ordinated marketing communications activities. Taste trials and point of purchase events together with sales promotion activities have been predominant. During this time new Philadelphia variants have been successfully introduced and marketing communications have been used to maintain the brand both in terms of awareness and market share. Indeed the revitalisation of the brand contributed to its market share rising to over 56% at one point.

Brands need to be sustained in order that they are fresh in the minds of buyers and clearly mean something of value to them. Marketing communications is responsible for communicating this meaning and at the same time providing a rationale for the perceived value and the premium price. This premium pricing is important, as the above-average profits that each major brand supports need to be reinvested in product development and innovation, in order that the brand has continuity and a long term value to the brand owners and the consumers.

Long term values

Marketing communications is necessary to build a brand over the long term. Over this time the value of the brand can increase and provide benefits associated with market leadership, often related to economies of scale and efficiency.

The strength of a brand can be measured or determined in a number of ways. Each of the following factors can be weighted, as the context in which a brand is presented will vary.

(a) *Market Share & Leadership* - is the share rising or falling?

(b) *Market Characteristics* - what are the growth characteristics of the market

(c) *Stability* - what is the level of brand loyalty?

(d) *Internationality* - international brands are normally worth more than purely domestic brands because risk is spread across more than one market.

(e) *Trends* - how able is the brand to sustain itself and to resist price cuts during recession and market downturns?

(f) *Support* - is the marketing spend appropriate for the brand? Money and resources are not enough: it is how they are deployed that really matters.

(g) *Protection* - is the brand protected by patent, copyright or trademark to prevent imitation and brand dilution?

Brands have an immense strategic value to an organisation and resources are required to build and sustain these important assets. Some of these assets have a value which is placed on a balance sheet. Companies may be purchased at a price well above their share value the difference reflecting the goodwill and market valuation of their brands. Rowntrees' accounting value was £4m in 1991 but the company was purchased by Nestle for £11m, the difference being accredited to the KitKat, Black Magic and Yorkie brands, amongst others.

Future of branding

It has been suggested that the future of brands is in doubt. Others are adamant that brands have a strong future. Some supermarkets have decided to restrict the amount of shelf space devoted to own-label brands as research shows that consumers want a wider choice of manufacturer's brands. This may be evidence that the brand will continue to play an important role in the medium term.

Marketing communications is increasingly recognised as an important area where not only efficiencies are to be made but effectiveness substantially improved. Management commitment to a brand is necessary if long term values are to be realised and the organisation's net worth is to be enhanced.

32 BRANDING AND MARKETING COMMUNICATIONS

> *Tutorial note.* The depth of understanding that students have of the branding concept will be significant indicator when answering this question. Branding as a strategy is central to marketing communications and a rounded understanding is important.
>
> *Examiner's comments.* Too few related their knowledge to marketing communications strategy.

Branding is an important *consumer marketing tool* and companies such as Nike, Cadbury's, Procter & Gamble, Virgin and British Airways have developed sophisticated means of managing and developing their brands. Many business-to-business organisations are starting to recognise the power of branding and are utilising the approach themselves.

A brand is a term, logo, name, symbol or design that identifies the product or service within particular markets. It may be that these elements are combined together in some way to provide a *distinguishing facility* within a competitive environment. Branding therefore is a primary means of *differentiating* a product or service. As product content, quality and facilities continue to converge, the importance of distinguishing one product from another becomes more and more important. Branding allows for the development of competitive advantage and adds value to the core product. This value may not be understood and or appreciated by all members of the population, but what is important is that members of the target audience appreciate and value the brand and its associated values.

Branding brings many advantages to both consumers and a brand's owners. These are set out in Table 1. However, it is only through *communication* that the essence of a brand is conveyed and maintained. Therefore, marketing and corporate communications are absolutely essential for effective branding to be developed.

British Airways have used branding to help achieve the corporate goals. BA use branding at a *corporate level* by differentiating the airline from all other airlines. They also use product

Answer bank

based branding to differentiate particular routes and ancillary services. The recent launch of their cut price airline 'Go' is significant in that the name (symbol, mark) of British Airways is not immediately associated with the primary means of identification. One might assume that the brand values of the parent company are not to be associated with those of the start-up fledgling airline. When British Gas wanted to launch a credit card and move into the financial services market the name (mark, symbol) of British Gas was not appropriate in that the wrong values and cultural associations were tied into British Gas that might have prevented or impeded a successful launch. They selected the name Goldfish and used a variety of different means to distinguish and separate the brand form the parent.

Customer benefits from branding	*Supplier benefits derived from branding*
★ Assists the identification of preferred products ★ Can reduce levels of perceived risk and so improve the quality of the shopping experience ★ Easier to gauge the level of product quality ★ Can reduce the time spent making product based decisions and in turn reduce the time spent shopping. ★ Can provide psychological reassurance or reward ★ Provides cues about the nature of the source of the product and any associated values	★ Permits premium pricing ★ Helps differentiate the product from competitors ★ Enhances cross-product promotion and brand extension opportunities ★ Encourages customer loyalty/retention and repeat purchase buyer behaviour ★ Assists the development and use of integrated marketing communications ★ Contributes to corporate identity programmes ★ Provides for some legal protection ★ Provides for greater thematic consistency and uniform messages and communications

Table 1

Benefits of Branding
Source: Fill (1999)

Conversely, *Virgin* have *developed and extended* the Virgin brand into many different markets, mainly because of the strength of the equity associated with Virgin. The marketing strategy of Virgin to enter new markets and to develop new products, often simultaneously, has been possible only because of the strength of the Virgin brand. Marketing communications strategy therefore has been based around maintaining and developing the strength of the Virgin brand.

There *are* different types of brand and numerous listings and topologies of brands.

(a) There *are manufacturers' brands* such as IBM, Cadbury's and Ford, *retailer* brands such as Marks and Spencer, Tesco and Sainsbury's and Generic brands as practised in the pharmaceutical industry where a very low price and the absence of promotional materials is the prime characteristic.

(b) Brands however are a reflection the relationship between the corporate body, the product itself and the competitive context within which it is positioned. As a result of these variables a number of different brands types can be identified.

   (i) Pirelli, Gillette and Kwik-Fit have a single product group offering so that the name of the organisation is the same as the lead name of individual products.

   (ii) Companies such as Lever Brothers have followed a multi-brand strategy so that products in the company's portfolio are branded without reference to the parent company. Marketing communications therefore are required to maintain this policy and to build values associated with each and every product in different ways. Should a single brand experience a crisis then the other brands in the portfolio need not be damaged, unlike the Family brand approach as followed by Kellogg's and Cadbury's where the organisation's name is a visible and imperative part of the name of each and every product in the portfolio.

Marketing communications needs to build the strength of the brand over the long term and it needs to be flexible in order to adapt to changing market conditions. However, many of the long-term successful brands such as Shell have been able to maintain core values and develop a level of consistency in their communications. Brands carry a measure of **goodwill**, which can be the prime attraction of predators. When Nestlé bought Rowntree, the value of brands such as KitKat led to a price far in excess of the traditional asset value of the company. A view of the future stream of earnings a brand is likely to generate is a major factor when determining the take-over price. The Rolls Royce brand is extremely attractive with strong equity and future earnings potential. Volkswagen have just paid a price premium to snatch the purchase of Rolls-Royce away from fellow German company BMW.

Branding is part of marketing communication strategy and needs to be developed and nurtured over the long term. It can be extremely effective and provide competitive advantage through increased customer satisfaction and retention.

33 INTERNET

> *Comments by the senior examiner.* This question asks for an *evaluation* and therefore students are expected to write a more discursive answer and to critically examine the Internet. A report or memorandum format was not required.
>
> *Examiner's comments, summarised by BPP.* About 40% of UK students and 30% of international students tackled this question. High marks were earned by UK students and relatively poorer ones by international students. Good answers stuck closely to the question asked - ways in which the Internet is being used - and will be used - by suppliers, customers and internally in organisations. Ideas that were realistic were rewarded. Unfortunately, some answers copied previous lists of advantages and disadvantages of the Internet generally, rather than the specific uses. General answers were less well rewarded.

What is the Internet?

The Internet is a world-wide network of computer networks. These are linked together so that users can search for and access data and information provided by others, linked through the different networks.

The World Wide Web is the multimedia element which provides facilities such as full-colour, graphics, sound and video. Web sites are points within the network created by members who wish to provide an information point for searchers to visit and benefit by the provision of information and/or by entering into a transaction.

Current uses and development issues

There are an increasing number of interactive uses that the Internet can be used for:

(a) Communication (information provision)
(b) Product development
(c) Facilitating transactions
(d) Fostering dialogue and relationships with different stakeholders

The attributes of the Internet that allow for these uses also need to be considered.

(a) High speed of interaction

Answer bank

(b) Low cost provision and maintenance
(c) Ability to provide mass customisation
(d) Global reach and wide search facilities
(e) Instant dialogue
(f) Multi-directional communications (eg: to suppliers, customers and regulators)
(g) High level of user control
(h) Customer (Visitor) driven
(i) Moderate level of credibility

Use with customers

The use of the Internet by organisations with their customers has in the initial years been focussed upon the business-to-business sector rather than consumer end users. Those customers that have used the Internet do so primarily in search of entertainment and information. Web sites have become increasingly sophisticated and are a useful means of meeting the needs of customers and organisations.

Businesses can communicate more cost-effectively with their customers and provide a wide range of facilities. The volume of customer traffic that can be handled is far larger and quicker than through traditional means. Sales literature, product designs and innovations, ideas, price lists, complaints, sales promotions such as competitions, and orders and sales can all be undertaken over the Internet. The objectives are essentially two-fold. The first is to generate the first steps of a relationship (or maintain one already established). The second is the collection of customer profile information to be added to the database. Names, addresses and other demographic and psychographic data can be collected without any human intervention and/or the associated costs.

The execution of financial transactions over the Internet has been a deterrent due to the fear of fraud and misappropriation of funds. More secure systems and protection devices are now becoming available and this will spur the growth of purchasing activities over the Internet in the future.

A further development is to integrate the Internet with other elements of the marketing and promotional mix. For example the Tesco and Sainsbury's initiatives to develop home shopping have met with limited success but further investment will generate new shopping patterns and purchasing behaviours.

Use with suppliers

The use of the Internet with suppliers will provide a more dynamic form of communication exchange. Problem identification, the formation of solutions and constant dialogue opportunities will enable suppliers to forge closer relationships in the marketing channel.

Marketing communications opportunities will arise where, for example, new products can be presented to suppliers much more quickly, sales literature and product specification data can be relayed instantly and, in some cases, advertising materials presented more effectively.

Sales order processing and lead management systems are already providing marketing channel members (and end-user customers) with greater efficiency and speed of information retrieval. Suppliers also benefit from being able to contribute to product modifications and fault-finding processes can be speeded up. Perhaps one of the more exciting opportunities the Internet provides is greater customisation - more tailored products for specific customers.

Use within organisations: intranets

Internally the greatest advance is the development of intranets. The provision of internal, password-protected communication networks allows for the rapid dissemination of corporate and marketing information. For global organisations this represents a tremendous step forward as an intranet can overcome time barriers and allow for the transmission of materials to all parts of a company instantaneously. It provides a wealth of information for members to keep themselves informed of company news.

The development and interest in *internal marketing* has been assisted by this new form of internal communications. The involvement of staff and the motivational opportunities afforded by intranet technology enable employees and management to work more closely together.

Future of the Internet

The future of the Internet is bounded only by imagination and technological advances. Essentially there will be greater interactive opportunities which will enable a range of stakeholders to interact with organisations as a community to provide information, education, entertainment, products, services and financial transactions quickly, efficiently and so release more time for leisure and recreational activities.

34 BUSINESS-TO-BUSINESS BRANDING

> **Examiner's comments.** The word 'branding' led to reams of information on branding but few candidates related it to the question set.
>
> Students **must** read the question properly before they start their answer. Pass marks were earned by relating branding to the business-to-business sector and seeing branding as a form of communication.

To :   The Marketing Director
From :   A CIM Diploma Student
Date :   8 December 1998
Ref :   Branding within The Business-to-Business Sector

1.0 Introduction

This report seeks to identify what branding is, establishes what business-to-business communications consist of and then attempts to consider how branding can assist this form of marketing communications in this sector.

2.0 What is a brand?

A *brand* is a design, name, sign, symbol or logo that differentiates one product from another and which is valued by customers. A brand is a composite of tangible and intangible elements mixed together in such a way that the resultant mix is not only meaningful but possesses values that are relevant and pertinent to customers.

Brands have many advantages for both the manufacturer and the buyer. Essentially, a brand *enables the brand owner to maintain some control* over how the products are sold through retailers and other distributors. It prevents the onset of commodification, allows for premium pricing, speeds purchase decisions, generates familiarity, reassurance and most importantly trust. It is through trust that loyalty can be developed, which in turn can bring increased profits and competitive advantage for the brand owner.

3.0 The business-to-business sector (BTB)

Branding has been an integral part of the consumer market for a long time. However, the BtB market is characterised by longer decision-making times, generally high involvement decision processes, the involvement of many people in the decision (DMU), large sums of money and potential risk. In the past, rational informative benefit based communications were regarded as important. However, the merits of using *emotional imagery* in the messages communicated to organisational buyers and by bringing together a number of identity cues under a brand umbrella has been seen to be attractive to many BtB organisations. In many of the markets in the BtB sector, competition is *priced based* and only through communication of the augmented product can the totality of the services and the value that a particular supplier can provide have the roots of branding started to be established.

Businesses buy benefits just as consumers do but they also willingly buy *relationships*. Branding provides for the establishment of a long-term relationship. Personal selling, sales support and packaging are part of the overall 'product' that organisations buy. When combined with guarantees and risk free finance deals, it appears that the embryo of a brand is under development.

In addition to the business benefits of branding, organisations have witnessed the value that some brands in the consumer sector have attained. The value of some brands far exceeds the total tangible asset value and adds to the appeal to create strong business-to-business brands. the recent takeover of Rover cars by BMW, the battle by VW and BMW to buy Rolls Royce and the value placed by Nestlé on Rowntree all testify to the value of the brand and the anticipated future income streams that reflect the overall strength of the brand. In addition, brands have a balance sheet value again an attractive option for many organisations.

4.0 Examples of business to business brands

The *Intel brand* has received a high level of promotional support and represents an attempt to develop a brand that has value for both the BtB and consumer sectors. Hewlett Packard has developed brand strength in the different markets in which it operates. IBM, Dell and Compaq have realised the benefits of brand strength when dealing with trade customers and the leverage it can bring in getting high distributor visibility or 'shelf-space'.

Newcourt Automotive Services is one of the largest leasing companies in the world. NAS supplies contract hire and leasing solutions specifically to business fleets. Through the provision of technology and consultancy Newcourt is beginning to establish a brand. Newcourt's strategy is to promote a consistent identity, values and a reputation that will help differentiate it from its competitors in the longer term.

Dexion is a strong brand in the partitioning and shelving market. Little known in the consumer world, Dexion enjoys a very strong position in the BtB market. What these two examples serve to demonstrate is that branding in the BtB sector has to be market specific otherwise funds are wasted. Therefore the identity cues used need to be managed tightly and focused upon the principal stakeholders.

5.0 The future of branding

The use of branding in the BtB sector will probably continue to increase as organisations seek to differentiate themselves, extend their brands into new products/markets and seek to find new ways of reach key members of DMUs. Some consumer brands are becoming much more flexible and allow their owners to stretch or extend into new markets, for example, Virgin. It is unlikely that this will be possible with BtB brands but opportunities to straddle consumer and BtB markets, as demonstrated by Intel, will be attempted by an increasing number of brands in the future.

35 TUTORIAL QUESTION: PROMOTIONAL BUDGETS

(a) There are four main approaches to building an advertising budget.

(i) *The affordable approach*

Basically this is a production-oriented method which relies on calculating gross margins, determining required net profit, taking out all other costs and expenses and then what is left is the advertising budget. The advantage of this approach is that the financial situation is under control but the major disadvantage is that there is no reference to reality and there is no scope to change as market conditions change. It also totally ignores the effect of advertising on demand. There is as little point in spending money on production when there are difficulties involved in selling the goods as there is in promoting products that cannot be produced.

(ii) *The objective and task approach*

This method takes the opposite view to the affordable approach. The objectives are looked at first and then the funds required to meet them are calculated. The major disadvantage with this method is that the objectives and tasks must be very detailed and accurate. It also makes forward financial planning very difficult. Its advantage lies in the assurance that all eventualities have been built into the budget.

(iii) *Competitive parity*

Competitive parity, as the name implies, uses the competition as a benchmark, in the sense that the more the competition spend then the more their competitors are forced to spend. This can involve detailed research and this is time consuming. Another danger is the presumption that spending more money on advertising equates with success but there are other factors to take into account including pricing, distribution and the other elements of the promotional mix.

(iv) *Percentage of sales*

This is the easiest to calculate. Either historical or predicted figures are used and an agreed percentage is allocated against these sales figures. The advantage here is that the method is clear to everyone in the organisation and it means that control is made easy. Problems arise when sales are falling and the percentage figure is forecast on these reduced figures. If reduced sales figures are of concern to the organisation then it ought to think carefully before reducing its advertising spend accordingly.

Other possible methods are less widely used.

(i) The *historical approach* entails establishing a level of expenditure which is acceptable to managers and sticking to it. This is comfortable and easy for managers and may work well in a stable market and economy. The dangers are that more than is necessary will be spent or that the organisation will have no idea how to respond to changing conditions.

(ii) *Experiment and testing* involves setting up different expenditures in different test markets which are equally matched in other respects. The resulting levels of awareness and sales achieved can then be measured and compared. The disadvantages of this method are that it is difficult and time-consuming to set up.

Answer bank

Experiment and testing may, however, be the only viable scientific approach in a very uncertain situation. It will limit the amount of expenditure wasted on unsuccessful approaches and, once results are known, will allow resources to be applied in the most effective manner.

(iii) *Modelling and simulation* use computers and mathematical techniques to build models that allow marketing managers to forecast the performances of different media plans and advertising expenditure. This is highly scientific and with *accurate* input data about costs, consumer response and so on it may give very reliable results. The problem is that in practice it is extremely difficult to obtain accurate input data and to set up the relationships between variables in such a way that the predictions will be borne out. This is because much depends on subjective or qualitative considerations and many external, unpredictable factors have to be taken into account.

(b) *Ten steps in applying the objective and task method*

Step 1 Define marketing and promotion objectives
Step 2 Determine the tasks to be undertaken
Step 3 Build up expenditure by costing the tasks
Step 4 Compare the results against industry averages
Step 5 Compare the results as a percentage of sales
Step 6 Reconcile differences between steps 3, 4 and 5
Step 7 Modify estimates to meet company policies
Step 8 Specify when expenditures are to be made
Step 9 Maintain an element of flexibility
Step 10 Monitor actual results against these forecasts

36 TUTORIAL QUESTION: INTER AND INTRA-MEDIA DECISIONS

(a) Media choice is governed by a number of factors arising from the different properties of the various media options.

The *nature* of the medium in its own right is an important consideration. People purchase magazines for their entertainment value, or because they serve as an information source. The fact that the magazines carry advertising may be of little importance to the reader. However, in terms of information value, editorial stance, style, language and personality, the magazine environment will tend to rub off onto the advertising and particular magazines will be chosen for their compatibility with the products and services being promoted.

Similarly, the *positioning* of adverts within television, radio or cinema contexts can make a difference to how they are perceived. An advert scheduled in the middle of a TV game show will deliver an audience with a different mind set from one scheduled in the centre break of a documentary.

Another consideration is the way in which *people use media*. For instance, many popular radio stations are used as a background to other activities (driving a car, talking to friends, carrying out activities at work or in the home). People are generally unlikely to be giving their main attention to listening to the radio (unless it is 'talk radio'). By contrast, reading a newspaper is a main activity in its own right. Whether the medium is used as sole activity or minor activity will affect the ability of that medium to deliver the advertising it contains.

The amount of *time* spent with the medium can be a factor. Daily newspapers are a relatively quick read in the busy environment of the working week. Saturday and Sunday papers are a more leisurely read in the relaxed environment of the weekend.

Some media options lend themselves to particular *creative opportunities*.

(i) A number of recent TV ads have taken advantage of the 'pause' button on the video recorder.

(ii) Television and cinema allow advertisers to use the power of sound and vision together to create an impression. Special effects originally created for film or pop video production can be used to give adverts an up to the minute feel.

(iii) Other characteristics that must be considered when judging a medium on its *creative* scope are as follows.

(1) Potential for colour advertising
(2) Potential for movement and sound
(3) Space and time limitations
(4) Reprographic standards

Booking and production *lead times* may rule out the use of certain media. Magazine space is generally booked months in advance. Television and cinema commercials with high production values will take months to prepare, film and edit.

As well as taking into account the inherent features of each medium, media channels must be evaluated *quantitatively* for their ability to deliver against criteria such as coverage, frequency and cost.

(b) (i) A media schedule is the formal listing of which adverts are to appear where.

(ii) A very small budget may dictate that advertising is limited to certain key times of the year (eg pre Christmas; peak sales periods). A large budget which allows for year round advertising is usually allocated in one of two ways.

(1) A *burst campaign* concentrates expenditure into promotional bursts of three or four weeks in length.

(2) A *drip campaign* allows for a continuous but more spread out presence.

37 BUDGET PROCESS

> **Examiner's comment**. This is a relatively easy question. It asks for a display of knowledge (what are the methods) and then asks for a proposal (evaluation and reflection).

To: Marketing and Sales Departments - Pantella Hair Care
From: Marketing Manager
Subject: Marketing Communication Budget Determination

As part of my new role for Pantella I wish to review the methods used to determine our marketing communication budgets. Following on from this I will outline proposed methods for determining budgets in future. I welcome your comments prior to our next departmental meeting.

Methods of budget determination

Before presenting the methods that are used by different organisations I need to point out that the theoretically optimal model is marginal analysis. By determining the point at which an extra pound sterling spent on communications generates an extra marginal pound sterling in profit it is possible to state that the optimal budget has been achieved. However, this is difficult if not impossible to determine in the real world for a number of reasons. The

Answer bank

main drawbacks are that we do not have perfect and timely information and sales are driven by a variety of factors not just communications (or advertising as first proposed).

The main real world methods are these.

1   *Percentage of last year's sales (or next years)*

    This method involves calculating the budget as a percentage of last year's sales. For example, this may be 5% or 10% but it is not customer orientated, it is retrospective and does not take into account any support that brands may need. For example, to counteract particular competitive behaviour, to launch a product or revive a declining brand.

2   *Case rate*

    This method uses a standard rate which is applied to each unit of sales. For example, case rate × no of sales = budget

    This raises the question of how the rate is actually calculated and once again is retrospective and doesn't consider the market conditions or that an increase in the marketing communication budget could actually increase sales.

3   *Affordable*

    Under this approach we need to work out all the other costs, and after assigning an amount for profit, what is left can be spent on communications. This approach appears to be adopted by product-orientated organisations and those that perceive communications as a cost rather than as an investment. Best avoided in my opinion.

4   *Share of voice*

    This approach requires a measurement of our market share and the total spend on marketing communications by all players in the market. Therefore, share of market and share of voice statistics can be determined and the relationship between the two expressed as a ratio. For example, we hold a 12% market share and the total communication spend (above-the-line) for the market was £87m last year. Therefore, the SOV should be around 12% of £87m or £10.44m. Although this does ensure we have an appropriate 'share of voice' it does not consider our objective to increase market share.

5   *Advertising to sales ratio*

    Closely allied to the SOV concept is the A/S ratio. In each market there is an average ratio of sales to communications spend. In engineering sectors this may be 0.2%, in food 4% and in fragrances 12.3%. The point is that in our sector the A/S ratio is about 15% so we need to understand whether the Pantella brand's A/S ratio is under, on or over the 15% and be able to justify the result.

6   *Media inflation*

    This simply takes prior year budget and adds the media inflation rate. This does not consider competitor activity by our organisation.

7   *Objective and task*

    This is considered in more detail later.

Proposal for determining promotional budgets for Pantella

So after considering the above I would like to propose the objective and task method of budget determination, in association with other bench marking methods such as SOV and A/S ratios.

Objective and task method works by identifying each communication objective for the forthcoming year. For example, 'raising awareness by 15% in our target market in the next six months' and the appropriate promotional tasks assigned to achieve it. For example, our TV work, print magazines and instore promotions need to be costed. If the resultant figure is not acceptable internally then the objectives need to be reworked or a different promotional strategy determined.

Whilst the objectives and tasks approach needs to be used for both the push and pull areas of our promotional work, one of the main benefits of this method will be that it will enable us to measure our results more productively and control the implementation of each campaign more effectively.

By using the other approaches (SOV, A/S ratio, competitive parity) as a series of bench marking opportunities it will be possible to have a feel for competitive conditions and to retain competitive performance. It is also possible to buy data from PIMS. This is a large database through which we would be able to understand the sector's performance and to invest in communications in such a way that might generate an optimal return on investment. This last point needs to be explored in greater detail before any commitment is made.

38 EVALUATE REPOSITIONING

> *Examiner's comments, summarised by BPP.* This question is intended to pull on the wider reading and preparation students should have undertaken. To pass the answer, students had to display reasonable understanding of positioning, comment on the objectives and the effectiveness of the campaign. Some attempt had to be made to the style/layout that might be required for a short article.
>
> The biggest single failing in answers was a reliance on description or a lack of any comment on the effectiveness of repositioning.

Proposal for Article

To :   The ABC Marketing Journal
From :   CIM Diploma Student
Title : *The Repositioning of X*
Date :   9 June 1998

Rather than just present a standard answer, I have chosen to set out the structure of a suitable response to this question and interlace it with possible brand orientated comments.

A good response lies with the key words in the question. These key words are 'evaluates' and 'reposition' and these constitute the framework for the answer. The actual structure for the answer is given in the last sentence yet it is amazing how many answers failed to utilise this simple aid.

The answer should commence with a simple descriptive scene setting. For example:

For a long time Lucozade was seen as a restorative health drink which was only administered to sick children and nursing mothers. Indeed the messages transmitted during the early phase of the brand's life conditioned its audience to perceive the drink in exactly this way. It was positioned such that the only legitimate way to consume the product was if you were sick.

The problem associated with this was that the positioning restricted the number of people who could consume it. As a result the brand began to lose market share as competitor products took advantage of the niche (or hole) that Lucozade had forged for itself.

This then sets the scene and provides the context for the answer.

Answer bank

The next section is needed to confirm what positioning is. A formal definition would have been sufficient.

According to Kotler, positioning is the 'act of designing the company's offering and image so that they occupy a meaningful and distinct competitive position in the target customers' minds.'

Ries and Trout argue that it is not what you do to a product it is what you do to the mind of the prospect. These comments clearly suggest that the positioning of products is a communication based activity, one that relies on the relative impact of a number of similar products and how they are perceived. Lucozade was positioned very clearly and to a defined audience but the illness market was not large enough to sustain profitability and the well being of the brand.

Having set out what positioning is, it is then necessary to consider what the owners did in order to correct the falling market share and how repositioning the brand was to be a successful remedy.

Market research was undertaken to try to understand the attitudes people had towards the brand and to other soft drinks in the market. Results indicated that attitudes towards the brand and the taste were largely positive but the most interesting result was that people never made it their first choice purchase and never bought it for their own consumption. It was always a brand that was bought for others, and those others were normally sick. The brand strengths revolved around the drink's taste and restorative and energising powers. The research also revealed that there was a gap in the market for a high energy sports drink.

The only sensible course of action was to communicate a new set of parameters so that the new (desired) target audience could frame the brand, understand its benefits and values and perceive it in a new way.

It is at this point that the second requirement concerning the objectives and the campaign design should have been considered.

This repositioning exercise therefore required a new creative approach in order that the brand be perceived in a totally new way, one which capitalised on the strengths of taste and restorative powers. To appeal to the new sports drink market required an entirely different set of messages, a new communication paradigm to use the current vernacular.

It was decided to use a sports personality to endorse the brand. Daley Thompson was selected partly because of his successful career and partly because he was recognised and liked by a huge cross section of the population. To utilise his impact both television and magazine advertising were selected as the primary media. The advantages of this combination were:

(a) They reached mass audiences

(b) It permitted the use of colour which allowed the strong orange colour of the bottle contrast with the label colours which are red and yellow

(c) The sports orientation could be reflected in the action and motion that television presented.

Having explained, reasonably briefly the objectives and the campaign the concluding section needs to deal with the third requirement, the apparent effectiveness.

The success of the Lucozade repositioning can not be underestimated. Market share was restored, profits increased and the average age of the consumer was reduced by nearly 50%. In addition to this, retailers were pleased with the campaign. Many of whom stock the drink in the refrigerators next to a whole raft of other soft drinks. Brand extensions are both a compliment and a testimony to the strength of brand. Needless to say, the Lucozade brand has experienced a number of subsequent successful extensions, all of which contribute to brand equity.

39 EVALUATE EFFECTIVENESS

> *Examiner's comment.* This is an actual student answer presented at the June 1999 diet of examinations. It was written by a student for whom English is not their first language. I have tidied up some parts of the answer and removed elements that I do not want replicated.
>
> It is not a model answer but it is an example of general good practice, including structure and sticking to answering the question set. Note the balance between the descriptive scene setting and the part that deals with the effectiveness measures and issues.
>
> Questions like these are often perceived by students as attractive (if they have reviewed campaigns) but unfortunately many answers are descriptive and make no attempt to consider the effectiveness issues.
>
> The answer presented here does not focus on the background to the campaign and indeed it could be argued that a more explicit context analysis would have been helpful. For example, was this the first campaign or has there been a previous 'Charity Show'?
>
> Anyway, the good point about this answer is the greater proportion of time was spent on the effectiveness elements, criteria and overall outcomes. Note how some of the positive and negative points are drawn out. The answer could be improved by elaborating upon some of the key points/outcomes, as just listing them is not sufficient.
>
> When preparing for your exam, ensure that you know the nuts and bolts of what happened and when but please look at effectiveness measures, use criteria that make sense and consider the outcomes of the campaign in the light of the objectives set.

'The Star Charity Campaign' 1999

Introduction

A very good morning to you all and thank you for taking the time to attend this presentation. Today, I will evaluate the effectiveness of the Star campaign.

Slide 1

Title and Presenter's Name

Slide 2

1.0 *Situation analysis*

1.1 Located in Singapore, this campaign is held every two years in conjunction with the national welfare campaign.

1.2 The organiser is the Singapore Welfare Department and the main sponsor of the operation was the Television Corporation of Singapore (TCS).

2.0 *Target market*

2.1 General public, business groups, entertainment industry and government authorities

Slide 3.0

3.0 *Objectives*

3.1 To increase the awareness of charity donation by 10% among the Singapore public.
3.2 To create a more socially conscious image of Singapore as a whole
3.3 To raise S$30million during one month, to help the unfortunate in Singapore.

Answer bank

Slide 4

4.0 *Strategy*

4.1 Through a combination of both push and pull strategies it was decided to reach members of the Singapore public (pull) and organisations (push). The former used a massive advertising and promotion campaign and the latter focused on the use of persuasive personal selling. The campaign was built around the use of famous artists and entertainers.

4.2 It was decided to standardise the media and creative work and use a positioning strategy that enabled the campaign to deliver a clear message. Key words in the message were 'caring, national and love'.

Slide 5

5.0 *Critical assessment of the overall effectiveness of the campaign*

Positive

5.1 There was great support from the various Government bodies and local artists which helped to stimulate the campaign.

5.2 It appears that the public was well aware of the campaign and a great deal of (unquantified) positive support for the campaign was generated.

5.3 The big impact of the campaign was partially generated by the effective choice of media and the creative proposition.

5.4 It would appear that the methods used by which donations could be made (telemarketing) were effective and efficient.

5.5 Good methods of planning and control enabled targets to be met on time.

Slide 6

Negative

5.6 There are still various minority groups who chose not to participate.

5.7 The positioning of the event was slightly confused.

5.8 There was some risk associated with the demonstrations and performance by the entertainers and artists recruited to the campaign.

Slide 7

Criteria for Assessment

Financial

Donations received - per day/week/month
Growth - comparison with previous campaign
Number of participants - restaurants, Government agencies, private sector etc
Size of audience watching the 'Charity Night' show.
Number of donation/pledging telephone calls

Other

The campaign franchising effort
Awareness levels
Recall measures
Market penetration levels
Satisfaction levels achieved by donors

Slide 8

Method of Assessment

Both pre and post campaign test were undertaken in order to evaluate the results.

Type of test	Objective of test
Recall test	Campaign message
Awareness test	Existence of the campaign
Retail audit	Level of sales against target
Consumer panel	Critical views and opinions for planning future campaigns
Observation	Audience reactions to the show
Survey	Satisfaction levels and objectives achieved

Conclusion

The campaign was very successful and achieved most of the objectives that were set. Lessons were learnt for the future and perhaps a more integrated marketing communications campaign would be more effective and enable further improvements in donations made to be achieved.

40 MEASURING EFFECTIVENESS

> *Tutorial note.* Our examples are taken from the Institute of Practitioners in Advertising, *Advertising Effectiveness Awards.*
>
> *Examiner's comments, summarised by BPP.* Three examples were required to answer to this question. This was a tall order yet the question proved to be particularly popular. Those who attempted the question did so fairly well. The main fault was the very few criteria suggested. A good answer started by saying why effectiveness was important and went on to set out the marketing and communications objectives which are the basis of measuring effectiveness. The good examples described suggest that many teachers are successfully using real case studies and this approach is encouraged.

REPORT: MEASURING ADVERTISING EFFECTIVENESS

(a) *Importance of measurement*

It is vital to be able to measure the effectiveness of advertising or of any form of marketing communications. In the final analysis advertising can only be justified by proving its effectiveness. Lord Thomson, the famous physicist, stated that if you wanted to understand a process then firstly you had to measure it. Measuring the effectiveness of advertising is not an easy task because the process of marketing communications is a complex business. This process can be effected by a range of variables, not all of which are within the control of the company.

Increasingly as pressures on budgets increase it is necessary to measure advertising effectiveness in order to justify the marketing communications expenditure.

(b) *Criteria for measuring effectiveness*

(i) *The meeting of marketing objectives*

(1) Sales volumes.
(2) Profitability.
(3) Market share.
(4) Levels of awareness.
(5) Number of new accounts.

Answer bank

    (ii) *The degree of integration*

        (1) How consistent are the messages?
        (2) Do the methods link together?
        (3) Are strategic and tactical issues addressed?
        (4) Are cost savings possible?

    (iii) *Cost effectiveness/investment*

        (1) Is the campaign cost effective?
        (2) Can it be justified financially in the short term?
        (3) Can it be justified as a long term investment?

(c) *Example A: Andrex toilet tissue advertising*

Andrex has 30% of the toilet tissue market. No other brand has held a share of over 12%. Besides expanding its *market share* there has been a substantial increase in the market. It is unusual that a commodity product such as toilet paper should develop a 'superbrand'. Andrex has been assisted by the consistent appearance of a Labrador puppy since 1972. Andrex has another distinguishing feature: it is a premium product, in fact the most expensive toilet tissue available. The remarkable factor about Andrex is that it has sustained its effectiveness over a 20 year period in which its market share has grown and it has retained its premium prices. Research has shown that the Andrex puppy advertisement is eight times more efficient than the average TV commercial.

(d) *Example B: Save the Children campaign*

Every year for a single week in April the Save the Children Fund appeals for donations and on average it generates £600,000. The annual appeal in 1991 was remarkable in that it generated an amazing £5.5 million in the midst of a biting economic recession. The creative team established a rate of exchange between life in the UK and life in Africa and came up with the appeal to:

SKIP LUNCH, SAVE A LIFE

The strategy was to *maximise the low budget* by buying 'distress' media space. Advertising was designed to provoke responses. The launch of the appeal was a media success story. BBC, ITN and the national press carried the message Skip Lunch, Save a Life.

(e) *Example C: Häagen Dazs ice cream*

In 1991 Häagen Dazs became the most talked about ice cream brand in the country. The campaign to launch the product was designed:

(i) To develop a super premium ice cream sector in the UK
(ii) To become the ultimate ice cream in the market
(iii) To command a premium of exactly £1 over its rivals
(iv) To become a purveyor of a mood of 'sensual intimacy'

The budget was limited and the agency decided to break away from television and spend the bulk of the money on weekend colour supplements of the upmarket press. They chose titles which had a regional bias to the South of England which coincided with the ice cream's distribution. The advertising first created consumer excitement, then there was extensive editorial coverage, then trade excitement and consequently more and more consumer excitement. Communications effectiveness is measured by sales volumes, market share, levels of awareness, and cost effectiveness.

41 MARKETING COMMUNICATIONS EXPENDITURE

> *Examiner's comment.* This question was phrased in such a way that it could have been answered in one of two main ways. The first of these is the role and strategic impact of marketing communications whilst the other was to consider how the marketing communications budget was strategically important. Either interpretation was equally acceptable. The answer that follows attempts to consider both of these approaches.

Using our Money Wisely on Marketing Communications

by

A Marketing Manager

The amount of money any company spends on marketing communications, and advertising in particular, is absolutely crucial. Are the communications working, are they effective, are we getting good value, could we get it more cost effectively? These are all good questions, which that all management teams must ask themselves regularly and be able to respond to when challenged.

What I intend to do here is to provide some information about how we decide how much to spend on marketing communications. Before we look at these specific areas it is useful to consider what marketing communications is and what it is supposed to do. Then it will be possible to look at the different approaches to budgeting or *setting the right appropriation*, as it is called when considering the overall amount of investment in communications.

If you think about the key areas where, each and every day, we communicate with various audiences, it should come as no surprise that marketing communications is important to our success and can cost a great deal. Broadly, we communicate with the following.

- Customers
- Dealers
- Employees
- Shareholders
- Financial advisers
- Suppliers
- Local communities
- Competitors
- Media
- Many other interested parties

Of course the level of interaction will vary in intensity with each of these audiences throughout each year, depending upon a number of variables. However, marketing communications is about creating and sustaining a *dialogue* with each of these stakeholder audiences but *not just with our customers*. We need to *inform* audiences about new developments within the company, about new products and services and about what we as a company believe and value. We need to *persuade* audiences, especially customers and potential customers, we need to *demonstrate how we are different* and of value to each of them and we need continually to *remind and reassure* our customers not only about who we are but also about our products and services so that they will keep coming back to us.

BA invested over £60m in their corporate rebranding exercise in order to be identified as a global, not British, airline. Kellogg's, Nestle, Cadbury's, Unilever and the many other *fmcg* manufacturers invest millions each year on advertising in order to maintain and/or grow their market shares. Organisations in the business-to-business sector spend much less on advertising but more on personal selling and sales support. The area where the investment is made is not important to this paper. We are, however, interested in the effective and efficient use of limited resources.

In order to inform, differentiate, persuade and/or remind, we need to invest and allocate some of *our finances to marketing communications*. Choosing the right level of investment is important but unfortunately it is not a science. Yes, we have learnt over the years and we have a good idea about what the right level of investment might be. Some companies allocate a percentage of sales as the appropriation whilst others just take last years figure and add a percentage for inflation. Others allocate what they can afford whilst a few just guess. All of these methods have flaws in that they are neither customer-focused nor designed to do the right job.

Some other techniques involve investing the same as our competitors. Well, which competitor and how can we be sure that we are achieving real competitive parity? The Advertising/Sales Ratio provides an industry benchmark in order that we can understand whether we are investing above or below the industry average. For example, 1996 the A/S ratio for female fragrances was 8.7%, for cold treatments 14.2% and for cars 2.3%.

This ratio has proved useful but it does not provide the answer we are looking for as it focuses only on advertising. As we also use sales promotion, direct and interactive marketing, public relations, the sales force plus all the internal marketing communication activities, there are severe limitations to this approach. However, if our communications are predominantly above-the-line then this might be a useful method strategically.

It was reported that Procter & Gamble wanted to reduce their amount of advertising from 25% to 20% and use the 'savings' to fund price-offs in order to compete more effectively (on price) with their own-label competitors. A counter view from the company was that they wanted use their advertising and media expenditure much more efficiently yet maintain their overall visibility. This was a strong strategic approach and it courted much criticism and debate. Which ever way this policy is interpreted it is the strategic perspective that is interesting and significant.

By gauging the percentage of our communication spend against the total spent by all others in the market we are able to determine what is known as *Share of Voice*. These figures can be compared to our *Share of Market* and through analysis determine how much we should spend to achieve the market share we set ourselves. Whilst this is intuitively appealing there are some real difficulties in making this work and it does not really apply to our growing market.

PIMS (*Profit Impact of Marketing Strategy*) is a database system that uses actual data from real organisations across a variety of industries and market sectors. Through analysis of the database it is possible to determine what return on investment can be achieved based upon a number of variables. Depending upon whether a company is market leader, *number 2* or just another player it is possible to make judgements about, for example, the level of above and below-the-line promotional expenditure, or the right amount of trade communications.

We can use a number of these methods and compare the outcomes. We also determine what it is we want to achieve (*goals*) and how we think our various push (trade), pull (consumer) and profile (corporate) communication strategies will work. We then determine the actual (real) costs of putting it all into action and then make changes as necessary. This objective and task approach is perhaps the soundest technique of them all but it does require a great deal of time and accurate prediction in order to make it work.

Pedigree Petfoods said that after the tins and the cost of the meat the third most important factor to be measured and evaluated was the cost of the media and level of discounts used to advertise their dog and cat food products. This further serves to demonstrate that the level of communication spend can be a very significant part of an organisation's activities and needs a strategic perspective.

To be wise when spending or investing money is important. Our company is important and in order to grow and thrive in the next century it will be even more important not only to make good use of marketing communications but to also invest in communications in order that we maintain dialogue with the right audience using with the right message at the right time.

42 COMPETITOR'S ADVERTISING SPEND

Memorandum

To: Marketing Manager

From: CIM Student

Date: 12 December 1998

Ref: Advertising Spend Levels and Competitor Awareness

Introduction

In most markets competition is inherent, it is a natural feature of business life. Just as a boxer might land a punch on their opponent, so it would be naive not to expect a return punch or some retaliation.

Competition in fmcg markets for example can be extremely fierce where margins are invariably low. Advertising is the primary promotional method used to reach mass audiences but although the cost per thousand (cpt) may be low, the total campaign spend on a grocery product may be worth several millions of pounds in media time/space alone.

It is also worth observing at this stage that reference to the term spend levels can be misleading. Advertising is essentially an investment activity. Investment in advertising is undertaken to build the value of a brand (an asset for the balance sheet) in order to generate a suitable return and assist profitability (profit and loss account). However, for the purposes of this memorandum I shall continue to use the term spend.

The significance of knowing a competitor's spend levels

Understanding the level of a competitor's spend on advertising is just as important as understanding how their distribution works, who their channel members are, what their prices/discounts are and how their product is configured. All areas of a competitor's marketing mix need to be understood and monitored if we are to compete successfully and advertising is no different.

The level of advertising spend provides an indicator, not much more, of the probable strategy a competitor is pursing. For example, new products need heavy investment in order to achieve suitable levels of awareness and distribution. Established brands tend to spend less on communication and advertising in particular, with more being put into sales promotions. Here the goal is to spend just enough to sustain the competitive position. In 1997, Procter and Gamble slashed their worldwide media budgets by 20% with the intention of putting the resource into price cuts in order that they could compete more effectively with own label brands.

Answer bank

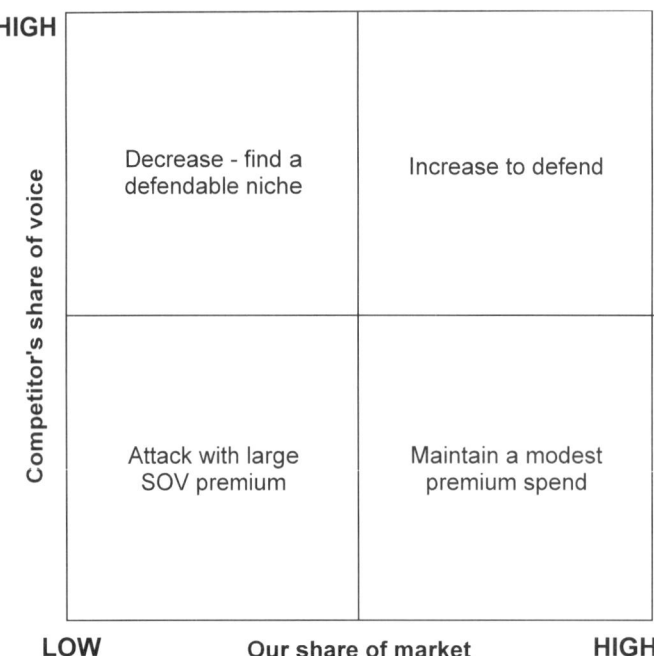

Some research (Schroer, 1990) suggests that by understanding the advertising spend relative to a competitors market share, it is possible to determine whether advertising spend should be varied.

The same research suggests that if the market leader (by share) underspends by some 25 to 30% and the number two player is able to increase its advertising spend (as a premium) then it is possible to become market leader. This approach has not been empirically proven but and may not be valid because of the difficulties involved in gaining access to suitable information. However, the principle is interesting as it consolidates beliefs about the relationship between spend and market share.

Four methods

One of the more basic methods of determining spend levels is competitive parity. By spending the same as our competitor(s) it is believed (by some) that optimal levels are achieved automatically. However, this ignores issues of different resource availability, strategy and brand value.

There are a number of methods used by organisations to determine their advertising spend. None of them can be regarded as correct although in practice the historic and accumulated experience is always a prime indicator of the ball-park spend that an organisation is likely to incur. It should also be understood that trying to establish an optimum figure is virtually impossible. Optimal implies having full and complete knowledge of the market, competitors and the returns that will be generated through advertising. Clearly this is not the case.

1   **Percentage of last year's sales (or next years)**

    This method involves calculating the budget as a percentage of last year's sales. For example, this may be 5% or 10% but it is not customer or competitor orientated, it is retrospective and does not take into account any support that brands may need. For example, to counteract particular competitive behaviour, to launch a product or revive a declining brand.

2   **Share of voice**

    This approach requires a measurement of our market share and the total spend on marketing communications by all players in the market. Therefore, share of market and share of voice statistics can be determined and the relationship between the two expressed as a ratio. For example, we hold a 2% market share and the total communication spend (above-the-line) for the market was £30m last year. Therefore, the SOV should be around 2% of £30m or £600K. Although this does ensure we have an appropriate 'share of voice' it does not consider our objective to increase market share.

3 Advertising to sales ratio

Closely allied to the SOV concept is the A/S ratio. In each market there is an average ratio of sales to communications spend. In engineering sectors this may be 0.2%, in food 4% and in fragrances 12.3%. The point is that in our sector the A/S ratio is about 15% so we need to understand whether our brand's A/S ratio is under, on or over the 15% and be able to justify the result.

4 Objective and task

The objective and task method works by identifying each communication objective for the forthcoming year. For example, 'raising awareness by 15% in our target market in the next six months' and the appropriate promotional tasks assigned to achieve it. For example, our TV work, print magazines and instore promotions need to be costed. If the resultant figure is not acceptable internally then the objectives need to be reworked or a different promotional strategy determined.

Whilst the objectives and tasks approach needs to be used for both the push and pull areas of our promotional work, one of the main benefits of this method will be that it will enable us to measure our results more productively and control the implementation of each campaign more effectively. It will also enable us to compete more successfully as our resources are being channelled more accurately into satisfying our objectives.

By using other approaches (SOV, A/S ratio, competitive parity) as a series of bench marking opportunities it will be possible to have a feel for competitive conditions and to retain competitive performance. It is also possible to buy data from PIMS. This is a large database through which we would be able to understand the sector's performance and to invest in communications in such a way that might generate an optimal return on investment. This last point needs to be explored in greater detail before any commitment is made.

43 CURRENT CAMPAIGN

> *Tutorial note.* There were three main hallmarks of a good answer to this question.
>
> (a) The ability to describe a current strategic marketing communications campaign in an exciting and relevant way.
> (b) The ability to set out and justify a range of effectiveness criteria especially linked to business success.
> (c) The ability to apply these criteria to the described campaign in a well judged manner.

REPORT

To: British Telecommunications 'It's Good To Talk'
From: Abbott Mead Vickers BBDO
Date: 3 December 1996
Ref: Measuring campaign effectiveness

1 Introduction

The 'It's Good to Talk' campaign for British Telecom's Personal Communications Division won the Grand Prix in the 1996 IPA Advertising Effectiveness Awards. It

Answer bank

produced startling business results, an estimated £297 million increase in sales, almost all of which equates to profits. In addition a new phrase 'It's good to talk' entered the English vocabulary.

Marketing magazine summed up the success of the campaign in the following quotation.

> 'Perhaps the word campaign does it an injustice, ... it's actually a piece of social engineering.'

This report describes the essence of the campaign and seeks to evaluate its effectiveness.

2 Description of the BT campaign

(a) *Situation analysis*

This is the third major campaign since the privatisation of British Telecom. It has proved to be the most successful, especially as it has taken place under difficult conditions including the following factors.

(i) An increase in competition from Mercury and the cable companies.
(ii) Changes in technology (the growth in use of faxes and e-mails).
(iii) Pressure by Oftel, the regulators to force BT to reduce a basket of charges.

In spite of these changes there remained a strong tendency amongst men to make minimum use of the telephone. Men viewed the telephone call as functional. Women were seen by some men as wasting money by long telephone calls. Men therefore acted in part as 'gatekeepers' controlling the use of telephones in their households.

(b) *Objective setting*

As BT's market share was decreasing one of the ways of retaining revenue was to use the power of advertising to stimulate the number of calls per customer. In particular the campaign had to have two major objectives.

(i) To change the attitudes of men to the personal and social value of telephone calls.
(ii) To tackle the perceptions of the relatively high cost of using the phone.

(c) *Strategy development*

A bold and innovative strategy was required to achieve these twin objectives. The campaign was developed around the powerful phrase 'Its Good to Talk'. This was particularly directed at the first objective and employed TV to present little vignettes, for example of a mother feeling neglected on her birthday. These were related by the actor Bob Hoskins, a very sympathetic character to male audiences.

The second objective was achieved by comparing BT charges to the cost of other everyday items such as a pint of beer.

(d) *Tactics*

Because of the audience size and the nature of the creative solutions television was chosen to present the vignettes. Bob Hoskins was portrayed as 'one of us' rather than a BT spokesperson. A national press campaign echoed and extended the TV campaign.

To reduce price perceptions a simple but powerful poster campaign was mounted starkly showing the relatively low price of BT calls compared with everyday items.

BT invested £44 million in these two campaigns between May 1994 and June 1995.

3 Criteria to judge effectiveness

The measurement of advertising effectiveness is a complex process. It is not possible therefore to state a simple set of criteria to judge campaigns. However, advertising can be seen as a marketing communications tool and marketing communications serves marketing objectives which in turn serve business objectives.

(a) The main criteria is the achievement of business objectives.

(b) Communication is a social tool most often concerned with influencing attitudes and behaviour patterns.

(c) Advertising has come to be recognised for its strategic contributions rather than being seen as having only short term influence.

(d) Media effectiveness is clearly important because of the costs involved.

(e) Creativity, though difficult to define, lies at the heart of the measurement of any advertising effectiveness.

(f) *Leverage* is the name given to the power to exert maximum effect from the combination of communications techniques used.

(g) Lastly, highly effective campaigns usually have a high degree of innovation of one kind or another.

These criteria can therefore be summarised as:

(a) Meeting business objectives
(b) Changing behaviour
(c) Strategic impact
(d) Media impact
(e) Creative impact
(f) Leverage
(g) Innovation

4 Evaluation of the BT campaign

The BT 'It's Good to Talk' campaign has been successful in meeting all of these criteria especially BT's business objectives.

(a) *Business objectives*

BT was able to demonstrate a significant increase in call duration and was able to achieve increased sales of £297 million compared with an advertising spend of £44 million.

(b) *Changing behaviour*

A noticeable shift in male attitudes to less than functional calls has taken place and there is now more realism about the cost of BT personal calls and residential services.

(c) *Strategic impact*

Because of competitive pressures and legal restrictions BT has to be bold in its strategy. Advertising has proved to be the key to unlock the strategic goal of increasing sales revenue. Because the infrastructure is in place most of the increase in sales has become an increase in profits.

(d) *Media effectiveness*

TV was effective in presenting the vignettes of life. Posters were ideal in giving simple price comparisons.

(e) *Creative impact*

The campaign succeeded in generating massive coverage in the media.

(f) *Innovation*

By being bold and innovative the campaign was proven to be successful A more cautious approach may not have worked.

*Changing mens behaviour
Prior to the campaign*

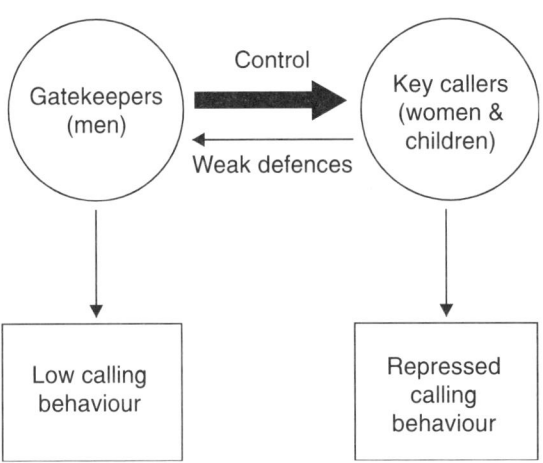

After the campaign

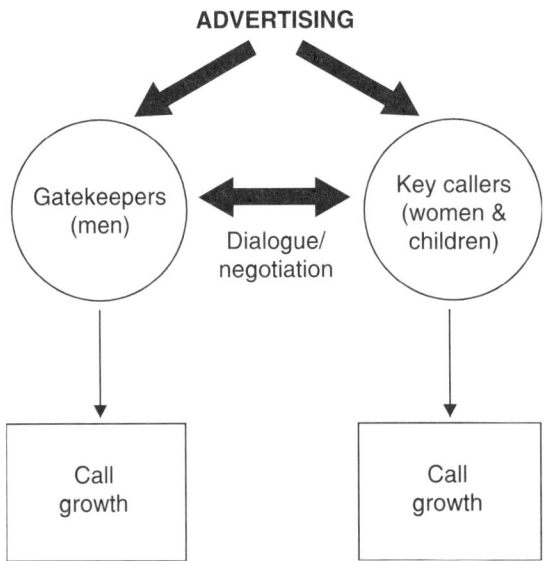

Conclusions

It is clear that the 'It's Good to Talk' campaign has been hugely successful in meeting BT's business objectives in very difficult trading conditions. It has been possible to describe other supporting criteria of measuring effectiveness. On these grounds too the BT campaign is judged to be successful. The award of the UK industry's top advertising prize to BT can therefore be seen to be justified.

44 PUBLIC INTEREST

> *Examiner's comments, summarised by BPP.* Better students were able to really evaluate the effectiveness of the campaigns they described. The same students were also clearly sensitive to the ethical issues involved.

Situation analysis

In 1994 a campaign by the Health Education Board for Scotland won an advertising effectiveness award from the Institute of Practitioners in Advertising. The award was a special prize in the 'given for a new campaign that resulted in a significant short term effect on the target audience's behaviour.

(a) Smoking remains the largest single cause of preventable illness in Scotland with over 10,000 smoking-related deaths per year.

(b) The overall prevalence of smoking in Scotland is at a higher level than in Great Britain as a whole.

(c) Without intervention the Scottish smoking problem is likely to become relatively worse until the end of the decade.

(d) A disproportionate number of smokers among the C2DE category also tend to be *heavy* smokers.

(e) Avoidance, denial, a fatalistic attitude and a resistance even to *try* to quit are common defence mechanisms among smokers.

(f) The Health Education Board for Scotland has to tackle a wide range of health issues but targeted smokers for this successful campaign.

Communication objectives

In its adult anti-smoking campaign the Health Education Board for Scotland has the following objectives.

(a) To remind smokers of the consequences to their health
(b) To motivate smokers to give up smoking altogether
(c) To contribute to a reduction in the prevalence of smoking
(d) To encourage the self-initiated kicking of the habit

The Health Education Board for Scotland concluded extensive research to test alternative approaches and found that:

(a) The purpose of advertising is not to impart the benefits of quitting
(b) A humorous tone would be rejected as trivialising the subject
(c) Empathy and practical help were needed

Communication strategy

To achieve these objectives the following strategy was adopted.

(a) Quitting is a complex process including many stages (see appendix).

Answer bank

(b) A new solution was required using both 'carrot' and 'stick' to tackle different stages of the quitting process.

(c) A two pronged strategy was designed combining both:

    (i) Hard-hitting messages to raise conscious of the health risk

    (ii) An aid to quitting via 'Smokeline', a free telephone helpline

(d) The campaign:

    (i) Created awareness of the Smokeline

    (ii) Generated responses to the Smokeline.

Advertising execution

The Health Education Board for Scotland used a mix of media.

(a) Television, in three bursts, with the carrot and stick message topping and tailing other commercials.

(b) Posters to maintain a hard-hitting message on the consequences of continuing to smoke.

(c) Smokeline: the free telephone helpline promoted through advertising.

(d) A booklet only available to callers to the Smokeline.

All elements of the campaign carried the strapline: 'You can do it. We can help'. In other words smokers were encouraged to give up by themselves, but with a helping hand.

Monitoring and control of effectiveness

The effectiveness of the campaign was monitored in four key areas.

(a) *Smokeline response*

    (i) Callers to Smokeline averaged 2,500 week during the first year.

    (ii) There was a direct correlation between number of calls and TV commercials.

    (iii) An estimated 6% of regular adult Scottish smokers made contact.

    (iv) The accompanying booklet had to be reprinted after only four months.

(b) *Changing attitudes*

Research carried out during the campaign demonstrated that:

    (i) There was an increased desire to quit smoking

    (ii) There was a decline in the weight of smoking

    (iii) Cutting down was regarded as a positive move towards quitting

(c) *Quitting smoking*

    (i) One year after the initial call to Smokeline 24% of the original smokers became non-smokers.

    (ii) Quit rates increased with increasing advertising exposure.

    (iii) Based on the quitting rate, minus the natural smoking decay rate, it was estimated that over 8,000 ex-smokers could be attributed to Smokeline.

(d) *Cost benefits*

The total campaign cost £650,000 and the saving to the Scottish economy in terms of health savings and reduced lost working days due to smoking-related illnesses is estimated at nearly £2 million. The profit generated by the campaign, taking into account advertising costs, is therefore £1.35 million.

Ethical issues

There are a number of ethical issues involved in any government advertising campaign and especially those involved in health education.

(a) Is it the job of government to try to prevent adult members of the public carrying out a lawful activity?

(b) Concurrently with the anti-smoking campaign the government is also receiving substantial receipts by way of taxes on tobacco products.

(c) Tobacco companies, within certain limits, are allowed to spend massive sums promoting their products. The tobacco advertising expenditure far outweighs that spent on health education by the government.

(d) If there are over 10,000 smoking related deaths per year in Scotland why is something more drastic not done?

(e) In additional large amounts of national health funds are being used up in treating smoking-related diseases. Should tobacco companies contribute directly to this treatment?

(f) If this campaign was so successful in Scotland why is it not being applied to other parts of the United Kingdom?

Appendix

The process of quitting smoking

1	Consciousness raising	I look for information related to smoking
2	Self-liberation	I tell myself I am able to quit smoking
3	Social liberation	I notice that public places are set aside for non-smokers
4	Self-revaluation	My dependency on cigarettes makes me feel disappointed in myself
5	Environmental revaluation	I stop and think that smoking is polluting the environment
6	Counter conditioning	I will do something else instead of smoking when I need to relax
7	Stimulus control	I remove things from my place of work that remind me of smoking
8	Reinforcement management	I am rewarded by others if I don't smoke
9	Dramatic relief	Warnings about health hazards of smoking move me emotionally
10	Helping relationships	I have someone who listens when I need to talk about my smoking

Answer bank

45 AN ACTUAL STUDENT'S ANSWER

> *Comments by the senior examiner.* I have chosen to reproduce an answer actually written by a student in the examination, including all spelling and grammatical errors. I will make comments about the answer and advise how it could be improved. This answer earned a pass but there is much room for improvement and many lessons to be learnt from this response.
>
> Students do necessarily have to provide material other than that specified as a requirement in the question. For example, the question makes no mention of budgets, strategies and promotional methods. It may be that in order to answer the question students may wish to refer to these elements and display the depth of their knowledge and understanding. However, there are severe time restrictions in the examination and I wish to encourage students to focus their answers upon those parts of the question actually stated.
>
> *Examiner's comments, summarised by BPP.* This question was the second most popular for international students. It was answered by 60% of international students and less than 30% of UK based students. A wide range of interesting campaigns was chosen and some reasonable results were achieved. The key to high marks was the ability to specify evaluation criteria. Clearly, this required a detailed and not superficial knowledge of the campaign.

Outline Report on the RSPCA's Communications Campaign

1   *Introduction - The Campaign*

   The RSPCA is currently running a direct mail campaign sending information and requesting for a questionnaire to be completed and returned as well as requesting for a donation.

   The mailing is in 3 colours, black, white and green, has the look and feel of recycled materials and interestingly, includes what they call "an inexpensive pen" to be used to complete the questionnaire and a prepaid reply envelope.

   The questionnaire asks about awareness of cruelty, whether it has been witnessed and general facts about the RSPCA which may or may not have been known. They also give information about the volume of cruelty cases/workload etc and ask whether this was higher/same or lower than expected.

2   *Campaign Objectives*

   The objectives are as follows.

   To increase awareness of the RSPCA and its work with animals
   To improve understanding that they don't just work with domestic pets
   To gage current levels of awareness
   To gage levels of concern about these issues
   To improve their database
   To generate income from donations

   The objectives are many, however, being a registered charity with relatively low budgets they are making the best use of their approach and therefore their budget. They are not in a position to be able to use many differing approaches for each objective.

3   *Target Audience*

   The audience targeted were:
   people with established links with the RSPCA
   previous known donators
   people known to be sympathetic to animal concerns
   families known to own pets
   people known to have been sympathetic to other charitable organisations

4   *Effectiveness*

Although the true effectiveness is yet to be known (as the campaign is still running) my evaluation of its effectiveness is as follows:

Positive: presentation looks inexpensive

pen enclosed - would people feel guilty not using it?

reply envelope (encouraging use of stamp)

effective use of resources 'feel'

powerful stories and pictures

Negative: pen damaged envelope in post

lots of different messages and lots of different questions - information overload

targeted at people already likely to have donated id not to RSPCA then to other charity - are they getting fed up?

possibly upsetting or could cause offence

assumptive close about donation means that non-donors are unlikely to return questionnaire.

5   *Conclusion*

Whilst I understand the considerable budget restraints charities have to contend with I feel the effectiveness is lost in that there are just too many messages. Information overload results in messages just not being heard.

I also believe that they should target outside the obvious with a campaign to change attitude - so that they become people likely to support.

They also need to get research on these people - linking a questionnaire with a donations misses this vital area. All they are likely to get is info about supporters' views and understanding.

> *Tutorial note.* Now read the analysis of this answer by Chris Fill, the senior examiner, on pages (xv) to (xvii).

46 TUTORIAL QUESTION: BRANDING

(a) The reasons for branding are as follows.

(i) It is a form of *product differentiation*, which makes customers readily identify the goods or services and thereby helps to create customer loyalty to the brand. It is therefore a means of increasing or maintaining sales.

(ii) *Advertising needs* a brand name to sell to customers and advertising and branding are very closely related aspects of sales promotion; the more similar a product (whether an industrial good or consumer good) is to competing goods, the more branding is necessary to create a separate product identity. An example is pet-food (eg Whiskas v Choosy).

(iii) Branding leads to a readier *acceptance* of a manufacturer's goods by wholesalers and retailers.

(iv) It facilitates *self-selection* of goods in self-service stores and also makes it easier for a manufacturer to obtain display space in shops and stores.

(v) It reduces the importance of *price differentials* between goods.

Answer bank

(vi) Brand loyalty in customers gives a manufacturer more *control over marketing strategy* and his choice of *channels of distribution*.

(vii) Other products can be introduced into the brand range 'piggy-back' on the articles already known to the customer (but ill-will as well as goodwill for one product in a branded range will be transferred to all other products in the range). Adding products to an existing brand range is known as *brand extension* strategy.

(viii) It eases the task of personal selling.

(b) According to Guilding and Moorehouse, seven factors are relevant.

(i) *Leadership:* how dominant is the brand in its sector:

(ii) *Market:* what are the growth characteristics of the market?

(iii) *Stability:* 'well established brands that enjoy consumer loyalty will receive higher strength scores'.

(iv) *Internationality:* international brands are generally worth more than national ones, as they are not vulnerable to one market, and a brand might be in another stage of its life cycle in an overseas market.

(v) *Trend:* a trend indicates a brand's ability to sustain itself. Reductions in sales volume reduce profit, but also make price increases harder to justify.

(vi) *Support.* Marketing expenditure can support a brand, but it must be of the right quality (eg a successful re-positioning).

(vii) *Protection* (eg patent protection, copyright, imitation etc).

(c) Branding is sometimes not considered relevant to products:

(i) That cannot achieve mass sales, because branding and the subsequent advertising would cost too much

(ii) Whose attributes cannot be evaluated by consumers

It is very difficult to think of good examples, however. Things like tap water, electricity, gas, and very common foodstuffs perhaps fall under (ii) in the UK (at present). Point (i) may have been true in the past but it is very questionable today. For example BPP is a distinctive and valuable brand, but the BPP Group does not achieve 'mass sales' in the conventional sense of the phrase.

47 EXAMPLES OF PLC

> *Examiner's comment.* This is a deceptive (not trick) question. Students saw the words product life cycle and leapt into an answer describing the concept but failed to focus on the promotional strategy with any depth of understanding. This should be an easy question but many failed to capitalise on the opportunity.

Memorandum

To: Marketing Manager
From: Marketing Assistant
Re: The Use of the Product Life Cycle concept (PLC)

Introduction

In this memorandum I shall set out what the product lifecycle (PLC) concept is and then determine whether the PLC is of any use when formulating and implementing promotional strategy. I hope the following points are of interest.

Definition of the PLC

The PLC is an attempt to explain and map the sales and profits that a product generates throughout its life time. The analogy drawn is that rather like a human being, a product is born, grows, matures and then declines towards death (or with drawl from the market place). As a result of defining these four stages in a products life, it has been suggested that it requires different strategies and tactics at each stage, in order that it flourish and achieve its potential.

This analogy is intuitively appealing and has been used a great deal to explain and interpret events. Whether it has a role to play in defining strategy is debatable, as will be seen later.

When the PLC was first proposed it was intended to refer to the life of generic products such as cars or telephones. However, it has become popularised to refer to particular products, brands and even fashion and more short-term events. The original idea therefore was that the strategies and tactics that evolved from the PLC were industry related rather than orientated to an individual product.

Four distinct phases of the PLC exist.

1	Introduction	the product's launch onto the market
2	Growth	rapid growth of sales volume as the product becomes known
3	Maturity	the product is in a mature competitive market - is no longer considered new
4	Decline	shrinking sales and profits, as the market declines and products are supplanted by new technology.

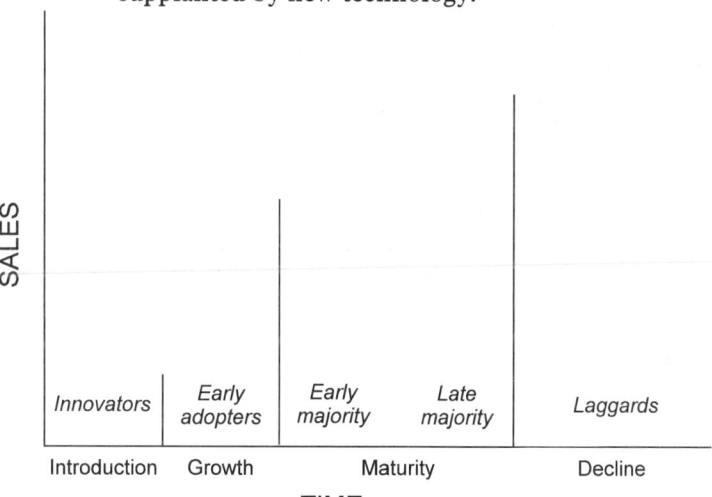

For the purposes of this memorandum I will refer to the PLC as a means of interpreting the lifecycle of individual products.

The PLC and developing promotional strategy

According to the theory each of the four stages have different strategic requirements and the focus here will only be on the promotional aspects.

Answer bank

Promotional Activities	Introduction	Growth	Maturity	Decline
Strategic focus	Strong push then pull for awareness	Pull to differentiate	Pull and push to sustain loyalty and exposure through reassurance	Some pull to remind core users
Public relations	x		x	
Advertising	x	x	x	
Direct marketing		x	x	x
Personal selling	x	x	x	x
Sales promotion	x		x	

The table above sets out the strategic focus for each phase and the main promotional activities to be considered. What the table does not show is the way the promotional tools are used to support a push as opposed to pull approach. One particular benefit of the PLC is that it is possible to overlay the various stages of the process of diffusion. Through this it is possible to identify the different types of buyer involved with the product at each stage and through this fine tune the appropriate message and media.

Introduction

For consumer brands this phase is critical as the primary need is to secure trade acceptance (and hence shelf space) and then build public (target audience) awareness. Sunny Delight was developed by Procter and Gamble in consultation with major multiple grocers. When the product was launched the multiples accepted the brand as had been developed partly to their specification, or least to particular category needs including price, ingredient and packaging/size specifications.

Digital TV has just been launched and there is strong competition between the two main players, Sky Digital and OnDigital. Both are using heavy weight advertising campaigns although both have resorted to sales promotion activity by giving away the set-top decoders free of charge where previously the price had been set at £200.

Growth

During growth promotional activity is used competitively to build market share. Customers are normally willing to buy having been made aware, their problem is one of brand choice. Marketing communications should therefore be used to differentiate and clearly position product such that it represents significant value for the customer. The mobile phone market has experienced tremendous growth in the UK in recent years. The four main players have sought to maintain (grow) their respective share of the growing market. Advertising and dealer support have been of paramount importance in meeting these needs.

Maturity

Once the rapid growth in a market starts to ease the period of maturity commences. The primarily characteristic of this stage is that there is little or no growth. The battle therefore is to retain customer loyalty and to do this sales promotions are often used to encourage trial by non-users of a brand and as a reward for current users.

Hoover have had to reposition themselves due to the market entry by Dyson with a technically superior product. Sales promotions alone therefore may not be sufficient and a whole repositioning programme may be necessary to sustain a brand in competitive conditions.

Decline

As sales start to decline it is normal practice to withdraw a great deal of promotion support. Direct marketing and a little well targeted advertising to remind and reassure brand loyals is the most commonly used.

Usefulness of the PLC

One of the main difficulties with the PLC is that the market is always interpreted in retrospective. It is very difficult to anticipate when different stages will be encountered and a lot depends upon the timing of the availability of sales figures. Returning to the original idea of the lifecycle, all children enter stages of puberty and adolescence but the timing will vary and their needs will often depend upon their personality and those of their parents. The same can be applied to products. The timing of the movement between stages will vary and the needs of the parent company (brand strategy) will also influence the promotional strategies that are implemented.

The PLC can help to:

1   Understand variations in demand
2   Account for different profit cycles and hence assist budgeting and control
3   Assist understanding of a products development
4   Assist teaching and understanding of marketing problems.

However, the PLC should not be used as a self-fulfilling prophecy and should not be used to develop marketing communication strategy in isolation of other tools and methods. Yes it can be of some limited general use but competitive conditions and environmental factors are constantly changing and the PLC is not rigorous enough to incorporate the complexities facing brand management.

48   LOYALTY SCHEMES

> **Examiner's comments**. This was the most popular question of the exam. Few candidates scored well. There was a failure to discuss the growth in these schemes. Many examples were used, but students should avoid the obvious Tesco/Sainsbury examples. The best answers pointed out the differences between loyalty and retention schemes.

Introduction

The growth of *customer retention and loyalty schemes* has been quite marked in recent years. There is a difference between the two although it is apparent that many commentators see these and *relationship marketing* as one and the same. This can be misleading as there are substantial differences between them.

The idea that consumers can display loyalty towards a brand or product in the same sense that they are loyal (or not) to partners and sports teams is questionable. However, this has not prevented the explosive increase in card based loyalty schemes, and especially those developed by the UK supermarkets, most notably Tesco and Sainsbury's.

Growth of customer loyalty schemes

The reasons for this growth are many and varied although it has to be said that *none of the schemes would have been possible without the increase in computing power* and the huge reduction in computing costs that have occurred since the end of the 1980s. *Database* technology and the ability to fuse different types of customer related information has helped transform marketing communications. Channel power has moved from manufacturers to retailers who are now able to collect and store information at the point of sale, about their customers and their product purchases.

Answer bank

A major influence on the development of these schemes has been the realisation that the *costs associated with searching for new customers far exceeds the costs associated with keeping current customers*. This may seem obvious, but it is only recently that many markets have become mature and stationary. Many new markets, such as the mobile phone market have experienced such high levels of customer loss or churn, that it is now important for the organisations in these markets to hold on to as many customers as possible, cross sell more products and so improve levels of profitability.

A further reason for the growth of these schemes has been the general strategic shift in communication spend from above to below the line. Advertising is still an important part of the communication mix but rising media costs and media and audience fragmentation have driven organisations to shift increasing proportions of their spend below the line. Customer retention initiatives represent a form of sales promotion and whilst there are many different variations the central theme of reward for continued patronage continues to be a favoured approach.

AirMiles

British Airways developed the AirMiles scheme from the overcapacity identified on certain flights. The scheme allows BA the opportunity to reward their more loyal customers with free air travel, at little cost to themselves. The business travel segment is an important market and by encouraging regular fliers to collect AirMiles, BA were adding benefit to the purchase decision and in doing so added value and competitive advantage to flying with BA. The global alliances that BA has since developed allows travellers the opportunity to collect AirMiles on a number of different carriers and flights. This further protects against overcapacity, provides for customer retention and perhaps contributes to an element of loyalty and the development of a competitive relationship between carriers and travellers.

UK supermarket loyalty schemes

Following the lead of Tesco, Sainsbury's offers its Reward Card scheme which awards customers with points when a purchase is made. These points can be exchanged for cash off a purchase or accumulated into a voucher which can be used to purchase a variety of different products, one of which is AirMiles.

This scheme along with the others in the sector appear to be effective. What may be happening, of course, is that rather than loyalty being demonstrated it is more a means of added convenience. The schemes provide a reason to return to the same store and so reduce the amount of experimental shopping (visiting rival stores). Indeed the stores actively encourage people to shop more often at their store rather than the once a week/fortnight big shop. The 'thank you' or even incentive is the collection of reward points.

One of the traps that need to be avoided is that these loyalty/retention/reward schemes should not be relied upon alone to provide the growth that the Sainsbury's, Safeway and Tesco seek to satisfy their shareholders. In-store ambience, ease of parking/access, display, store layout, range of goods, pricing and the overall shopping experience are significant contributors to customer retention levels and overall levels of customer satisfaction.

Effectiveness

The strategic significance of these loyalty schemes should not be underestimated. Sainsbury's held off for a long time before following Tesco's lead with a Reward Card. The implication is that these schemes represent not an advantage necessarily but more of a competitive requirement. Once a loyalty or reward scheme is established in a market by one organisation it appears that all other players need to offer a competitive scheme. Competitive advantage rests with the first entrant, whereas competitive parity becomes the imperative for the others. This can be further evidenced by the proliferation of retention schemes offered by High Street retailers such as Boots and W.H. Smith and the store card schemes offered by the majority of national retailers.

These schemes appear effective and may represent good value for promotional spend. One of the alternatives is to spend the 'reward money' on advertising. The measurement and overall effectiveness of advertising has been questioned for a long time whereas Retention schemes are easily measurable and the impact clearly visible.

49 CUSTOMER RETENTION

> *Examiner's comments*
>
> Most students gave the two answers required. Good answers differentiated loyalty from retention; they went on to explain where value was added. It was not enough to describe two schemes. These schemes needed to be assessed for their ability to add value.
>
> It was evident that many students failed to read the question properly.

To: The Marketing Manager
From: CIM Student
Date: 7 December 1999

Ref: Customer Retention Schemes

1.0 Introduction

This report explores the suggestion that the development of a customer retention scheme might add value to our marketing communications. To do this I will discuss issues concerning loyalty and retention and then provide two examples where in my opinion the communications strategy has been improved as a result of including the retention scheme.

2.0 Customer Retention

In many consumer markets the number of customers who switch to competing brands is very high. As the level of profitability appears to be directly linked to the number of customers retained it is important for organisations to minimise the number of customers lost each period. 20% of customers provide 80% of profit and according to Kotler, the bottom 30% absorb 50% of the profits.

Financially therefore, it is imperative to control the levels of retention/defection. A brand's health is also indicated by the level of retention as this can be regarded as a surrogate measure of customer satisfaction, albeit a crude one. The UK mobile telephone market is subject to a rate of customer churn (defection) of around 30% but this is spread fairly evenly across the four main players. This figure has been reduced through the introduction of new products such as pay-as-you-go services which introduced new customers to the market and provide an element of stability.

Customer retention is not customer loyalty. These terms are often interchanged but regular purchase may be indicative of convenience and instrumental buyer behaviour which is based around satisficing and the search for valued rewards such as Air Miles and Reward Vouchers.

Loyalty in its true form means that customers might need to make sacrifices in order to remain loyal to a brand. This rarely happens, as consumers readily switch brands among their repertoires and are prepared to trial new retail brands (grocery multiples) if levels of customer convenience and satisfaction fall below acceptable thresholds. Retention should be regarded as a matter of overall product acceptability or at least satisfaction across salient attributes.

Management are now in a far stronger position to manage levels of customer satisfaction and retention through technology. Through customer profiling and profitability analysis based upon transaction data collected through POS systems and reward cards it is now easy to shape the product offerings to meet customer needs more accurately. To a large extent, many supermarket reward schemes are based on the use of their data in this way.

3.0 Impact on Communication Strategy

The development of a customer retention programme could have a number of benefits. It would serve to direct the attention of staff towards the need to be vigilant about standards and the need to drive up satisfaction levels. In that sense it could be part of an integrated marketing communication programme. A retention scheme would also serve as a focal point of a pull based strategy and perhaps reduce the level of fragmented communication activities. Retention schemes are to a large extent customer focused and enable rewards to be offered to different types of customers and in doing so reflect their levels of involvement with the brand. British Airways reward their frequent fliers through a tiered scheme according to the benefits sought by their customers. For example, Blue members are more interested in Reward (for their custom) with a little lounge service, whilst Silver members are interested in service, exclusivity and reward in roughly equal proportions. Finally, Gold members are more interested in exclusivity and service, reward for them is not important.

Our communication strategy would be enhanced as it would enable us to use our resources more effectively and reduce the level of our above-the-line spend. Through the use of direct marketing techniques we can personalise our communications and introduce a more customised approach to our entire operations. Tesco have developed their direct mail operations so that it is now a powerful and important part of their marketing communications. By understanding individual buying patterns and preferred products it has become possible to develop targeted sales promotions, delivered through direct mail, which serve to retain customers and improve satisfaction levels.

One of the difficulties however, is that customer expectations rise, competitors imitate schemes and there is a need to be innovative and find new ways of retaining and satisfying customers. This requires resources and an organisational culture which, if to be successful requires the development of good internal marketing communications.

All of these activities have the potential to affect our corporate image so we would be better able to change our positioning and develop a more robust and contemporary corporate brand. Tesco have moved from a market position based upon relatively inexpensive products and poor value to one that represents excellent value and quality across their operations and has enabled them to become market leader. Their above the line work reinforces the Tesco brand and little effort is spent communicating product offers and particular discounts.

4.0 Conclusion

The development of Customer Retention schemes is an important part of many consumer marketing communication plans. To maintain and grow levels of profitability it is necessary to keep a greater number of customers. To do this properly it appears that an organisation's communication programme benefits from schemes that rewards its customers and deliberately seeks to add value to staff, customers and all those associated with the programme.

50 TUTORIAL QUESTION: DIFFERENCES

(a) *Arguments for standardising communications*

   (i) Economies of scale can be generated. A single worldwide advertising, packaging or direct mail execution will save time and money.

   (ii) A consistent and strong brand image will be presented to the consumer. Wherever users see the brand, they will be reassured because the messages received will be the same.

   (iii) A standardised communications policy allows for easier implementation and control by management.

   (iv) Good communications ideas are rare and should be exploited creatively across markets.

   Arguments against standardising communications

   (i) Any standardisation policy assumes consumer needs and wants are identical across markets. This may be a false assumption, as the example below illustrates.

   (ii) Centrally-generated communications concepts may prove to be inappropriate for the specific culture of the local market.

   (iii) Media channel availability and infrastructure varies widely from country to country.

   (iv) A country's level of economic and educational development may prevent a standardised approach. For instance, a press campaign featuring detailed copy would be a non starter if literacy levels were low.

   (v) Legal restrictions may prove to be a stumbling block. For example, France does not allow any advertising of alcohol on television; cashback sales promotion offers are not allowed in Italy or Luxembourg.

   (vi) Standardisation may encourage the 'not invented here' syndrome, so that local management become lacklustre about creative ideas and communications policies imposed from above.

(b) The following dimensions are of particular relevance to the *international marketing* communicator.

   (i) Verbal and non verbal communications
   (ii) Aesthetics
   (iii) Dress and appearance
   (iv) Family roles and relationships
   (v) Beliefs and values
   (vi) Learning
   (vii) Work habits

(c) (i) Press may not be appropriate in countries where levels of literacy are low.

   (ii) TV ownership may not be widespread. There may be no commercial stations.

   (iii) Outdoor tends to rely on visuals and it is therefore a good international medium.

   (iv) Cinema is experienced in different ways (drive-ins etc). The quality of films (and hence the audience) varies considerably.

   (v) Radio is mainly a support medium across the world. Commercial stations may not be available.

   There are many other valid points that you could have made.

Answer bank

51 TWO COUNTRIES IN THE KITCHEN

> *Tutorial note.* The hallmarks of a good answer for this question covering international marketing communications strategy are:
>
> (a) the choice of two contrasting companies;
>
> (b) an understanding of the cultural, economic and media differences and their importance;
>
> (c) an ability to explain the relevance of the differences to the marketing of consumer goods;
>
> (d) a sensitivity to growing internationalism.

MARKETING COMMUNICATION STRATEGIES DIFFERENCES BETWEEN BRITAIN AND JAPAN

1 Introduction

For the purposes of this question I have chosen to contrast two countries, the United Kingdom and Japan. Though they are both developed countries they are representative of two different cultures, a western culture and an eastern culture. There are also considerable differences in economic conditions and in media availability. All these factors influence the manner in which a consumer goods manufacturer designs a marketing communications strategy.

Contrasting with this many products have become global in character. Interestingly this applies particularly to Japanese consumer products such as those made by companies like Sony, Sharp, Canon and National Panasonic as well as to automotive brands such as Honda, Toyota and Mitsubishi.

A marketing maxim to guide selection of strategies is:

> TO THINK GLOBAL
>
> AND ACT LOCAL

The firm and its national environment

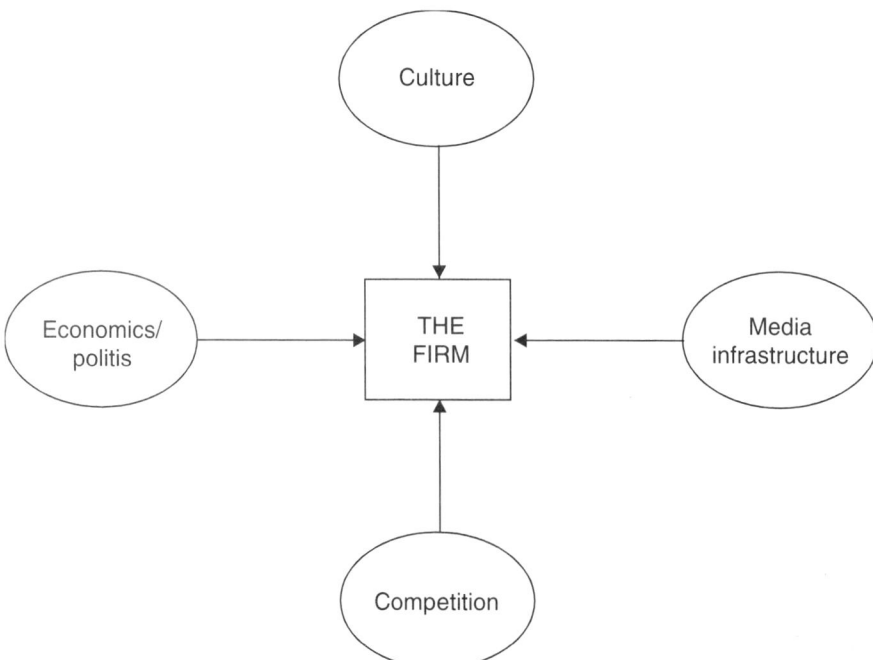

From this diagram the firm can be seen to be in an environment surrounded by a number of factors. These factors such as culture, economics and media availability, are largely outside the firm's control and they are likely to differ from country to country. If they vary and cannot be controlled the firm must adapt its strategy from country to country

3 The communications process

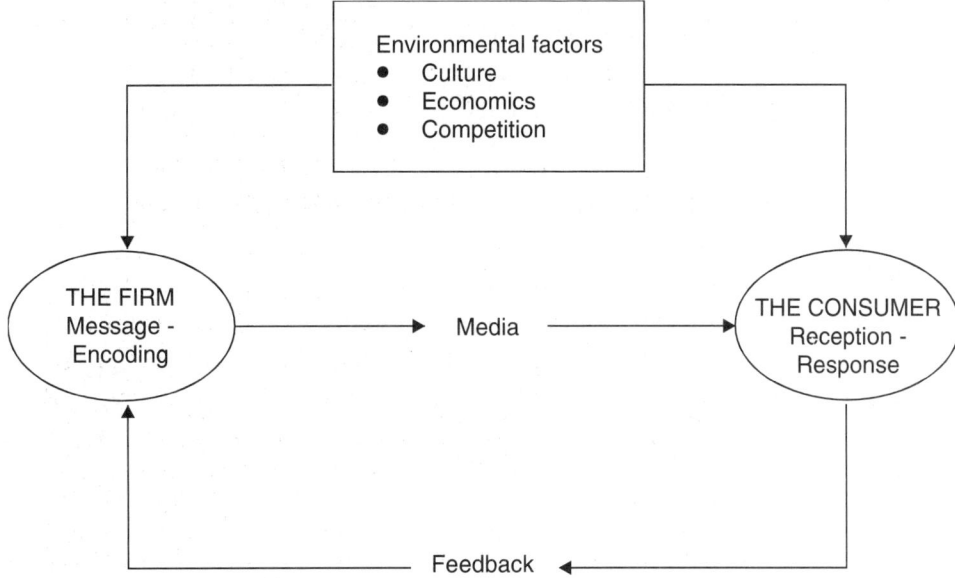

It can be seen from this diagram that one of the key strategies that has to be changed is that concerned with marketing communications. The uncontrollable variables of culture, economics and media availability impact directly on both the firm and its customers.

4 Cultural differences

The *eastern culture* is considerably different from the western culture in a number of important respects.

(a) Attitudes and beliefs
(b) Religious traditions
(c) Lifestyle and demography
(d) Verbal and non verbal communications
(e) Habits and traditions
(f) Gender roles
(g) Family behaviour
(h) Gender roles

There are many contrasts between the UK and Japan in respect of these areas. For example, Japan is still a very male dominated society. Recent campaigns for Sainsburys and OXO showing men cooking would be inappropriate in Japan.

Similarly, campaigns in Japan often feature the problems of living in the same household with three generations of a family. This is a situation which is becoming much less frequent in the UK.

Verbal and non verbal communication patterns can also influence advertising methods. Japanese characters often take up more space to write a simple strapline than English ones do.

Products in Japan often carry long product descriptions whereas this is less common in the UK.

Religion in Japan plays more of a part in dictating what is acceptable and many UK commercials in the UK would be seen as too risqué for the Japanese market. This would particularly apply to campaigns with overt sexual connotations.

Answer bank

5 Economic differences

Japan has an economy which is in many ways more developed than the United Kingdom. Factors that we need to consider are as follows.

(a) What is the level and trend in per capital income?
(b) Is the balance of payments favourable or unfavourable?
(c) Is inflation under control?
(d) Are the exchange rates stable?
(e) Is the currency easily convertible?
(f) Is the country politically stable?
(g) How protectionist is the country?
(h) Who controls distribution channels?

Traditionally Japan has been a more controlled economy than the United Kingdom. Import restrictions have kept Japan's balance of payments favourable.

Companies are controlled by the large Japanese banks and the economic wealth has trickled down so that standards of living are high.

This makes Japan attractive to manufactures of luxury goods such as whisky and Rolls Royce cars. However, western goods such as Coca Cola and McDonalds have still managed to penetrate the Japanese market.

Seeking a Japanese business partner is one way of entering the market. Such a partner will be able to advise on marketing communications strategy.

6 Media differences

Japan has a very complex media scene where television often dominates advertising campaigns. TV provides strong national coverage.

There are a few national daily newspapers but the regional press is very strong. Radio advertising is also strong.

Consumer products must be effectively targeted and this involves choosing a media that is relevant, available and cost effective, has appropriate lead times and provides effective representation.

7 Marketing consumer products

Any effective marketing communications strategy must take account of individual country's cultural, economic and media differences to ensure that it is appropriate and sustainable.

Whilst there is an increasing push towards internationalisation of campaigns (with successes such as De Beers and Pizza Hut) it must be remembered that each target market has specific characteristics to be planned for.

52 WITH OR WITHOUT?

> *Examiner's comments, summarised by BPP.* This was a relatively popular question with 40% of international students. This contrasts sharply with only 20% of UK students. Those that did attempt it did relatively well. Tea and coffee afforded candidates a reasonable opportunity to explore various communication issues and demonstrate their strategic knowledge. The concept of breaking into a saturated market appeared to be less well understood. Very good answers were able to demonstrate an intimate knowledge of the cultural/social and market conditions in their chosen country and draw strategic linkages between the different components of the question.

Answer bank

REPORT

To: F W Smith - Managing Director of Super Beverages Ltd
From: T Leaf
Date: 4 June 1997
Ref: UK tea and coffee market conditions

1 *Executive summary*

This report suggests that the tea and coffee *market* in the UK is large but competitive. There is a range of target markets, depending upon convenience or real product preference.

Cultural and social trends are considered: the indications are that the market is unlikely to decline but consumption may be static.

Growth within the market is dependent upon brand switching, which is difficult and can be expensive to achieve.

The *retail structure* reflects concentration in five main supermarkets for the convenience market. The independent sector deals with specialist beverages and each sector requires an entirely different marketing communications strategy.

The availability of a wide range of sophisticated *media* allows many opportunities to reach target audiences.

The report concludes by recommending that entry will depend upon positioning and brand development.

2 *Situation analysis*

This report has been prepared in order to assist you with your decision about whether or not to enter the UK market for tea and coffee. Various aspects of the market are considered, in particular the social and cultural trends, the retail structure and media opportunities.

3 *Target end users*

There are a number of segments that could be investigated further to determine the depth of potential.

- Convenience coffee users
- Real coffee users
- Tea bag users
- Real tea users
- Specialist tea users

The majority of tea is consumed by users spread across the socio-economic profile with coffee users skewed more to the ABC1 profile. Real coffee has become more popular in recent years, particularly in the 30 to 45 age range.

Opportunities may exist to position a new instant coffee or tea product by real differentiation. The market is currently dominated by a number of key brands, who use taste and smell (rich aroma), lifestyle (up-market and affluent) and usage (tea bag shape) as the principal means of differentiation. However, the market is relatively static and experiencing little real growth.

4 *Cultural trends*

Traditionally tea is drunk at the end of the afternoon and first thing in the morning and coffee is drunk at the end of a lunchtime or evening meal. These traditions are giving way as new products such as decaffeinated coffee and specialist teas become

Answer bank

more popular. There are no significant regional differences to the consumption of either drink although more tea is drunk than coffee.

Consumption of tea in the UK is probably high in comparison to other European markets and from that point of view the UK market is attractive to new entrants. However, margins are tight and profitability is only likely to be generated by developing niche markets or by finding a new market segment.

5   *Social trends*

It is estimated that by the year 2000 over 50% of the UK population will be over retirement age (65). This may mean that the number of cups of tea consumed may well continue to rise. Tea is a relatively low-involvement product decision and it is important to establish brand loyalty, as taste deters switching.

The traditional family unit continues to be eroded as divorce rates continue to climb and the number of single parent families also increases. At the same time there is an increasing awareness of the need to eat a healthy diet, take more exercise and lead a more sympathetic lifestyle. Because of this decaffeinated coffee products have taken a substantial foothold in the UK market.

Associated with this point about lifestyle is the increased attention being given to green and ethical issues. In particular the exploitation of third world workers has been highlighted by a number of pressure groups and in this sector there has been negative publicity directed at tea producers in India.

6   *Retail structure*

The retail structure has changed dramatically over the past 10 years. Five major supermarkets dominate 65% of food purchases. Manufacturer and own-label branded tea and coffee products are bought from these outlets, in packages that suggest a purchase cycle of 2 to 3 weeks. Tea bags are packaged in card based cartons; instant coffee is distributed in glass jars, which adds to weight and cost. To secure sufficient market coverage it will be necessary to gain a listing with at least one of these main supermarkets. A strong promotional support package will be expected, incorporating trade allowances, joint promotions and price deals to remain competitive and provide strategic leverage.

There are a number of specialist retailers who deal with high quality teas and coffees for those segments who prefer high grade, unbranded products. Depending upon the target market, attention will need to be paid to negotiations with central buyers for the supermarket sector or a variety of individual buyers in the independent sector.

7   *Media factors*

The UK is a media rich country and the choice of media opportunities is expanding. With 98% of the population having access to at least a single television, it is possible to reach a mass market to develop a branded product.

There are numerous newspapers and consumer magazines in which advertising is possible. The development of a branded tea or coffee will be based partly around suitable print formats to reach different target audiences.

In addition to this, billboards, transport and cinema media will be an integral part of mass market campaigns.

With a purchase cycle of 2 to 3 weeks it will be necessary to generate and maintain top-of-mind awareness. Whilst this will incur high absolute costs the relative costs associated with reaching each member (or 1,000 members) of the target market will be quite small.

To promote tea and coffee in this market it will be necessary to use peripheral cues as consumers are not particularly interested or involved. The use of long copy formats is not a requirement and so the media used to prompt awareness and preference will favour television and billboards rather than print.

The are a number of trade magazines, such as *The Grocer*, in which it will be necessary to communicate with the central supermarket buyers and, more importantly, the independent specialist buyers who run their own retail outlets will have access to this publication. Unlike the consumer market, these buyers are highly involved and it will be necessary to provide detail about the product and its constituents and origins if credibility is to be established.

8 *Conclusion and recommendations*

The UK consumes huge quantities of tea and increasing quantities of coffee. The instant beverage market is driven by a number of major brands so successful entry will be dependent upon accurate positioning and communication with the target segments.

53 GLOBAL CAMPAIGN

> *Examiner's comments, summarised by BPP.* This was not a popular question. Possibly this was because not many students at the diploma level are involved in global strategies even though they may work for international companies. However, this is an important topic in the syllabus and it is one which is reinforced by the International Marketing Strategy syllabus. The question called for a short report on the advantages and limitation of global campaigns. Whist reference to particular campaigns adds value to an answer what was mainly required was a listing of the main advantages and limitations of global campaigns.

REPORT

Subject: Advantages and pitfalls of global advertising strategies
Prepared for: Managing Director
Prepared by: Marketing Manager
Report date: June 1995

1 *Executive summary*

To date our company has organised its advertising on a country-by-country basis. We have even used different agencies in different countries because of their local knowledge.

In the past the bulk of our sales have been in the domestic market but now increasingly our sales are shifting abroad and we are starting to manufacture abroad.

It is now an appropriate time to review our global advertising strategy and to decide which direction we should go in. In this short report I will list the advantages of a global campaign strategy and also identify some of the possible pitfalls.

Finally I will give some recommendations which may be summarised as:

THINK GLOBALLY - ACT LOCALLY

2 *Advantages of a global campaign*

The extremes to which global campaigns may be taken are exhibited by McDonalds and by Coca Cola. Here the campaign and message is designed and controlled centrally. IBM in its corporate branding campaign has designed a standard campaign centrally and uses it throughout the world. IBM is concerned to present a high-impact consistent image. The only difference from country to country is the sub titles in the local language but the message is the same: 'IBM: solutions for a small planet'.

Answer bank

In fact this IBM campaign indicates one of the main reasons for considering a global campaign that is standardised. We are living in a shrinking world - a global village - a small planet.

Other advantages of such a standard global campaign are as follows.

(a) Worldwide consistency
(b) Economies of scale in production and media
(c) Greater buying power
(d) Suits international customers
(e) Used in international media
(f) There is a convergence of tastes internationally
(g) Faster communications between countries
(h) Use of the information superhighway
(i) Easier management control

3 *Possible difficulties of a global campaign*

These are powerful reasons for considering a standard global campaign, especially as there are claimed to be cost savings. However, on talking to similar companies to ourselves, it appears that the traffic is not one way and that there are a significant number of difficulties as well.

(a) There are language and translation difficulties. Tremendous mistakes have been made.

(b) There are cultural and religious differences which will influence the way we would market the product.

(c) There are also differences in the state of technological development between our different overseas sales regions. In the worst case they require completely different products.

(d) In a few countries we have been able to establish ourselves as a specialist niche player.

(e) Each country has its own distribution channels which will affect our advertising strategy.

Overall there is the human factor to consider. Our overseas companies and agents are used to having the power to make autonomous decisions. They know their customers and the local conditions. We are likely to demotivate them if we radically change the systems.

4 *Recommendations*

I am therefore recommending that we strive to achieve a balance. We should take greater control of the design and planning of our corporate international campaign but we should delegate as much as possible of the local execution and short-term sales strategies to our overseas centres. We really should follow the maxim - think globally, act locally.

54 ADVANTAGES AND DISADVANTAGES OF INTERNATIONAL AGENCIES

> *Examiner's comments, summarised by BPP.* Some students were clearly aware of the topical issues and were able to describe the advantages and disadvantages of international agencies. The best students were able to go on and describe the changes that the agencies are facing in the future.

Answer bank

Full service multinational agencies

Over the last forty years many companies have expanded their operations internationally. Initially advertising strategies would have been controlled centrally from the company's head office. With growing size and confidence a policy of 'Think globally - act locally' would be developed. One consequence would then be the appointment of local advertising agencies in each of the operating countries. In time, dozens or even (in the case of very large companies) hundreds of agencies, each with their own specialisations, could become involved. This obviously has many potential difficulties.

Fortunately over the same period as companies expanded their operations internationally so too have advertising agencies. Many international agencies have grown either by setting up branch offices overseas or by merging with or acquiring local agencies. Key among world wide agencies have been groups with headquarters in London eg Saatchi and Saatchi and the WPP Group (which includes J Walter Thompson and Ogilvy and Mather). Another mechanism for growing international advertising services is the formation of international networks or alliances of autonomous companies.

As the trend among advertisers has been towards international brands and global integrated campaigns, the need for the international full service agency has also grown. By 'full service' we mean the offering of a range of communication services: advertising, public relations, direct marketing. It has been suggested that agency structure tends to mirror the structure of their clients. This is shown below.

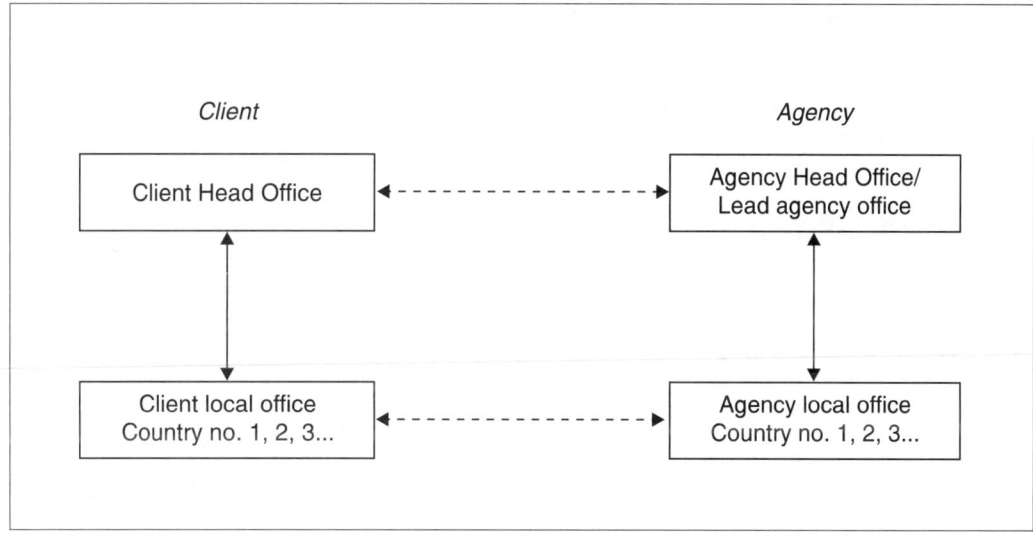

Advantages of multinational agencies

(a) Centralised control of all advertising effort
(b) Less duplication and dilution of effort
(c) Speedy response across markets
(d) Consistency of presentation
(e) Pooling of ideas and talents from throughout the agency
(f) Specialist resources can be made available
(g) Standardised working methods by the agency
(h) Reduced costs due to economies of scale

Disadvantages of multinational agencies

(a) Antagonism is caused at local level
(b) Possible loss of local knowledge
(c) Uneven quality in their different branches
(d) Bland campaigns can sometimes be produced

Answer bank

(e) Local cultures and styles may be lost
(f) Quality control can suffer because of complex logistics
(g) Campaigns are tailored to suit the conventions of the agency
(h) Smaller clients suffer from lack of attention of senior local staff
(i) There is a tendency for large agencies to suffer from a high turnover of creative staff
(j) 'Not invented here' syndrome

The changes they are facing

Multinational full service advertising agencies will face many changes in the next five years.

(a) International client companies are likely to continue to grow, placing even more demands on their multinational agencies.

(b) Forms of transnational media such as satellite television and the Internet will pose challenges in terms of media status.

(c) Media buying and selling power is becoming more concentrated. This has lead to the continuing growth of international media independents.

(d) Advertisers are likely to become more sophisticated and more demanding of their agencies.

(e) Agencies will need to become more accountable. There is some movement to payment by results systems.

(f) There is likely to be a continuing concentration of ownership of agencies with fewer larger global organisations.

(g) There will be a growth of agency branches in developing countries such as Russia, Eastern Europe and China.

55 MINI-CASE: BRITISH GLASS RECYCLING COMPANY

Examiner's comments.

(1) This question signals that the minicase will in future draw on a range of contexts. Students will be required to use material that reflect a variety of circumstances and that global brands can no longer be expected to be the base material.

(2) Students are advised that **this** question format will not necessarily be followed in future. Students must be able to prepare marketing communications plans for products and brands in the consumer and business-to-business sectors. In addition, students may be asked to prepare a plan for a major global brand, a small industrial product or for any type of product or service in unfamiliar contexts. **It does not follow that students will always be expected to produce a marketing communications plan.**

(3) The answer that follows contains elements that for some students are new or only vaguely familiar. I did not receive many answers with the content as set out here, although most followed the same structure.

Students are advised that it will be necessary to provide depth and judgement in their answers and that it is important to recognise the importance and significance of understanding the behavioural aspect of the buyer. In other words, an understanding of consumer behaviour will be an important part of the marketing communication strategy paper in future.'

In addition the examiner made the following comments about students' performance in the exam.

'More students gained higher marks than is normal ... too many failed to realise the significance of the trade sector and the need to enlist other members of the marketing channel, both vertically and horizontally.'

Answer bank

Strategic Marketing Communications Plan for BGRC 1999-2001

Contents

1.0 Context analysis

> *Examiner's comments.* Students may be more familiar with the term situation analysis. I prefer the term Context Analysis as it stresses the need to consider a range of elements that are *particular* to the development of a single communication plan. Many students either ignore the need to consider the current situation and those that do include it often make the mistake of reiterating detail from the question and focus on general marketing issues rather than the marketing communication issues.

1.1 The business context

The level of recycling activity in the UK lags behind the levels expected by the EU and the Government, and this is the prime force behind this marketing and marketing communications activity. The UK needs to increase the level of glass recycling from 30% to 50% by end of the second year of this plan, 2000.

There are some complications associated with the quality (and colour) of the glass collected from the public, which impacts on the level of recycling that is possible. Steps need to be taken therefore to control the quality and form of glass collection.

1.2 The customer context

There are two main types of customer involved with this plan.

(a) The *general public* contains a number of important subsegments. The attitudes of men towards the recycling of glass is deemed as negative. This attitude problem is of particular significance as these men act as *role models* for children and in order to encourage long term recycling habits it is necessary to communicate with children, families and men in the 25 to 34 age group.

(b) The other main customer group is *organisations*. The most important of these are restaurants, clubs, hotels and local authorities.

Both main customer groups have different motivations to be involved with glass recycling. Most people have limited knowledge about recycling and it may be that further education is needed about the ecological issues. Both perceived risk and involvement is low for this group.

For the business group, levels of awareness need to be raised and the *opportunities for cost saving* and *community contribution* need to be brought to their attention.

1.3 The organisation context

Assuming the culture of the BGRC organisation reflects the relatively young age of the company, and because of the nature of the business the company is involved in, it is likely that the attitudes and motivation of the workforce are vibrant, strong and committed to the recycling cause. These qualities can be harnessed through a coordinated internal campaign to generate suitable external messages.

The *financial resources* available for marketing communications is small, currently £500,000. It will be necessary to work with other organisations. Media selection will be crucial to any campaign.

1.4 Stakeholder context

As mentioned above, there is an opportunity to work with other organisations so that UK targets are achieved. BGRC are not solely responsible for the achievement of these targets but through working in partnership with other packaging companies, trade associations, manufacturers and other recycling organisations, a joint campaign should

Answer bank

be possible. There are many other stakeholders who need to be drawn into a campaign through a sense of responsibility for the environment.

An alliance with a major retail brand, such as one of the main supermarkets, would bring required financial resources and provide the partner with strong, credible identity cues.

1.5 Environmental context

This public is becoming more aware of recycling requirements. There are political, social and strong economic reasons for all countries to improve radically their environmental awareness and recycling activities. The EU has now provided some regulatory reasons and it may be important to incorporate these forces within the messages conveyed to different target audiences.

> *Note.* Students should be aware that plans need to be justified. Hence in the future, it will be expected that students will attempt to justify their objectives, strategy and message and media decisions, based upon their context analysis and their understanding of the (likely) attitudes, involvement and motivations of the target audience.

2.0 Promotional objectives

2.1 To develop an integrated promotional plan, we will have to incorporate key strands from the mission and overall corporate strategy.

2.2 Corporate objectives

The main objectives are to increase the size of the UK recycling market and to enable the organisation to grow. If we do this effectively and efficiently, we will improve the return on investment for its two main investors.

2.3 Marketing objectives for the distribution sector

(a) To increase sales by 65% over the next two years and to increase profitability by 10% in each of the next three years.

(b) To increase demand and the proportion of glass packaging which is made of coloured glass by 30% over each of the next 3 years.

(c) To increase the number of bottle collection points so that there is a ratio of 1 bottle bank for every 1800 people by the year 2001.

2.4 Marketing communications objectives for the marketing channel

To raise the level of awareness of the need to recycle glass and to communicate the benefits of this activity amongst 60% of the top manufacturers who buy glass-packaged products over the next two years.

To help develop a generic glass recycling campaign owned and paid for by the Glass Manufacturers Federation.

2.5 Marketing objectives for the consumer segment

To increase the level of glass recycling undertaken each week by households throughout the UK. Current levels need to be established through market research and changes in activity need to be based on this data.

2.6 Marketing communications objectives for the consumer segment

The need to increase levels of awareness of the benefits of recycling glass is paramount. Awareness levels need to increase by a minimum of 40% each year.

Answer bank

The attitudes held by men aged 25 to 34 towards glass recycling need to be changed, so that 75% of this group realise and accept the need to recycle glass, by the end of the year 2000.

To convince 80% of school children aged 8 to 14 of the need to recycle glass.

3.0 Marketing communications strategy

A combination 'push and pull' strategy is needed to satisfy the various objectives. It is worth utilising the visibility opportunities associated with the campaign to present BGRC as an environmentally aware and responsible company.

3.1 Channel/trade sector

A *push strategy* is necessary to convince other glass manufacturers (horizontal channel members) and users of glass packaging (vertical channel members) of the need and benefits of using recycled glass.

This approach is also necessary to reach other members of the marketing channel, such as local authorities, restaurants and owners of large entertainment sites. They must be persuaded of the need to recycle and to provide increased numbers of bottle banks.

The support of a national food retailer or other such organisation should also be sought through a push strategy.

3.2 Consumer segments

So that attitudes towards recycling be changed, a pull strategy is necessary to reach men aged 25 to 34 and school children aged 8 to 14.

3.3 Other stakeholders

It is also important to raise the visibility and credibility of BGRC and as such a small profile strategy should work off the back of the primary communications.

4.0 Promotional methods

An integrated campaign is necessary. Because of the complexity associated with these issues, the messages should be simple and easily understood by all audiences. Consequently a *generic* campaign to raise awareness and change attitudes should be based on a common theme that would embrace the trade sector as well.

4.1 The push strategy is to be led by a *direct mail campaign* targeted at all major glass packaging users with a view to establishing a 'glass recycling awareness day'. This should be tied into *general advertising* in the *trade press* to support the initiative. Personal selling activities by senior managers with a hit list of major public companies to enlist their support will be important. Public relations activities should then act as a lead force to create visibility.

Direct marketing should also be used to reach local authorities and major entertainment organisations to encourage greater participation and to offer trade discounts on the establishment of additional bottle banks. Personal selling will be required to support this activity.

Sponsorship should be sought through the use of a suitable agency and established networks. Approaches need to be made to all major food supermarkets.

4.2 *The pull strategy is to be based on awareness and education.* Because of the low level of involvement and the perceived risk present in the prime target audience (men 25 to 35), formal copy and reasoned argument may not be sufficient. Some form of peripheral cue will be needed to convey the need to recycle. To help deliver the message the media used must reach large audiences to build initial awareness will be necessary. Because of the huge costs, advertising through television cannot be considered unless a major sponsor is attracted.

A *poster campaign* signalling the importance of recycling supported by a door-to-door leaflet drop to targeted households should form the backbone of the campaign. In addition to the information and the reasons/benefits of recycling, the leaflet should urge households to look out for new bottle bank sites and to encourage them to contact their local authority to request information about their glass recycling activities. The essence *of the message* should be on *attitude change* and to increase the level of involvement people feel towards glass recycling. For example, it may be possible to use an animated character (like Hector for the Self Assessment campaign) to attract attention and drive new values which can be associated with the cause.

In the second year the poster campaign should focus on the build up to the 'Glass Recycling Awareness Day'. The animated character will be well known and as long as research shows that audiences perceive the character positively, it should be possible to continue using this device.

Local authorities and the main sponsor should work together to reinforce the campaign. They should be encouraged to provide educational packs for schools and leaflets to provide basic awareness and information.

Public relations will be an important part of the pull strategy and will be needed to gain press and television coverage in order to disseminate the message to a wide audience and provide interest and possible humour in order to attract men 25 to 34 and school children.

Promotional schedule

Activity	*1999*	*2000*	*2001*
Trade sector			
Trade Press Advertising	x	x	
Direct Marketing	x	x	x
Public Relations	x	x	x
Personal Selling	x		
Consumer sector			
Posters	x	x	x
Leaflet Drops	x	x	
Sponsorships		x	x
Schools Education Pack		x	
Awareness Day		x	
Local Exhibitions	x	x	x
Web Site	x	x	x

Note. In future examinations students will be expected to justify their media and promotional tools selections. For example, justification could be based upon the nature of the target audience in terms of their levels of involvement and perceived risk.

5.0 Budget

5.1 A budget of £500,000 is very small and in order to reach a high number of people in the target market, financial assistance in the form of sponsorship will be required.

Activity	*1999*	*2000*	*2001*
Push	50%	40%	30%
Pull	40%	50%	60%
Profile/contingency	5%	5%	5%
Market research	5%	5%	5%

5.2 Initially, the push strategy will be emphasised so that more bottle banks can be set up. The pull strategy will then be given primacy, so that the bottle banks are then used.

6.0 Control and evaluation

6.1 The control of the promotional activities will be based on a number of key activities. Variance analysis will be used on a quarterly basis to measure against actual and targeted performance.

However, the *primary means* of control and measurement will be based upon the objectives set for the programme (as listed above). To consider performance against these goals, a mixture of quantitative and qualitative measures are recommended and funds need to be assigned for this important part of the marketing communications activities, for both the trade and consumer segment based objectives.

Quantitative measures

These will be based on the marketing objectives and the extent to which they have been achieved/bettered. So, the number of bottle banks, the ratio of banks to people, the tonnage of glass recycled and the return on investment will provide the main basis of control and evaluation of the campaigns.

Qualitative measures

These will concentrate on the attitudes of the target audience including members of the marketing channel. To accomplish this informal feedback through the sales force and formal measures of the public's attitude should be undertaken regularly.

To evaluate the performance of individual parts of the campaign, marketing research studies need to be commissioned on a pre during and post campaign basis. In particular continuous tracking studies and focus groups should be held to evaluate the key variables, awareness, attitudes towards recycling must be undertaken.

7.0 Conclusion

This marketing communication plan sets out the objectives necessary for BGRC to achieve our growth targets in the UK by developing awareness, improving facilities and changing the attitudes of particular target audiences.

56 MINI-CASE: CAR COMMUNICATIONS

> *Examiner's comments.* This question illustrates the need for students to develop a strategic awareness and understanding. Students answering a question like this must resist the urge to write a communication plan because they are not an acceptable response and score very few marks.
>
> It is important that students be able to integrate their understanding of marketing communications and relate to the strategic issues that are often easy to identify as they are common across many markets namely. competition, market characteristics, internal issues and selected strategies and objectives.
>
> The answers presented here are *not* examples of answers expected by students and this form is *not* intended to be replicated in an examination. The responses illustrated here represent the style, structure and quality of the content that is expected. You should try to understand the depth and the way in which each element of marketing communications is interlinked with other elements.
>
> It would have been a better answer had a Summary been included. Space can be left and when the answer is written return to write a brief synopsis of the whole report/answer.

Answer bank

(a) *Assumption*

It is assumed that the manufacturer is a multinational whose resources are commensurate with its market standing. It operates across a number of market segments but needs a successful launch in order to maintain overall market share in the UK.

Introduction

The car is being launched into a price sensitive market. The marketing plan indicates that we will compete on differentiation grounds rather than price so the marketing communications need to support the differentiation platform and discounts and promotions need to be minimised.

The promotional triangle

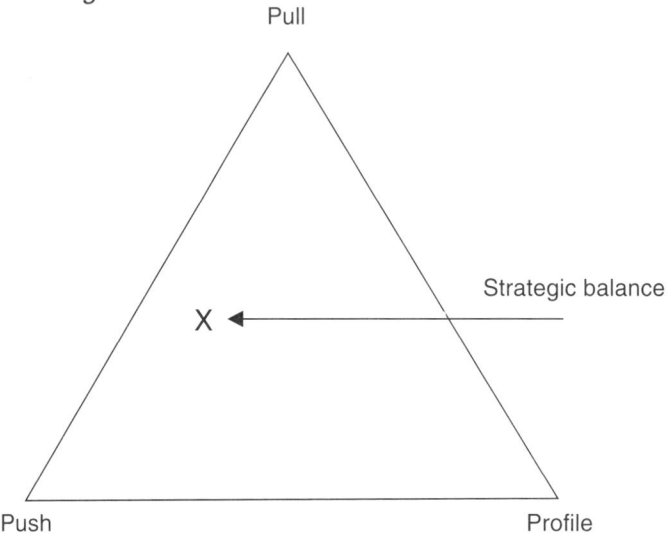

Promotional strategy

There are three main strategic opportunities, pull, push and profile strategies. All three have a role to play in the launch and development to of the Zen. However, the degree of strategic emphasis will vary through the life of the brand.

Pull strategies are those directed at end users, in this case car owner/drivers and this may include both private customers and fleet managers. It should be remembered that a sizeable proportion of the private market (family) market will consist of those who bought the previous model. Continuity of values and beliefs will be necessary.

At the time when private customers actively decide to change cars, levels of involvement become high. Normally attitudes in these situations develop based on information processed prior to a test drive or visit to a dealership. For those not actively engaged in changing their cars, involvement is low so attitudes can be shaped through the provision of emotional messages based on imagery aimed at social and ego motivations.

However, in order to communicate with a widely dispersed mass audience it will be necessary to use a variety of media and promotional methods. The first task will be to build awareness and this should be accomplished through traditional means. Therefore, television advertising will be required as the primary media supported by a 96 sheet outdoor programme. Working in combination it will be necessary to use a strong public relations exercise to build credibility for the brand. The synergistic effect should be to excite new and established customers and to promote a sense of loyalty amongst current fleet buyers. Strong informational based messages will be necessary to reach both the private as well as the fleet car buyers, although the latter will require a high level of personal selling and key account management skills.

Attendance at all the main stream exhibitions will be important as it is through these that publicity and goodwill can be generated. Not being at these events can stir a great deal of negative communications for the wrong reasons.

Push strategies

It would appear that dealerships are an increasingly important and integral part of the marketing process. Competitors are investing much more in this area and in order to avoid being perceived as disloyal/uncaring about our dealers it will be necessary to embark upon an improved dealer support programme. Therefore, it is recommended that we build up our engineering and marketing training programmes and actively involve these important stakeholders in our marketing communication programme. It is also advised that we seek to improve our customer and dealer ordering processes and build eCommerce facilities into our dealerships over the medium term. Whilst this will benefit the whole range of products and services and not just the Zen, it is important part of reducing costs, building customer benefits and enhancing levels of trust between all stakeholders.

Profile strategies

Due to the increasing similarity between products in each market segment, the standardisation of quality and the reluctance to enter into price based competition consideration should be given to the development of the corporate brand. Developing a corporate brand may give new opportunities to develop competitive advantage and might well provide a cost effective umbrella under which to launch new products, not only in the car market but in related and even in unrelated markets as well. BMW have established a strong monolithic type corporate brand but also operate bank services in Germany as well.

A profile strategy will be necessary in order to build strong internal communications with all employees involved with the development and launch of the Zen. If we are to be effective and efficient it will be necessary to develop integrated marketing communications. In order for this to be accomplished it is important that we blend our internal with our external communications. We need everyone associated with the Zen to share the same set of brand values and beliefs and to further develop or customer orientation.

Our reliance (and risk) associated with just operating in the car market might be reduced if we had a strong corporate brand that enabled us to move into new market sectors. However, the development of a corporate brand will take time and substantial resources and will also have implications for the level of service provision and dealer identification that we currently have in place. We do not have time or the resources to establish a corporate brand in order to launch the Zen. However, we should begin to develop a profile strategy in order that our internal/external communications improve our identity and the way in which we are perceived and hence the image held of us by various stakeholders, including our various suppliers.

The strategic balance

As suggested earlier it will be important to balance the thrust of the strategic communications as the Zen becomes established.

A push strategy is required initially in order that the dealerships are prepared when a national launch takes place. Engineering and customer training will be paramount.

Answer bank

Direct marketing, key account management, demonstrations, training and conferences will be used initially.

A pull strategy will be necessary at the point of the national launch. The aim will be to build awareness and desire to trial the car through visits to local dealerships. This will require the use of television advertising, public relations, attendance at exhibitions and direct marketing to current users.

A Profile strategy will be used to develop internal communications in time for the launch. As the Zen becomes established so we should develop the corporate brand and establish corporate brand values. This will enable us to reduce the level and intensity of the pull strategy and enable a reduction in the high costs associated with individual product brand awareness programmes.

(b) The key strategic factors that need to be considered when formulating the communication budget are as follows.

The communication strategy and objectives
Level of available resources
Competitive spend levels
Agency relationships and media buying effectiveness

The communication strategy

The pull strategy is intended to build awareness levels quickly. The use of television and outdoor work demands a substantial budget be allocated. As it is normal to expect the generation of 600 to 800 ratings a sum in excess of £5 million should be allocated for media expenditure.

The push strategy will be less demanding unless a refurbishment programme is anticipated. However, it will be necessary to take the dealers overseas for a preview of the Zen and to undertake a similar exercise for the motoring correspondents in order to generate the desired levels of credibility and desire in the target audience.

Dealers will need training and new literature will have to be prepared to support them and their customers.

Level of available resources

The Zen will be competing for a limited level of resources but it is probable that as the company is established and the Zen is an important part of the new generation of cars that a suitable level of funds will be released.

Competitive spend levels

It is important that the funds allocated are proportionate to the spend levels of competitors and the prevailing contextual conditions. The context is the launch of a new product by an established player in a price sensitive market. Traditionally car manufacturers spend large funds supporting their brands and supporting their dealerships. The share of voice will need to be carefully evaluated and a decision made in consideration of the support required. It is probable in these circumstances that the share of voice should be in excess of the expected share of market.

Agency relationships and media buying effectiveness

Where the pull strategy plays such a significant part of the early promotional activity, it is important that we are working with the best creative team. In addition we the media buying must be efficient and able to drive the largest media discounts. It may be that we need to centralise our media buying and consolidate our global media purchases. The relationships held with our agencies must be based on trust and commitment in order that we maximise are spend potential.

57 NETLINE TECHNOLOGIES

> *Examiner's comment.* I have deliberately broken away from setting a marketing communications plan as the task for the first question. Some students may have been surprised by this as they might have been taught the planning framework in a systematic or even rigid format. This new approach seeks to encourage students to think about and give emphasis to the strategic issues and move away from the predictability and sometimes sterile approach associated with the preparation of a plan. What this means is that students are expected to be able to consider the strategic communication issues associated with a particular scenario and articulate them in different ways.
>
> It should be noted that students may be asked to write promotional plans in the future.

To: Marketing Director
From: Marketing Communications Controller
Date: 8 Dec 1998
Ref: Key strategic marketing communication issues facing Netline Communications

1.0 Introduction

C-Guard represents a new product and it is likely to be copied within twelve months. Actions taken now will lay the foundation for the success of the product and for its ability to withstand future competition.

This report is in two sections. The first seeks to highlight the key strategic issues that impact on the marketing communications of C-Guard and the second sets out some *recommendations* in order that Netline successfully addresses these issues.

2.0 Key strategic issues

One of the problems associated with this part of the report is establishing the *key strategic issues*. General communication issues that can be identified but for the purposes of this report it is necessary to focus on the key strategic *marketing communications* issues. They are not presented in any particular order or priority.

1. The public's perception of the product and the values they place on the benefits of C-Guard

2. Marketing channel/franchisee related communications

3. The overall level of communication effectiveness and efficiency associated with the campaign

These three primary issues will now be explored.

2.1 The public's perception of the product and the values they place on the benefits of C-Guard

Public demand for C-Guard protection will be important in building the market and will be a significant factor in encouraging businesses to install the C-Guard system. In order that business-to-business clients be willing to install C-Guard, they should be persuaded that public opinion favours such facilities and that the annoyance factor of mobile phones needs to be addressed. Acceptance of the *product concept* is important, so it is crucial that initial communications convey appropriate messages (including the benefits of C-Guard).

The attitudes and perceptions of mobile phone users and non-users will be researched so that appropriate messages be conveyed and a dialogue established. Whilst further research is necessary to establish which of the many public 'areas' (or vertical market segments) have the greatest need/potential, it is important to develop C-Guard as the market leader and maintain its number one position.

Answer bank

2.2 Marketing channel/franchisee communications

A key strategic communication issue has already been resolved. Control over *brand identity* is not to be devolved to franchisees and responsibility will remain with Netline. However, the franchisees appointed to distribute C-Guard require support not only with training and installation issues but also with brand support and their communications with their employees and customers - the businesses who install C-Guard.

Communications in the marketing channel are potentially confusing. On the one hand, communications between Netline and franchisees might be generally informative and motivational whilst communications between the franchisee and their clients will probably be more emotive and persuasive in nature. This issue needs to be appreciated and suitable strategies put in position.

2.3 The overall level of communication effectiveness and efficiency associated with the campaign.

In order that the marketing communications for C-Guard are effective and efficient the total communication process should be highly professional. A number of areas that need to be addressed if the effectiveness and efficiency be maximised, for example, the international dimension of C-Guard's distribution, the financial resources to be appropriated, the agencies to be appointed, the goals to be achieved, the messages to be sent to different stakeholders and the media to be used to convey them.

3.0 Recommendations

In the light of the key strategic communication issues established earlier it is necessary to make some recommendations about how the issues can be overcome.

3.1 The public's perception of the product and the values they place on the benefits of C-Guard

Public perception, whether mobile phone users or not, is crucial to the success of the product. To help influence perceptions the development of a strong brand for C-Guard is imperative. Associated with branding is the position C-Guard is seen to occupy in the market.

A *pull communication strategy* is necessary, and the essential aspect of the strategy should be the *development of a brand*. Through branding, Netline will have the opportunity to communicate a consistent and relevant identity so that the public can recognise quickly and easily understand the values associated with the product. Branding will also enable the development of public attitudes and awareness, important in the first six months of the launch. A decision about the degree to which C-Guard and/or Netline is branded (*product* and *corporate brand* respectively) needs further consideration.

Associated with branding is the way in which C-Guard is perceived and positioned in the mind of the public and business customers. *Positioning* is important as once established it is a lengthy and difficult (expensive) to reposition. Care must be taken to associate the brand with relevant values and substitute products. Is the no smoking similarity and association a viable long term position for C-Guard?

3.2 Marketing channel/franchisee communications

A *push communication strategy* will need to be established. This strategy, aimed at communicating with members of the marketing channel, should seek to provide message consistency and reflect the desired level of quality in order that the overall values of C-Guard be reinforced. This will also assist the motivation of franchisees to work on the C-Guard brand, but it will also be communicated through to their business-to-business customers.

The development of strong franchise relationships will be important in order to establish market credentials and to withstand strong competitive activity in the future.

3.3 The overall level of communication effectiveness and efficiency associated with the campaign.

The effectiveness and impact that the campaign has will be a reflection of the degree to which the marketing communication activities are integrated. Management are responsible for these decisions and it is imperative that they make these decisions on a holistic rather than fractured or partial basis and that the CEO is seen to lead and endorse the integrated approach.

It may not be possible to achieve full scale integration at the outset but that should not deter from setting targets for the establishment of an integrated approach. This may be achieved on an incremental basis by first aiming to coordinate the messages conveyed through the promotional tools and then moving to a functionally coordinated marketing mix through a cultural shift and finally complete IMC.

To assist this process, it is necessary to ensure that the business philosophy, marketing strategy and promotional objectives be consistent with each other. Management play an important role coordinating, advising and controlling this aspect of the communication process. Internal communications will be important in creating internal identity with the C-Guard brand and the values associated with Netline's overall business development.

Marketing Communication Agencies need to be appointed who can not only provide and identify with the integration requirements but who have the necessary networks, experience and potential to assist the international development and distribution of C-Guard. Decisions about whether messages should be adapted or standardised in fresh international markets can be assisted by the contacts and experience of these important outsourced providers.

The *financial resources* will need to be allocated such that the Push, Pull and Profile strategy investment requirements are met. Use of the PIMS database may be of assistance in order to generate the best possible return on investment.

The *campaign* will require a substantial amount of *advertising* in order to create awareness and establish brand values. Management need to ensure that the media time/space purchased is bought at the best possible rate. It is probable that Netline need to appoint a media buying house in order to derive the best possible deal.

In addition to the advertising, all the promotional tools will be used at sometime in the campaign. For example, public relations will be important, especially at the launch to carry public opinion. Sales promotions will be required at certain times in the financial year to encourage businesses to install the system, direct marketing will be used to create associations and identity with C-Guard and personal selling will be required to set up franchises and for selling into business accounts.

To assist the goal for effectiveness and efficiency a marketing communications plan will need to be generated. This need not be overly rigid and a degree of flexibility will be beneficial. However, the use of the planning approach will serve to focus thoughts, help coordinate activities in line with the promotional goals and will act as a communication device so that all involved with the marketing communication activities are aware of what is happening and when.

4.0 Conclusion

C-Guard represents an important commercial opportunity and a chance to meet a real customer need. Marketing communications are important in order that these opportunities

Answer bank

58 DUTTON ENGINEERING

> **Examiner's comments**. Some candidates tried to write a marketing communications plan which showed they did not know what key strategic communications issues were.
>
> Candidates should have set out the issues and then dealt with each one. Many candidates failed to see that each point was linked by the integrated marketing communications concept. Few students attempted to work out a budget for marketing communications.

To: Dutton Management
From: Marketing Communications Advisor
Date: 7 December 1999
Ref: Marketing Communication Issues facing Dutton

Summary

Introduction

a **Key Communication Issues**

The Key Communication Issues (KCIs) facing the company are drawn from the change in marketing strategy and the need to harness the current culture and strong customer orientation that staff have. The search for new customers, in current markets, represents a significant shift away from the tight current customer orientation where the communication strategy (or approach) is based upon the need to retain customers through high levels of satisfaction. The practice of Customer Relationship Management has been successful and should not be abandoned. What is required is a complementary and integrated marketing communications strategy that builds on what the company already has.

KCIs will be:

1. The characteristics of the targeted market segments. What are the perceptions and attitudes of current non-customers towards Dutton and their current suppliers? Such information will be essential to the message and media decisions necessary to position Dutton.

2. How are competitors' communicating with the target market? Once again there are implications for the positioning strategy.

3. How many new customers are required and what will be their geographic spread? If a small number of new customers are to be located in a tight accessible region then there may be message and media savings.

4. One of the prime KCIs concerns the branding strategy. It would appear that Dutton have a certain reputation for innovation and management style. Is this Dutton brand to be developed as part of a corporate brand or is branding to be more product orientated?

5. Following on from the branding position decision are issues concerning the content of the messages to be communicated. This is partly derived from the positioning statement but the relative balance of rational and emotional message style will have a strong bearing upon how Dutton is perceived.

6. A further KCI concerns the media to be used to reach the target audience. It would seem that the use of new media technologies would be useful if the personalised customer focus is to be perpetuated. Issues concerning the configuration of the

Answer bank

promotional mix and the implications of possibly deploying a sales force need to be examined. If a small sales force is to be appointed, how will they interact with the current customers?

7   The revised communication strategy will represent an investment. Therefore, it will be important to determine the right level of human and financial resources that are to be used and consider where any new resources are to be obtained. For example, it may be possible to outsource the task to find new customers, to a field marketing organisation or employ agents. Alternatively, Dutton may wish to retain a high level of control over the search and new customer acquisition process in which case it may be better to employ a small sales force.

8   The final KCI concerns the need to plan and integrate the new marketing communications strategy. It appears that this aspect of planning and consequent liaison with other outsourced providers (eg advertising agencies) will require a set of skills that the current management team may not possess. This could mean the recruitment of a senior marketing manager or a current manager taking on new responsibilities. This decision will also impact on the culture of the organisation.

b   Recommendations for Dutton's Marketing Communications Strategy

Once the KCIs have been addressed it is important that any responses and answers be implemented as necessary. These recommendations are presented as a means of indicating the scale and direction of the communication strategy, based on the information provided. However, further research would be advisable.

9   In order to maintain and build upon their reputation for customer care, Dutton should be positioned as a Corporate Brand whose identity is based around the care concept.

10 In order to develop new business it would appear that the recruitment of a traditional field force selling team would not be compatible with the current culture or business philosophy. Outsourcing the operation or appointing agents may be more appropriate. However, new business can also be developed through the use of eCommerce facilities and this would also be of benefit to the current customer base. It is recommended that Dutton develop an eCommerce facility and project their identity through new technology.

11 It is also recommended that an integrated approach be adopted. This would allow for the following:

(a) A consistency of messages reflecting a coherence between the philosophy and culture of the company.

(b) The maintenance of current customer goodwill.

(c) Lower media and management costs.

(d) Potentially higher impact of all communications (product, price, place and promotion).

(e) The continued involvement of staff as an integral part of the communication activities.

12 One member of the senior management team be assigned to be responsible for Dutton's overall communications, both internal and external. This will involve the development of the eCommerce facility and the appointment of a suitable local agency to be responsible for the creative and media planning work.

13 A sum of £115,000 be allocated to marketing communications over each of the next two years. This represents 5% of this year's turnover. This figure needs to be revised as

necessary, although further investment will be required to develop the eCommerce facilities and associated activities. Once installed there will be substantial transaction cost savings, some of which could be redeployed into eCommerce.

Conclusions

Dutton are in a strong position to develop and to exploit their market position to generate new business. Through the use of an integrated approach to marketing communications and the incorporation of eCommerce facilities, Dutton should be able to leverage their current strengths in order to grow the company.

Test your knowledge

Test your knowledge

1. What factors have influenced the development of direct marketing?
2. What matters might you consider when developing the packaging for a new product?
3. List eight criteria against which a model may be evaluated.
4. What is the 'product' in internal marketing?
5. What are the thirteen principles of the British Code of Sales Promotion Practice?
6. What are the advantages of personal selling?
7. List three technological developments that have affected or will affect marketing communications.
8. What are response hierarchy models and what are their drawbacks?
9. What are the six groups in the DMU?
10. List seven methods of determining advertising expenditure.
11. List five types of internal communications.
12. Give some examples of measures of advertising effectiveness.
13. List five factors that influenced the growth of advertising.
14. Explain the mnemonic SMART.
15. Why is it important to study buying behaviour?
16. What are the advantages of press as a medium?
17. What does the British Code of Advertising Practice say about decency and truthfulness?
18. Explain the mnemonic SOSTT + 4Ms.
19. What are the strengths and weaknesses of direct mail?
20. What are the disadvantages of outdoor as a medium?
21. What categories of advertising are specifically covered in the British Code of Advertising Practice?
22. List the main types of segmentation variable.
23. What is the main disadvantage of PR?
24. List ten potential publics.
25. What are the three main ways in which a sales force can be organised?
26. How can sales promotions be evaluated?
27. What formats might be taken by a creative brief for an advertising agency?
28. Give two definitions of direct marketing.
29. What is CAVIAR?
30. What issues and developments are likely to affect marketing communications in the future?
31. List all promotional influences on the customer.
32. Explain Mary Goodyear's five levels of advertising development.
33. What is the TGI and what does it measure?
34. Integration of marketing communications is possible at what three levels?
35. What is a brand? What are four types of brand?

Test your knowledge: answers

1 You might have mentioned the following.

   (a) The disintegration of the nuclear family as the dominant group in the population.
   (b) Technology which allows banks of data to be collected and sorted, especially by retailers.
   (c) The growth in use of credit cards and debit cards.
   (d) The rise in the cost of TV advertising.
   (e) The development of global markets and the breakdown of cultural boundaries.
   (f) Better educated consumers and lower brand loyalty.

2 In brief, design, shape, size, colour, graphics and name.

3 Williams listed eight criteria against which a model could potentially be evaluated, as follows.

   (a) Simplicity   (e) Explanatory power
   (b) Factual basis   (f) Prediction
   (c) Logic   (g) Heuristic power
   (d) Originality   (h) Validity

4 The product is the marketing strategy and the details of the marketing plan. These must be 'sold' to people in the organisation.

5
   (a) Legality   (h) Truthful Presentation
   (b) Spirit   (i) Substantiation
   (c) Fair competition   (j) Limitation
   (d) Consumer interest   (k) Suitability
   (e) Consumer satisfaction   (l) Administration
   (f) Fairness   (m) Responsibility
   (g) Public interest

6 (a) Personal selling contributes to a relatively high level of customer attention since, in face to face situations, it is difficult for a potential buyer to avoid a salesperson's message.

   (b) Personal selling enables the salesperson to customise the message to the customer's specific interests and needs.

   (c) The two-way communication nature of personal selling allows immediate feedback from the customer so that the effectiveness of the message can be ascertained.

   (d) Personal selling allows a larger amount of technical and complex information than could be communicated using other promotional methods.

   (e) In personal selling there is a greater ability to demonstrate a product's functioning and performance characteristics.

   (f) Frequent interaction with the customer gives great scope for the development of long-term relations between buyer and seller, making the process of purchase more of a team effort.

7 Examples are the Internet, digital TV and multimedia.

8 Response hierarchy models attempts to predict the sequence of mental stages that the consumer passes through on the way to purchase. Examples are AIDA (Awareness, Interest, Desire, Action) and the DAGMAR model (Unawareness, Awareness, Comprehension, Conviction, Action).

The drawbacks are that such models do not describe many simple purchases where the consumer may not go through the staged process and that in some situations buyers may go through the stages in a different order.

9 (a) *Users*
   (b) *Influencers*
   (c) *Deciderss*
   (d) *Approvers*.
   (e) *Buyers*
   (f) *Gatekeepers*.

Test your knowledge: answers

10   (a) As much as you can afford
     (b) Historical basis
     (c) Matching competition
     (d) Percentage of sales
     (e) Experiment and testing
     (f) Modelling and simulation
     (g) Objective and task method

11   Possible answers include the following.

     (a) In-house magazines and employee newsletters
     (b) Employee relations videos
     (c) Formal employee communications networks and channels for feedback
     (d) Recruitment exhibitions/conferences
     (e) Speech writing for executives
     (f) Company notice boards
     (g) Briefing meetings

12   Possible answers are:

     (a) Number of orders
     (b) Number of enquiries
     (c) Responses from creative development research
     (d) Pre-testing results
     (e) Tracking studies data (omnibus survey results, or panel research data).

13   Factors include:

     (a) The growth of settlements
     (b) The invention of printing
     (c) The Industrial Revolution
     (d) The development of national and global businesses
     (e) The invention of broadcasting
     (f) The development of advertising agencies
     (g) The growth in competition

14   SMART is a mnemonic for the qualities of objectives. Marketing communications objectives need to be:
        Specific
        Measurable
        Achievable
        Relevant
        Timed and targeted

15   (a) The buyer's reaction to the organisation's marketing strategy has a major impact on the success of the organisation.

     (b) If organisations are truly to implement the marketing concept, they must examine the main influences on what, where, when and how customers buy. Only in this way will they be able to devise a marketing mix that satisfies the needs of the customers.

     (c) By gaining a better understanding of the factors influencing their customers and how their customers will respond, organisations will be better able to predict the effectiveness of their marketing activities.

16   Press has the following advantages.

     (a) Nationals reach large numbers of people
     (b) A variety of contents are available from the deeply serious to the frivolous
     (c) Copy lead times are generally short
     (d) A choice of reproduction options (black and white, glossy colour)
     (e) It may be possible to target special interest groups very closely
     (f) Readers are loyal
     (g) Local impact is possible

17   The code's definition of *decency* states that advertisements should not contain any matter that is likely to cause grave or widespread offence in the light of standards of decency and propriety currently acceptable in the UK, or, any material that might be found distasteful because it reflects or gives expression to attitudes or opinions about which society is divided. Whether the latter is the case, the code states that advertisers' should carefully consider the effect that any apparent disregard of the

Test your knowledge: answers

sensitivities involved may have upon their reputation and that of their product, and upon the acceptability, and hence usefulness, of advertising generally.'

The code states that, as far as *truthful* presentation is concerned, 'No advertisement, whether by inaccuracy, ambiguity, exaggeration, omission or otherwise, should mislead consumers about any matter likely to influence their attitude to the advertised product'. The code makes the distinction between matters of fact and matters of opinion, stating that advertisers should be able to substantiate any material presented as a matter of fact in their adverts and that they should not claim that an account that an advert gives of facts is true when there exists a division of informed opinion on the issue. Matters of opinion must be recognisable as such. Subsequent sections of the code explain in detail how this is to be achieved in specific cases such as political claims, quotation of prices, availability of products and so on.

18   The mnemonic is the one used by Paul Smith to summarise the planning process.

Situation	(Where are we now?)
Objectives	(Where do we want to go?)
Strategy	(How do we get there?)
Tactics	(Details of strategy)
Targets	(Target markets/audiences)
+	
Men	(and women required to do the job)
Money	(financial resources/budget)
Minutes	(timetable of activities)
Measurement	(monitoring effectiveness)

The order of the letters represents the logical order of the planning process.

19   Strengths are as follows.

   (a)   The advertiser can target down to individual level.

   (b)   The communication can be personalised. Known data about the individual can be used, whilst modern printing techniques mean that parts of a letter can be altered to accommodate this.

   (c)   The medium is good for reinforcing interest stimulated by other media such as TV. It can supply the response mechanism (a coupon) which is not yet available in that medium.

   (d)   The opportunity to use different creative formats is almost unlimited.

   (e)   Testing potential is sophisticated: a limited number of items can be sent out to a 'test' cell and the results can be evaluated. As success is achieved, so the mailing campaign can be rolled out.

   (f)   What you do is less visible to your competitors than other forms of media.

There are, however, a number of weaknesses with this medium.

   (a)   It does not offer sound or movement, although it is possible for advertisers to send out audio or video tapes, and even working models or samples.

   (b)   There is obvious concern over the negative association with junk mail and the need for individuals to exercise their right to privacy,

   (c)   Lead times may be considerable when taking into consideration the creative organisation, finished artwork, printing, proofing, inserting material into envelopes where necessary and finally the mailing.

   (d)   The most important barrier to direct mail is that it can be very expensive on a *per capita* basis. A delivered insert can be 24 to 32 times more expensive than a full page colour advert in a magazine. It therefore follows that the mailshot must be very powerful and, above all, well targeted to overcome such a cost penalty. (In many cases, though, this is possible.)

Test your knowledge: answers

20 Disadvantages of outdoor include the limited number of prime sites, possible vandalism, long lead times between buying the space and the advert appearing, inflexibility, and the difficulty of achieving national coverage.

21 (a) Health claims
   (b) Hair and scalp products
   (c) Vitamins and minerals
   (d) Slimming
   (e) Cosmetics
   (f) Mail order and direct response advertising
   (g) Financial services and products
   (h) Employment and business opportunities
   (i) Limited editions of products
   (j) Advertisements aimed at children
   (k) Media requirements
   (l) Alcoholic drinks
   (m) Cigarettes and tobacco

22 A list of the main types of segmentation variable is given below.

   (a) *Geographic, eg* Continent (Europe), Country (United Kingdom), Region (South East), County (Lancashire), Town (Manchester), Postcode (WA14)

   (b) *Demographic*, eg Age (over sixty). Sex (male, female), occupation etc.

   (c) *Psychographic, eg* Social class (A B C1 C2 D E), Lifestyle (upwardly mobile), Personality (ambitious)

   (d) *Behavioural*, eg benefits required (quality, service, price). Usage rate (light, medium, heavy). Loyalty status (strong)

23 The main disadvantage is the loss of control over how the message is presented, or even what the message is. Editors can just as easily present a negative picture as a positive one.

24 Possible answers include the following.

   (a) Customers - existing, past and potential
   (b) Members of the public in general
   (c) The trade and distributors
   (d) Financial publics - shareholders, the City, banks, institutions and stockbrokers
   (e) Pressure groups
   (f) Opinion leaders
   (g) The media - as a special type of public as well as a channel of communication
   (h) Overseas governments, EU bodies and International bodies
   (i) Central and local government bodies, MPs and members of the House of Lords
   (j) Research bodies and policy-forming units
   (k) The local community
   (l) Trades Unions
   (m) Employees

25 Territorial organisation, product organisation and market/customer organisation.

26 Sales promotions can be evaluated:

   (a) In terms of take-up (number of coupons redeemed, number of competition entries etc)
   (b) By means of, say, omnibus surveys to measure awareness
   (c) Through household panel information or retail tracking information (eg Nielsen's Homescan)
   (d) By means of *ad hoc* research

27 A creative brief might take the following format.

   (a) *Background/Introduction*

   (b) *Target market(s):* at the very least, a listing of the target audience characteristics. It could also include an assessment of what audiences currently think about the product or service.

   (c) *Advertising objectives*

   (d) *Advertising proposition.* This links with (b) above, and answers the question 'What do we want our audiences to think?' The proposition should be summed up in a short sentence or two, stating in laymen's terms the response that is desired from the audience on seeing the advertising. Some agencies call this the brand promise.

Test your knowledge: answers

- (e) *Support.* This is the backup for the advertising proposition. It would include the information or attributes that might help to produce the desired response. Support might take the form of factual benefits that a product possesses which differentiate it from the competition, or it might include findings from research.

- (f) *Tone of voice.* Should the advertising be authoritative, serious, friendly, modern in approach?

- (g) *Mandatory inclusions.* Typical examples of these would be 'pack shot must be included', or 'parent company logo must be easily identifiable in end freeze frame.'

28 Possibilities are as follows.

- (a) The Institute of Direct Marketing in the UK define direct marketing as 'The planned recording, analysis and tracking of customer behaviour to develop relational marketing strategies'.

- (b) The Direct Marketing Association in the US define direct marketing as 'An interactive system of marketing which uses one or more advertising media to effect a measurable response and/or transaction at any location'.

29 CAVIAR stands for Cinema and Video Industry Audience Research, which gives details of cinema-going habits, video viewership and other media usage.

30 Possible answers are:

- (a) Shifting demographic profiles
- (b) Changes in spending patterns
- (c) Improved social values
- (d) Fragmentation of the media
- (e) Increased levels of technology both inside and outside the home
- (f) Globalisation
- (g) New regulations
- (h) Economic cycles

31 Your list should include the following.

- (a) Word of mouth
- (b) Sales promotion
- (c) Public relations
- (d) Merchandising
- (e) Direct marketing
- (f) Exhibitions
- (g) Internal marketing
- (h) Corporate image
- (i) Packaging
- (j) Sponsorship
- (k) Advertising
- (l) Personal selling
- (m) Branding

32 Goodyear identifies five levels of advertising development along a continuum from the unsophisticated to the sophisticated.

- (a) At the least sophisticated level of advertising, the emphasis is on the manufacturer's *description* of the product. Messages are factual and rational with much repetition. Product or pack shots take prominence.

- (b) At the next level, consumer choice is acknowledged so emphasis switches to the product's *superiority* over the competition (eg products that wash whiter, feel softer).

- (c) At the mid point on the continuum, consumer *benefits* are emphasised rather than product attributes. Executional devices may include the use of celebrity endorsements or role models may give demonstrations, for example a dentist endorsing toothpaste products.

- (d) At a more sophisticated level, brands and their attributes are well known, so need only passing references (perhaps by way of a brief pack shot or logo). The message is communicated by way of *lifestyle narrative* (eg Gold Blend couple; Bisto family).

- (e) At the most sophisticated level, the focus is on the *advertising* itself. The brand is referred to only obliquely, perhaps at a symbolic level (eg Silk Cut; Benson & Hedges). Consumers are believed to have a mature understanding of advertising, and are able to think laterally in order to decode messages.

Test your knowledge: answers

33 The TGI (Target Group Index) is a national product and media survey which collects information from 24,000 adults each year. The TGI measures the following.

   (a) Heavy to light usage for over 3,000 brands in more than 200 FMCG product fields; additionally, usage of over 450 other brands in banking, building societies, airlines, holidays, cars, grocery and other retail outlets.

   (b) The 1,400 or so brands with more than a million claimed users, broken down demographically and by media.

   (c) The readership of more than 200 newspapers and magazines.

   (d) The weight of viewing of ITV and Channel 4, and half-hourly viewing behaviour.

   (e) The weight of listening to commercial radio.

   (f) The level of exposure to outdoor media and the cinema.

   (g) The full range of standard demographics together with special breakdowns such as terminal education age, and working status.

34 (a) Integration with business strategy
    (b) Integration with marketing strategy
    (c) Integration of the promotional tools

35 'A successful brand is a name, symbol, design or some combination, which identifies the "product" of a particular organisation as having a sustainable differential advantage.' (Doyle)

   Four types of brand are as follows.

   (a) *Individual* brand name. This is the option chosen by Procter and Gamble for example, who even have different brand names within the same product line, eg Bold, Tide. The main advantage of individual product branding is that an unsuccessful brand (eg Strand cigarettes) does not adversely affect the firm's other products, nor the firm's reputation generally.

   (b) *Blanket family brand* for all products, eg Hoover, Heinz (originally 'Heinz 57 varieties'). This has the advantage of enabling the global organisation to introduce new products quickly and successfully. Also the cost of introducing the new product in terms of name research and awareness advertising will be reduced (eg Honda lawn mowers).

   (c) *Separate family names* for different product divisions, eg the US based company Sears sells electrical appliances under the name Kenmore, and women's clothing under the Kerrybrook brand. This is obviously the option for the global organisation with 'inconsistent' product lines where the family brand name above is not appropriate. But within each 'family' the advantages identified in (b) still apply.

   (d) The *company* trade name combined with an *individual* product name (eg Kelloggs - Corn Flakes, Rice Crispies etc). This option both legitimises (because of the company name) and individualises (the individual product name). As in (b) above it allows new 'names' to be introduced quickly and relatively cheaply.

Diploma in Marketing

June 2000 paper

9.51 Integrated Marketing Communications

3 Hours Duration

> This examination is in two sections.
>
> **Part A** is compulsory, based on a min-case and worth 40% of total marks.
>
> **Part B** has six questions, select three. Each answer will be worth 20 marks totalling 60% of the whole for the paper.
>
> **DO NOT** repeat the question in your answer but show clearly the number of the question attempted.
>
> Rough working should be included in the answer book and ruled through after use.

DO NOT OPEN THIS PAPER UNTIL YOU ARE READY TO START UNDER EXAMINATION CONDITIONS

PART A

Woodstock Furniture

Woodstock Furniture is a privately owned company located in a fashionable area in London. The company makes bespoke, high quality kitchen and bathroom furniture. Kitchens account for 80% of sales and the average order value is £25,000.

The general kitchen furniture market in the UK is worth over £800 million but of this the bespoke market is only worth a static 1 %. Woodstock's sales have fluctuated over its 22 years of trading and currently stand at £1.7 million per annum with net profit at 6.9%. However, the balance sheet is weak and there is little opportunity to attract finance for promotional investment. Staff are very supportive of the company, appear to identify strongly with the customised approach and many have been with the company since its start up. However, many of the internal systems and procedures are old, slow and in need of updating - perhaps a reflection of the slower, detailed craftsmanlike culture that identifies the Woodstock Furniture Company.

In recognition of some of the problems facing the company, the management has developed a marketing plan which seeks growth of 15% per annum to be achieved by market penetration and in particular, the attraction of new customers. It now needs a marketing communication programme to develop a strong corporate brand. The problem is that profit margins are small and there is little to invest in developing the brand and competing with well known high street outlets.

The competition, as Woodstock see it, have huge resources which can be used to invest in promotional campaigns to drive awareness and action. For example, these companies have authentic web sites, unlike Woodstock's site which is little more than an online brochure. Many of the large national standardised companies can produce promotional literature in large production runs and are happy to ignore wastage. Using expert photography of 'pretend' kitchens, the quality and impact of the literature is high. Woodstock's smaller budgets dictate that photographs of real customers' kitchens are required, which seldom look perfect and can even appear amateurish. It costs £4 to produce each of the Woodstock brochures so vetting of each request for literature is important to avoid those people who ask for brochures but buy nothing. A high conversion rate is necessary and although 50% of quotations are converted into sales, Woodstock cannot afford this figure to be lowered.

Woodstock's customers do not want the standardised kitchen units provided by the larger, more dominant players in the market They want kitchens made to measure and which complement the character of their homes. They look for attention to detail, design, craftsmanship and support when commissioning bespoke companies such as Woodstock. The target market is affluent, often has more than one home and-relies on word of mouth recommendation when drawing up a shortlist of possible providers. For many, price is not the key issue - rather it is the capability to craft suitable furniture to match the required decor and house style. This requires a high degree of trust, which successful companies in this market are able to reciprocate and in turn generate commitment. Many of Woodstock's customers are celebrities but because discretion and privacy is important to them, they often refuse to allow their names (and kitchens) to be used for Woodstock publicity. However, customer loyalty is extremely important with over 60% of new business being driven from existing customers.

In recognition of this, Woodstock now believes that it is in the business of craftsmanship and the design and construction of customised furniture rather than the business of making and installing kitchen and bathroom furniture. It has improved levels of support and service (having, for example, introduced annual maintenance contracts) and has high levels of customer satisfaction. The marketing plan states that prices are to be raised to capitalise

Test paper: June 2000

on premium pricing opportunities and the high levels of demand inelasticity. The marketing plan involves forming relationships with architects and developers and creating cross promotions and alliances with firms operating in similar markets, such as conservatories, studies and staircases.

Source: *Adapted from an article in the Sunday Times, 15th August 1999.*

PART A

Question 1

As a Marketing Adviser you have been asked to help the company achieve its objectives. In particular you are to prepare an Integrated Marketing Communications Plan for Woodstock Furniture covering the next two years. It is important to justify your recommendations and state any assumptions made in order to prepare the plan.

(40 marks)

PART B - Answer THREE Questions only

Question 2

Many marketing communication campaigns make use of opinion leaders and opinion formers. Using examples to illustrate your points, explain how and why these personal influencers might be used.

(20 marks)

Question 3

For many organisations, business to business marketing communications have been transformed, by the development of the Internet and related digital technologies. Prepare notes for a meeting at which you are expected to argue the case for the development of Internet based marketing communications for a business or company of your choice.

(20 marks)

Question 4

Write a report for your Senior Managers, explaining how marketing communications can contribute to the development of EITHER a consumer OR business to business brand. Use examples to illustrate your points.

(20 marks)

Question 5

Many marketing communication campaigns are influenced and shaped by competitive and wider external environmental forces. Using examples, explain how such forces might influence and shape the marketing communications for a brand (or brands) of your choice.

(20 marks)

Question 6

As Marketing Communication Manager for a global financial services organisation, you have decided to ask your assistant to attend a meeting with your full service agency. Prepare a briefing note advising your assistant of the key media concepts to be considered when developing media strategy.

(20 marks)

Question 7

In 1999 British Airways decided to reverse a decision concerning the design of their corporate identity used on the tail fins of many of their aircraft. The controversial designs were said to be disliked by overseas customers. At the same time, the redesign had been criticised by many staff who had been in conflict with the organisation about a cost cutting campaign introduced previously by management at the airline.

Prepare a report in which you identify the main theoretical elements of corporate identity/branding and use examples to illustrate how corporate communications can be used to reach important internal and external audiences. Use organisations of your choice to answer this question.

(20 marks)

Answers

**DO NOT TURN THIS PAGE UNTIL YOU
HAVE COMPLETED THE TEST PAPER**

Test paper: suggested answers

Question 1

Integrated Marketing Communications Plan

for

Woodstock Furniture Co Ltd

Prepared by

A CIM Student
June 2000

Contents

Executive Summary

Introduction

Context Analysis

Promotional Goals

Marketing Communications Strategy

Promotional Methods

Budget and Management Control

Evaluation

Executive Summary

This marketing communications plan for Woodstock Furniture Company seeks to build on the business and marketing strategies and over the next two years develop the Woodstock corporate brand. Funds are limited and this plan seeks to develop the brand by repositioning it away from the high street competitors as a high quality craftsman brand. This will be achieved by making the brand aspirational and will use a range of promotional tools designed to reinforce the craftsman position and by stimulating word-of-mouth communications.

Introduction

This Integrated Marketing Communications (IMC) plan has been developed for the Woodstock Furniture Co (WFC) based on the information provided in the briefing document. It covers a two year period and is designed to build on the marketing strategy which has already been put into position. WFC needs to develop its corporate brand and this plan sets out the way in which this is to be achieved, the costs and the timing associated with the activities.

Test paper: suggested answers

Context Analysis

In order to understand the situation facing WFC it is necessary to understand the context within which the communications are to be implemented. The following analysis sets out some of the key communications related issues facing the company.

Business Context

The company's performance has been quite variable over the past few years. Revenue has grown to £1.7m and profits stand at £117,300. Market share is 21% and the corporate goal is to grow at 15% pa. This may be difficult in a static market but with property prices in London and the South East starting to level out more people may decide to withdraw their homes from the market and wait for prices to rise in the future. In the meantime they may choose to refurbish their kitchens. Kitchens are an important room for buyers when they consider a house purchase.

The competition from the high street brands is seen as a threat but in terms of materials, product quality and design they do not attract the more discerning customer, sought by WFC. The promotional materials used by these large brands pose a threat and serve to homogenise the market. As a result of this there has been a change to the organisation's view of its own business. It no longer perceives itself as a manufacturer and installer but as a craftsman based company who design and construct high quality furniture to match and complement the interior of a home. This decision represents a repositioning away from the high street retailer based competition and seeks to differentiate the Woodstock brand. This change in purpose needs to be communicated to relevant stakeholders and acts as the base for this communications plan.

Customer Context

WFC customers are characterised by their wealth. They are affluent and can afford to have kitchens and bathrooms crafted to complement their homes. It is important to them that they appoint companies who attend to detail and who are able to match the decor of their homes. The communications that are recommended here reflect the privacy that the target audience values. The purchase decision represents high involvement so it is important to develop positive attitudes prior to purchase. This will require the development of high levels of trust which needs to be converted into commitment to the WFC brand. The strength of the credibility and subsequent customer satisfaction with their new installation should help provoke positive word of mouth comment. Advocacy can be developed if post purchase communications maintain levels of purchase satisfaction and privacy.

Members of the target market take pride in their homes and have a modern outlook. This is demonstrated by their interest in new technology and innovations generally. It should therefore be quite feasible to communicate with them through the Internet.

The marketing plan specifies that alliances are to be created with other manufacturers in related markets (conservatories, studies) which represent a horizontal dimension. In addition, new markets are to be approached through the development of new relationships with architects and property developers in what is a vertical dimension. This will require suitable communications.

Stakeholders

The brief fails to mention other stakeholders in detail but WFC needs to identify key stakeholder audiences. These may be associated with the new markets (eg trading association for conservatory manufacturers) or financial institutions and venture capitalists in an attempt to attract investment. Communications with these audiences need to reflect the values and performance of WFC rather than product range or terms of business.

Organisational Context

The company needs to update its old systems and procedures and become more efficient. However, the values associated with craftsmanship must not be lost. Rather, they need to be incorporated in the style and format of communications with the various target audiences. One way of doing this is to build on the loyalty and affinity many of the staff have for the organisation. Their knowledge of the market and the organisation can be used to signal high value, prestige and their behaviour harnessed as a strong corporate identity cue.

One of the most critical factors is the small amount of financial resources available for marketing communications.

External Context

The wider external environment is relatively unimportant in this context. It is unlikely that changes in the political arena will impact on the company but changes in the economic conditions (eg changes in capital gains taxation, stamp duty) might affect decisions to invest in kitchen furniture. However, it is felt that promotional materials and the new position should not stress, or even mention price, as this is not a decision criteria for this target audience. Wider social influences are few and technological influences limited to the methods WFC can use to communicate with its target audiences.

Promotional Goals

Three main types of objective can be determined:

1 *Corporate Objectives*

   These refer to the revised mission which repositions the organisation as a craftsman based organisation which designs and builds high quality bespoke furniture. This needs to be understood and accepted by all employees within 3 months and 75% of all strategically significant stakeholders within 6 months.

2 *Marketing Objectives*

   These are that the company must grow at 15% per annum, that prices should be adjusted to reflect the premium position and that new marketing channels (vertical and horizontal based relationships) need to be developed.

3 *Marketing Communication Objectives*

   The marketing communication objectives are to reposition the company and develop a corporate brand which reflects values of craftsmanship.

In order to accomplish this it will be necessary to first raise awareness (60% prompted) amongst the target customer audiences, then build positive attitudes towards the brand. This will be accomplished over the next two years.

In addition, communications need to reach architects and property developers (80% awareness) and links with other carefully selected manufacturers need to be established.

Marketing Communications Strategy

Owning a WFC kitchen should be regarded as a signal of achievement. However, the limited amount of funding restricts the amount and impact that the marketing communications can be expected to deliver. Therefore, a strong pull strategy is not realistic at this stage of development. The main weight of the campaign should be directed to a profile strategy and the generation of word of mouth communications. The essence of the profile strategy is to differentiate WFC on the basis of its total craft approach, employee skills and overall attention to the detail of customer needs. The brand needs to be repositioned as *aspirational* among successful entrepreneurs, sports personalities and other celebrities.

The strategy should be built first around the employees. These people need to be trained in customer service and management so that they carry and reflect the high values of the WFC brand. Whilst this is proceeding we need to reconsider the design elements of our corporate identity to ensure that it conveys the correct values that support the Woodstock brand, in all the ways that we project it (letterhead, workwear, vehicles etc.).

The next stage will involve the development of a suitable web site that seeks to provide information and be capable of collecting information about potential customers. A more extensive and interactive web site will be beyond the current resource levels and should be developed as a separate business strategy, at a later date.

A suitable set of consistent corporate identity cues need to be developed and conveyed through reasonable points of contact with customers and architects.

In order to reach architects and other specifiers a push strategy is also required. This includes appropriate sales literature which must include product specification (capabilities) information. High quality photography is not important, just the accuracy and completeness of the information provided.

Towards the end of the two year period aspects of a pull strategy might be introduced.

Promotional Methods

In order for the corporate brand to become established, a *word of mouth* campaign is to be developed, perhaps through a viral email campaign and selected kitchen based 'parties' (events) at special high profile locations.

Public relations activities are essential and could feed off the 'parties' by placing articles and editorial features about kitchens and related issues, in suitable magazines and newspapers. This is crucial to establish the values of the WFC brand.

Advertising in trade journals will be necessary during the first year. Placement in up-market consumer magazines is recommended towards the end of year 2 or possibly later as the word of mouth campaign may still be running.

Sponsorship may not be possible but should be considered for the longer term. An association with the arts, certain food manufacturers or fashionable yet well designed restaurants may complement the required positioning.

Personal selling remains an important part of the promotional mix. This is necessary not only to finalise customer orders but also to meet architects and to arrange horizontal alliances. In reality, there may only be a few people in the organisation responsible for personal selling but regardless of their status, these people need to be advised of the repositioning, given suitable promotional materials and trained in closing orders to increase the conversion ratio. Selling to architects and specifiers is very different to selling to end user customers. It may be worth considering the recruitment of someone with suitable skills and experience which can then be transferred internally.

Direct Marketing will be useful in the second year as names and addresses of potential customers build. The current format of the brochure needs to be revised especially with the technical data required by the specifiers. The craft approach needs to be reflected in a contemporary style.

It is important that these activities be coordinated, timed and delivered in such a way that the audience perceives a single consistent message, whether this be through the actions of employees or through the web site or sales brochures.

Test paper: suggested answers

Budget and Management Control

The budget available to WFC is approximately £85,000 for each of the two years of the campaign. This represents 5% of revenue and does not take into account higher margins or increased revenue in year 2. Cash flow needs to be monitored carefully to ensure there is no over commitment to the marketing communications strategy.

Promotional Tool	Q1	Q2	Q3	Q4	Q5	Q6	Q7	Q8
Public Relations	x	x		x	x	x		x
Email Campaign			x	x				
Direct Marketing						x	x	x
Advertising - Consumer								x
Advertising - Trade				x	x	x		
Employee Training & Communications	x	x			x			x
Corporate Literature and Sales Brochures		x				x		
Web Site Development	x	x	x					

Table 1.1 Schedule of Promotional Methods

Evaluation

The campaign should be evaluated not only at the end but also periodically through the campaign's life. The limited number of funds suggests that official recall and recognition techniques will not be possible. However, it should be possible to record informally where and how new customers and architects first heard of WFC. Once the Web Site is up the number of hits and the collection of names, addresses and other materials should be possible.

Finally, the campaign should be tracked against the objectives listed above. It is through some understanding of the level of awareness and the attitudes held about the Woodstock brand that the true worth of the campaign will be understood.

Question 2

Introduction

My response to this question will be based around an understanding of communication flows and then an appraisal of opinion former and opinion leader concepts.

Multi-step Flows of Communication

The flow of communication in a campaign was first considered to be linear in that information flowed from a source through a channel to a receiver who then provided feedback. This interpretation proved to be inaccurate in that it failed to account for the many variables that can impact on the communication process. One of the main variables is the influence of other people, shaping and redirecting the flow, content and intended meaning of messages.

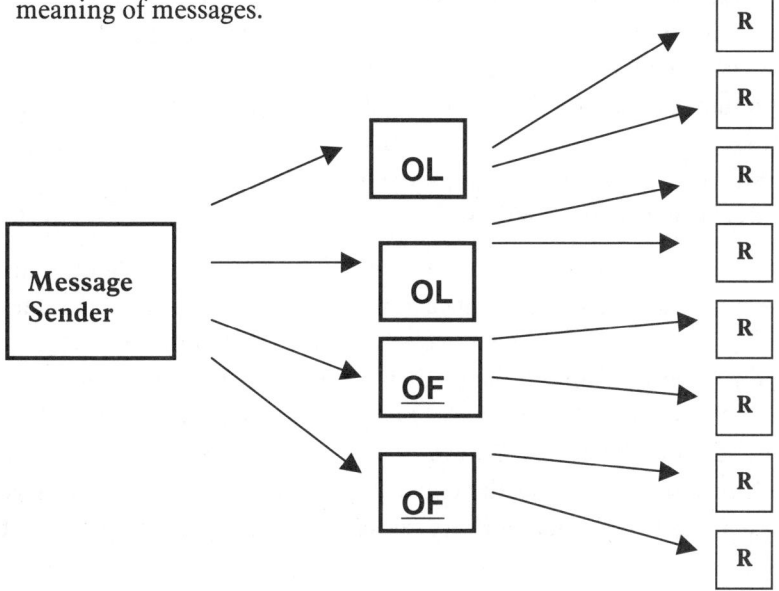

Figure 1.1 The Two-Step Model of Communication

The Two-Step Model (see Figure 1) and multi-step flow models of communication reflect the potential impact that these individuals might have on communications.

Types of Influencers

There are two main types of influencer, opinion leaders and opinion formers. The first are usually members of a peer group who have a particular interest and knowledge about a product category or area of interest. They may be friends, family or work colleagues to whom others (opinion followers) turn for advice and reassurance when contemplating a particularly significant purchase. They believe the information they receive is both credible and unbiased when considered in the light of many commercial messages.

Opinion Formers on the other hand are people who are designated as expert and knowledgeable about a particular topic or subject. Very often these people are public figures and it is the nature of their work that bestows the perceived expertise. Opinion formers therefore help shape the thoughts of others by providing information and advice that opinion followers value and believe is credible. Pharmacists, motoring journalists and qualified accountants for example, can provide credible information about medicines, cars and taxation issues respectively for those active in the decision making process. This information may be communicated person to person or through broadcast or print media.

In a marketing context this is an important factor because if it is possible to identify and direct marketing communication messages to those people that are capable of influencing other people then the implications for the efficiency and effectiveness of marketing communications activities is enormous. A popular advertising format is to use a slice of life approach where typical members of the target market are observed discussing issues and one of the characters uses the sponsors product to resolve the difficulty (soap powders, shampoo (for dandruff removal) and furniture).

Opinion leaders provide information for a number of reasons. People like to talk about their product purchases because it can relieve post purchase tension, bestow status on them and provide a means of advising and showing care for others (in this case those considering a similar purchase). Whilst it is difficult to isolate opinion leaders and target them directly, many are known to be innovators or part of the early adopters group within the process of diffusion. These people are actively interested in their topic/area and seek out information in advance of the general population. Identification therefore is helped because they are more likely to attend exhibitions, access specific web sites and read the specialist press. For example, when Sony launched the mini disc they targeted specialist music equipment retailers and held premium prices. The hi-fi enthusiasts (opinion leaders) were keen to buy the latest technology (regardless of price) and they then told others (followers) about their discovery which fed further demand which then allowed Sony to release the product through other high street (mainstream) outlets.

Opinion formers provide information because they are required to do so either because it is part of the job or because they have been contracted to do so or because it is a means of maintaining their own position. Some forms of sponsorship and celebrity endorsement can be regarded as opinion forming if only because they might be regarded as supporting the central act or object of the sponsorship itself. So, David Ginola may act as an endorser for L'Oreal haircare products but he is not known as an expert in haircare, he is seen as supporting the brand, in return for a specific (financial) reward. Opinion formers pass on information because it is part of the job and may only be known to a discrete number of people.

Conclusion

Recognition of the role that opinion leaders and formers can play in assisting the marketing communication process is important if the potential of a brand, and especially new brands and product launches, is to be fulfilled.

Question 3

Introduction

In business-to-business (b2b) markets organisational buying behaviour is more complex than that observed in consumer markets. This is because of the increased number of people involved in the decision making process and the nature of the relationships between organisations. As a result of this and other factors marketing communications in the b2b market is traditionally characterised by the predominance of personal selling and the relatively little use of advertising. In fact it is the complete reversal of business to consumer based promotional activity (b2c) where mass media based communications have tended to be the most important route through to the target audience.

The development of the Internet and related digital technologies has introduced new ways in which audiences in both sectors can be reached. There are many other ways in which organisations can benefit from these developments but these notes will concentrate on communications in the b2b sector.

Very briefly, the Internet and digital technologies can lead to faster communication, more information, lower costs, more effective transactions, a reduction in sales force personnel costs, improved relationships with intermediaries, the development of new/revised types of intermediary, potential for improved levels of customer satisfaction, speedier problem resolution, greater accuracy and less noise in the communication system, provision of exit barriers for intermediaries and an improved use of the communication mix. I will not go into these in detail but will highlight some of the points made.

In the b2b sector the development and maintenance of profitable relationships is important. Part of marketing communications role is to develop these relationships by reducing perceived risk and uncertainty. It also needs to provide clarity and provide fast, pertinent and timely information in order that decisions can be made.

Loyalty

Loyalty between organisations can be improved therefore by targeting information and customised messages at the right people within the partner organisation. Speed of response to customer questions and the clarity of the information provided is important for the development of trust and loyalty.

Productivity

Productivity should be increased as electronic communication not only saves time but also shortens the time between order and delivery.

Reputation

The reputation of our organisation should be enhanced considerably, not only through our web site but also through the way we are perceived to meet the needs of our customers. Subject to the actions of our competitors in this area we may also have a competitive advantage.

Costs

The costs of our communications can also be considerably reduced. Just as sales literature and demonstration packs take time to prepare, even longer to change/update and are quite expensive with a great deal of wastage, brochure ware on the Web site is fast, easily accessible and adaptable. One step further into Web site development will enable us to collect names and addresses, respond to email questions and provide rich data for our sales force. If we develop the Web site still further, then eCommerce transactions will enable routine orders to be completed quickly and at a lower cost, freeing up the sales force to visit established customers more often and opportunities to open new accounts and manage those accounts that are strategically important, more attentively.

Marketing Communications Mix

Digital technologies enable the collection of data for use through on and offline sources. So our direct marketing activities can be improved, our sales promotions targeted to provide real and valued incentives. Even our public relations activities can benefit by placing suitable material on our web pages.

Effectiveness

Finally, digitally-based communications can improve the accuracy of the information we provide and also enable us to measure the effectiveness of our marketing communication activities. However, we must not forget that offline communications are going to still be important and these new communication formats should be considered as an addition to rather than a substitution of our current marketing communications.

Now, whilst I have set out the advantages we must be aware of some of the drawbacks.

Traditional Customers

Internet access for some of our smaller business partners may be restricted and they may prefer to continue having face-to-face contact with our sales force. This we must respect and so deploy our new marketing communications mix carefully and not impose it on unwilling organisations.

Investment /Set Up costs

The set-up costs will be expensive and an appropriate investment approach needs to be adopted. Some parts of this technology can also lock us into relationships which might be difficult to get out off, should conditions change. In effect these are barriers to exit for each party.

Legal and Security

There will also be some legal and information security issues that we need to address in order to reduce any risk our partners might perceive.

End Notes

In order to conclude and summarise our marketing communications with business partners will improve through improved efficiency and effectiveness which in turn will be reflected in the nature and quality of the relationships we hold and ultimately be reflected in our overall performance and meeting our corporate goals.

Improved trust, commitment and a higher propensity to share information must lead to increased business performance. The development of the Internet based communications is a strategic decision that needs to be thought through in terms of the impact it will have on the way we and our partners do business. This in turn will require significant changes in the way we currently communicate and do business in the b2b market.

Test paper: suggested answers

Question 4

To: Marketing Management
From: A CIM Student
Date: 13 June 2000

Reference : The Contribution of Marketing Communications to Brand Development

1.0 Introduction

The development of a strong brand is important for business performance. The role of marketing communications in the branding process is also important and one that should not be underestimated.

According to Doyle, a brand is a name, symbol, design or some combination which identifies the 'product' of a particular organisation as having some differential advantage'. Brands can apply equally to products and organisations. This report will examine the role marketing communications has in developing a brand, whether it be for an organisation or product, in the business-to-business sector (b2b).

2.0 What are the Benefits of a Brand?

Before examining the impact of marketing communications it is necessary to establish the benefits that branding can bring. There are numerous advantages and they apply to both customers as well as the brand owner. Fill (1999) cites the following benefits for customers.

- Identify preferred products
- Reduce levels of perceived risk and so improve the quality of their shopping experience
- Determine levels of product quality
- Reduce shopping time
- Derive psychological rewards of status, ownership, etc

Benefits to brand owners include the following:

- Normally allows for premium pricing
- Helps differentiate the product from competitors
- Enhances cross-product promotion and brand extension opportunities
- Encourages customer retention and possibly loyalty
- Promotes the development of integrated marketing communications
- Contributes to corporate identity programmes
- Provides some form of legal protection

What emerges from this is that branding is important because if brands are managed properly then marketing performance is likely to improve.

3.0 The Strategic Perspective of Branding

From a strategic perspective, there are three key aspects of branding, differentiation, added value and integration.

Differentiation

Brands provide the means by which a product can be seen to be different from a competitor's product. Branding is a method of separation and positioning so that customers can recognise and understand what a brand stands for, relative to other brands.

Added Value

The second key aspect is that of added value. Brands enable customers to derive extra benefits as one brand can provide different advantages to another. These advantages might be in the form of rational attribute based advantages (eg whiter, stronger or longer) or they may be more emotionally based advantages derived through the augmented aspects of the products (eg the way you feel about a brand).

Integration

For a brand to be maintained and to work it is important that the communications used to develop and maintain the brand are consistent and meaningful. Part of the essence of integrated marketing communications is that all the tools used to support a brand and the messages that are used to convey brand values must be consistent, uniform and reinforcing. Therefore, successful branding is partly the result of effective integrated marketing communications.

4.0 The Role of Marketing Communications

Marketing communications plays a vital role in all three of these strategic aspects. Marketing communications is the means by which products are turned into brands, by which customers can see how the product is different and understand what a brand stands for and what its values are.

Black and Decker discovered that they were losing sales in the trade sector because their products were perceived to be more suitable for consumers and the do-it-yourself market. Their response was to develop a separate brand for this particular trade sector. They used a new name 'Matika', identified the product range through the colour yellow and made it available through different trade channels. The promotional materials and support documentation needed a different "tone of voice" to reflect a more rugged and stronger position. The messages were integrated in order to reinforce the desired positioning.

A b2b brand is often tied closely to the company itself as opposed to b2c brands which often take preference to the manufacturer or company name. For example, a Rolls Royce power turbine is branded Rolls Royce because of the perception of tradition, high quality, performance and global reach that are associated with the Rolls Royce name.

The marketing communications should be developed so that they incorporate and perpetuate the personality of the brand. So, all the Rolls Royce advertising materials should be in corporate colours and contain the logo. All copy should be in the house style and reinforce brand perceptions.

Conclusion

Marketing communications are the means by which products become brands. By communicating the strengths and differences of a brand, by explaining how a brand brings value to a customer and by reinforcing and providing consistency in the messages transmitted a level of integration can be brought to a brand.

Question 5

Introduction

The purpose of this answer is to explain the nature of the influences of the wider largely uncontrollable environment and to evaluate their possible impact on an organisation's marketing communications.

The externally driven forces acting on an organisation vary in size and immediacy. It is not possible to be specific about how a force might affect an organisation's marketing communications but it is possible to make some judgements about the form and general response an organisation should make. For the purposes of this report I will use the PEST framework after first examining the competitive forces.

Competitive Forces

The impact competitors can have on an organisation can be quite critical. Very often new entrants, a new marketing strategy, brand extensions, use of new technology or new products can cause an organisation to review the way it operates, its marketing strategy and/or its marketing communications strategy. One of the most significant forces is a competitor's communications which may either directly or indirectly refer to your brand. One of the responses that needs to be considered is a repositioning exercise or at the least a review of the way your brand is communicated (mix, message, media) and the way in which a brand is perceived, relative to the competition. For example, some manufacturers brands have felt it important to respond to the development and packaging of some competitive retail brands (Coca-Cola and Sainsbury's cola, Penguin and Puffin bars) by taking legal action to protect the way in which their brand is positioned.

A competitor may attempt to use particular product attributes to position themselves which may intrude upon another brand's position. The response will be either to reinforce the communication of the strength of the attribute or move to a new attribute that is thought to be of worth to the target audience.

PEST Forces

Of the wider external environment the Political, Economic, Social and Technological forces are the most prominent.

The **Political (and legal)** environment may change in such a way that an organisation is powerless to control or influence them in any meaningful way. Some industry sectors such as pharmaceuticals are active lobbyists and seek to prevent the introduction of policies and regulations that might harm the way they communicate with their audiences (and influence other aspects of their businesses) Changes in the EU regulations are threatening the use of certain types of sales promotion and direct selling. This will cause organisations to review their promotional mix and to find new ways of communicating. Advertising to children is under threat and if it becomes EU law, will cause organisations in the sector to adapt their communication strategy.

Comparative advertising regulations have changed recently such that Sky Digital launched a campaign that compares their brand to that of their main competitor On Digital. In response and recognition of the potential harm to the On Digital brand, the organisation has had to address the Sky Digital statements and so divert them from their brand building strategy.

Changes to the **economy** can influence levels of disposable income and in turn change perceptions about value for money. In times of recession, price driven promotional campaigns are (in general) perceived to be more effective, while a return to relative affluence can enable brands to return to communicating brand values that do not influence price. Many organisations tend to reduce the level of their above-the-line work during periods of economic downturn but recent research suggest that the brands that survive and recover fastest are those that continue to use advertising to build brands during the depressed periods.

The impact of **social** changes should of course always be incorporated in the marketing strategy. Such influences need to be reflected in the communications used by organisations if they are to be perceived sympathetically and be regarded as 'in touch'. Of course this is very applicable to fashion brands but social views about GM foods have been adopted by Iceland food group as a means of differentiating themselves from their larger competitors. Marks & Spencer, once high street market leaders failed to keep in touch with changing social trends (and the reactions of competitors) and the brand became outdated and of little value (relative to its past). This was reflected not only in the way the promotional mix was deployed but also in the clothing ranges and the style of products, which of course is an intrinsic part of the way a retail brand communicates. The response has been to revise the product strategy as well as use above-the-line and through-the-line strategies in a more contemporary way.

Of all the forces in the external environment, it could be argued that changes in **technology** can, and do, have the biggest impact. The development of the Internet and new methods of interactive communication have forced brands to have an on-line presence and dot.com identity. This requires a new strategic approach which some are mastering but others are not, such as www.boo.com, which went into liquidation. The balance between off-line and on-line communications is important as the need to drive site traffic is imperative for commercial success. During the late 1990s outdoor advertising experienced huge growth mainly as a result of on-line brands generating traffic and top-of-mind awareness as a run up to privatisation (www.lastminute.com) It is not just the Internet however that can impact on organisations. Developments in database technology have influenced the way in which organisations can undertake direct marketing and sales promotions. They have helped drive a move towards integrated marketing communications. The current developments concerning WAP facilities and mobile convergence will undoubtedly affect the way some consumer brands are positioned.

Conclusion

Changes in the wider environment can have a significant impact on the way in which a brand is communicated. These forces are not constant and brand managers need to monitor and keep abreast of the changes if they are to meet the challenges they present and enable their brands to be successful. An effective marketing information system can be of help but there is an overall need for organisations to be flexible and if possible anticipate changes so that their brand values can be retained.

Test paper: suggested answers

Question 6

To :   A N Other Marketing Communications Assistant
From :   A J Smith Marketing Communications Manager
Date :   13 June 2000

Ref : Media Concepts

Prior to your forthcoming meeting with our agency XYZ I would like to set out some of the key media concepts and then see how they are associated with media strategy.

Concepts

Two of the important concepts are Reach and Frequency. Reach refers to the percentage number of people in the target market who are reached once with the message. Frequency refers to the percentage who are exposed to the message two or more times within a given budget and time frame. Of course it is possible to develop both coverage and frequency but this will normally require separate campaigns.

Gross rating points, or ratings, are the number of impacts made in a campaign (simply put this is coverage x frequency) and is a useful measure as it indicates the total effect of a campaign. Very often the media plan will state the ratings to be achieved and this will relate to the cost of the campaign. Obviously the higher the ratings, which can be guaranteed by the media, the heavier our investment will need to be.

Now, as you know, our target markets around the world do not buy a single newspaper or magazine nor do they see a single television programme. Therefore our media plan should state the level of overlap between people who are likely to be exposed more than once to our campaign. This is referred to as duplication and the agency will have duplication tables so as to improve the efficiency of our investment.

The only other concepts are Opportunities–to-See (OTSs) which refers to the number of people who buy the vehicle (magazine, paper) but does not necessarily mean they actually see our message, Cost per Thousand (CPT) which is a measure of the cost incurred to reach each thousand people in our target audience. You might like to look out for the point that CPT can only be used to compare the media costs within a media vehicle not to compare costs across media (for example television and magazines). The final concept is flighting which refers to the pattern of advertising: is the advertising to be transmitted in a concentrated period of time (burst) or is it to be fed out over a longer period (drip)?

There are a number of other concepts which are not media specific. However, if we are to undertake a global campaign we need to be aware of target markets, and the local conditions that may impair or assist the way in which we communicate with our audiences.

Media Strategy

Media strategy is about trying to get the best fit between media vehicles and the target audience, at the lowest possible price.

The media strategy will be dependent to a large extent on what we are trying to achieve. If we are rolling out a new brand then awareness will be a prime objective. If awareness is the goal then a coverage based media strategy is likely to be more appropriate. Here we will be trying to make as many people as possible aware of the new brand. If our goal is to reposition or remind people about our brand then a frequency strategy may be more appropriate. When people are required to learn something about our brand we may need three hits with our message. The first to make them aware, the second to make the point and the third to remind them about the point in order for them to memorise it. Now this approach is questionable and we should be open to new views. The level of education and the social fabric in each of the geographical areas in which we operate varies and so the media strategy needs to be flexible and we should not necessarily dictate a rigid media approach.

What we can expect is that the media plan itself needs to be efficient and effective. We need to be sure that as far as media buying is concerned that the agency buys the media on our behalf at the most advantageous rates (discounts) that can be reasonably expected. If we are not happy with the rates we may need to centralise all our media buying into a media house (dependent or independent). This of course will impact on all our brands so we will need time to carefully consider this decision.

Most of these notes have concentrated on advertising but we need to be aware of the integrated nature of our campaign and the need to harmonise the activities of the other parts of the promotional mix. We will be using sales promotions and direct marketing together with our web site. The messages that these deliver must be the same in order to not confuse our target customers, many of whom travel and will see our messages in different locations.

The media strategy will need to take account of the message standardisation or adaptation debate. I think we need XYZ to update us on their views on this subject although I think our current globalisation approach is the best way forward.

Final Comments.

I hope these notes are of some help but you will come across a raft of others during the meeting. Overall, it is the strategic approach to media planning that is important and the degree to which XYZ tries to take an integrated approach to the media planning activities. Please look out for the level and quality of the skills and resources that they have available throughout the different country regions in which we have a presence.

Test paper: suggested answers

Question 7

To   Whom it may Concern
From : A CIM Student
Date: 13 June 2000
Ref: Report about Corporate Identity

1.0   Introduction

In this report I will explain the main concepts concerning corporate identity and proceed to explain how internal and external audiences can be reached using corporate communications. From this I will suggest that the development of Integrated Marketing Communications can be based around this orientation to multiple audiences and the need for consistent brand values.

2.0   Theoretical Aspects of Corporate Identity

It now appears to be generally accepted that Corporate Identity consists of three main elements, Corporate Personality, Identity and Image.

Corporate personality is about the nature and characteristics of the organisation itself. To a large extent it is made up of the dominant culture in an organisation and the strategies the organisation is pursing. Personality is about what the organisation actually is.

From this base, management select corporate identity cues which are used to signal particular aspects to selected target audiences. I will explain later about the range and types of cues that can be used. However, at this stage it is important to understand that identity cues can be planned and timed and they can also be unplanned and accidental and yet have a more damaging effect. Corporate identity therefore is how the organisation wants to be seen and understood.

Corporate Image is the perception each person has of the organisation as a result of interpreting the cues they receive. It is clear that people hold a variety of images of organisations and it is this multiplicity of images that represents a major challenge to those responsible for the management of corporate identity. There is a further aspect which is referred to as corporate reputation. This is the deeper, more ingrained set of images that accumulate through time and often through direct transactional experience with an organisation. Corporate image is about how the organisation is actually perceived.

The management of corporate identity can be considered in terms of reducing the gap between the way an organisation wants to be seen and understood, and the actual image that they have. These perception gaps may be large or small, they may affect a large or small number of stakeholders and they may be trivial or they may concern strategically important issues. The recent attempt to force management of Standard Life to float on the stock market (to demutualise their status) resulted in a publicly held debate through the news media. The image and understanding of the issues in favour of the action and the large personal windfalls were vigorously counteracted by the management who did not want this policy adopted. This required them to put forward their arguments in an attempt to correct their members' perception of the short and long term benefits.

These corporate communications are normally targeted at a range of different stakeholders and involve the transmission of a range of different messages. For example, the messages sent by Standard Life to the financial markets would have been orientated heavily towards encouraging them to resist the buy out and look to the long term interests of the organisation. The messages sent to their members would have stressed the financial implications but would not have been technically complex or obtuse. Messages sent to staff might have been geared to keeping them informed of events, to prime them of news that was about to break nationally and to keep them supporting the resistance.

This last group of stakeholders, the employees are increasingly being considered as an important, if not an essential part of the total communication process. With many organisations seeking to provide a high level of personal service as part of their brand's added value, it is absolutely vital that this group of stakeholders is informed, trained and has a strong customer orientation.

3.0 Corporate Identity Cues

The cues used by organisations to reach stakeholders are many and varied and should reflect the media vehicles stakeholders use. However, the diversity of cues can best be seen through the corporate identity mix as framed by Birkigt and Stadler.

- Behaviour
- Communication
- Symbolic

The behaviour of the organisation refers to the actions undertaken, what an organisation actually does, how it performs and how it reacts to environmental events. This also concerns how the people in the organisation interact with those externally and how they are observed to interact among themselves.

Communication refers to the visual and verbal messages which are more immediate and quicker to instigate than learning through behaviour. The style and tone of the promotional mix and the way the company presents itself is an important part of the overall corporate identity mix.

Symbolic cues refer to the logo and letterhead design, normally associated with corporate identity. In reality these symbolic aspects are used to harmonise and pull together the behaviour and communication aspects.

4.0 Internal Communications

Communications used to reach employees have changed a great deal over the past few years. In particular technological advances and the use of the Internet, coupled with Extranets and Intranets have enabled organisations to keep their employees informed. Many new corporate branding launches use video conferences to prime and to simultaneously inform employees across the world in many different locations. For example, British Airways used video conferencing for staff when launching their now infamous tail-fin design in 1997.

One of the main staff based communication issues is increasingly that management now appear to accept that employees play a critical role of interaction with those stakeholders who are external to the organisation. The quality of this interaction is perceived by customers as a means of determining what they think and feel about the organisation as a whole. It is during this service encounter that images are crystallised and the closer these two groups understand each other the stronger the corporate identity is likely to be. Many retail brands have put great emphasis on their customer service training and more recently financial services organisations have attempted to lift this aspect of their brands. B&Q use staff in their television (and print) ads as part of their positioning. This provides motivation and a means by which staff can identify with the brand. However, this needs to be managed carefully as the expectations customers have of B&Q (and their staff) are raised and need to be met in order not to cause customer dissatisfaction and disappointment.

The blend between internal and external communications, another indication of the role integrated marketing communications has to play, suggests that staff act as a strong cue that signals corporate brand values.

Topic Index

Topic index

Advertising agencies, 8
Advertising budget, 13
Affordable approach, 115
AirMiles, 142
American Marketing Association, 7
Andrex, 124
Article, 13, 14
Attitudes, 66, 71
Attributes, 66

BMW cars, 33
Boddington's beer, 33
Boddingtons, 77
Brand, 10, 12, 16
Branding, 12, 16
Branding and marketing communications, 107, 109
British Airways, 78, 109
British telecom's, 129
Budget determination, 117
Budget process, 13
Burst campaign, 13
Business-to-business market, 11
Business-to-business sector, 12
Buying centre, 59

Cadbury, 107
Carling, 91
Channel members, 12
Choice set, 56
Communication mixes, 34
Communications strategy, 24
Competitive advantage, 103
Competitive parity, 115
Competitors advertising spend, 14
Complex decision-making, 56
Conclusion and recommendations, 151
Conclusion, 69
Consumer buying behaviour, 7
  consumer, 56
Context analysis, 86, 88, 155
Corporate brand, 162
Crisis management, 53
Cultural and social trends, 18
Cultural trends, 149
Culture, 18
Customer retention schemes, 16

Decision making
Direct and Interactive Marketing, 34
Direct mail, 136
Drip campaign, 13

Effectiveness, 121, 142

Employees, 11, 12
Ethical issues, 16
Examples of business to business brands, 114
Executive summary, 149

Fill, Chris, 49
Ford, 107

Global advertising strategies, 18
Government campaign, 16
Government markets, 58
Growth of customer loyalty schemes, 141

Health Education Board for Scotland, 133
Heinz, 107
How might agencies adjust?, 70

IBM, 151
Inertia, 57
Information superhighway, 53
Institutional markets, 58
Integrated communication planning process, 5
Integrated comunications, 50
Integrated marketing communications, 4, 5, 43, 47
Integrated marketing, 5
Internal marketing communications programmes, 11
Internal marketing communications, 12, 100
Internal paper, 13
Internal report, 22
International agencies, 18
international communications strategies, 8
International communications, 18
Internet, 5, 12, 111
Introduction, 68, 69, 102, 113, 141, 163
It's Good to Talk, 129

Japan, 146

Kellogg, 107
Key communications issues, 23
Key strategic factors, 21
Key Strategic Issues, 22, 24, 163
Kotler, 55
Kwikfit, 107

Limited decision making, 57
Low involvement decision making, 57
Loyalty based schemes, 16

Topic index

Majaro, 28
Market conditions, 149
Marketing audit, 10
Marketing communication plan, 86
Marketing communications, 4, 11, 13, 22
Marketing communications budgets, 13
Marketing communications campaign, 13
Marketing communications expenditure, 14
Marketing communications plan, 11
Marketing communications strategy, 4, 11, 16, 18
Measuring effectiveness, 13
Media choice, 13, 116
Media factors, 150
Media schedule, 13
Memorandum, 12, 14
Mintzberg, 4
Mission statement, 11
Models, 60

New products
Not invented here syndrome, 145

Objective and task approach, 115
Objective and task method, 13
Objectives, 4, 5, 11, 156
Organisational buying behaviour, 7
Organisational environment, 59

Pepsi Cola, 64
Perceived risk, 7
Percentage of sales, 115
Perception, 68
Philadelphia Cheese, 108
Planned communications, 12
Positioning strategy, 10, 76
Positioning, 10, 79
PPP Healthcare, 33
Presentation, 5, 10, 13
Producer markets, 58
Product Life-Cycle, 16, 62
Professionalism, 59
Profile Strategies, 161
Promotional budgets, 13, 118
Promotional mix, 4, 10, 11
Promotional strategy, 16, 21, 139, 160
Promotional toolkit, 27
Public relations, 36
Pulford, Alan, 41
Pull strategies, 160
Purchasing agent, 58
Push Strategies, 161

QVC, 53

Reasons for possible incompatibility, 69
Report, 10, 11, 12, 13, 16, 23
Repositioning, 119
Reseller markets, 58
Resource utilisation, 103
Retail structure, 150
RSPCA, 136

Saatchi and Saatchi, 47, 153
Save the Children, 124
Segmentation, 10
Seven levels of integration, 41
Situation analysis, 88, 149, 155
Smoking, 133
Social trends, 150
Staff motivation, 102
Staff retention, 103
Stakeholder, 155
Strategic marketing communication campaign, 16
Strategic marketing communication, 16
Strategic marketing communications plan, 20
Strategy and objectives, 4
Strategy as pattern, 36
Strategy, 4
    success of, 57

Target end users, 149
Targeting, 10
Tea and coffee market, 149
Telemarketing, 5
The benefits of internal marketing communications, 102
The Business-to-business sector (BTB), 114
The future of branding, 114
Traffic generation, 52

UK supermarket loyalty schemes, 142

Virgin, 110

What is a brand?, 113
World Wide Web, 111
WPP Group, 153

CIM Order

To BPP Publishing Ltd, Aldine Place, London W12 8AA

Tel: 020 8740 2211. Fax: 020 8740 1184

Mr/Mrs/Ms (Full name)

Daytime delivery address

Postcode

Daytime Tel

Date of exam (month/year)

POSTAGE & PACKING

Study Texts

	First	Each extra	
UK	£3.00	£2.00	£
Europe*	£5.00	£4.00	£
Rest of world	£20.00	£10.00	£

Kits/Passcards/Success Tapes

	First	Each extra	
UK	£2.00	£1.00	£
Europe*	£2.50	£1.00	£
Rest of world	£15.00	£8.00	£

Grand Total (Cheques to *BPP Publishing*) I enclose a cheque for (incl. Postage) £ ☐☐☐☐☐☐☐

Or charge to Access/Visa/Switch

Card Number ☐☐☐☐☐☐☐☐☐☐☐☐☐☐☐☐

Expiry date ☐☐☐☐ Start Date ☐☐☐☐

Issue Number (Switch Only) ☐☐

Signature

		5/00 Texts	9/00 Kits	Tapes
CERTIFICATE				
1	Marketing Environment	£17.95 ☐	£8.95 ☐	£12.95 ☐
2	Customer Communications in Marketing	£17.95 ☐	£8.95 ☐	£12.95 ☐
3	Marketing in Practice	£17.95 ☐	£8.95 ☐	£12.95 ☐
4	Marketing Fundamentals	£17.95 ☐	£8.95 ☐	£12.95 ☐
ADVANCED CERTIFICATE				
5	The Marketing Customer Interface	£17.95 ☐	£8.95 ☐	£12.95 ☐
6	Management Information for Marketing Decisions	£17.95 ☐	£8.95 ☐	£12.95 ☐
7	Effective Management for Marketing	£17.95 ☐	£8.95 ☐	£12.95 ☐
8	Marketing Operations	£17.95 ☐	£8.95 ☐	£12.95 ☐
DIPLOMA				
9	Integrated Marketing Communications	£17.95 ☐	£8.95 ☐	£12.95 ☐
10	International Marketing Strategy	£17.95 ☐	£8.95 ☐	£12.95 ☐
11	Strategic Marketing Management: Planning and Control	£17.95 ☐	£8.95 ☐	£12.95 ☐
12	Strategic Marketing Management: Analysis and Decision (9/00)	£24.95 ☐		

SUBTOTAL £ ☐

We aim to deliver to all UK addresses inside 5 working days. A signature will be required. Orders to all EU addresses should be delivered within 6 working days.

All other orders to overseas addresses should be delivered within 8 working days.

* Europe includes the Republic of Ireland and the Channel Islands.

CIM - Diploma: Integrated Marketing Communications (9/00)

REVIEW FORM & FREE PRIZE DRAW

All original review forms from the entire BPP range, completed with genuine comments, will be entered into one of two draws on 31 January 2001 and 31 July 2001. The names on the first four forms picked out on each occasion will be sent a cheque for £50.

Name: _____   Address: _____
_____
_____

How have you used this Kit?
(Tick one box only)
☐ Home study (book only)
☐ On a course: college _____
☐ With 'correspondence' package
☐ Other _____

Why did you decide to purchase this Kit?
(Tick one box only)
☐ Have used complementary Study Text
☐ Have used BPP Kits in the past
☐ Recommendation by friend/colleague
☐ Recommendation by a lecturer at college
☐ Saw advertising
☐ Other _____

During the past six months do you recall seeing/receiving any of the following?
(Tick as many boxes as are relevant)
☐ Our advertisement in *Marketing Success*
☐ Our advertisement in *Marketing Business*
☐ Our brochure with a letter through the post
☐ Our brochure with *Marketing Business*

Which (if any) aspects of our advertising do you find useful?
(Tick as many boxes as are relevant)
☐ Prices and publication dates of new editions
☐ Information on Kit content
☐ Facility to order books off-the-page
☐ None of the above

Have you used the companion Study Text for this subject?   ☐ Yes   ☐ No

Your ratings, comments and suggestions would be appreciated on the following areas

	Very useful	Useful	Not useful
Introductory section (Study advice, key questions checklist, etc)	☐	☐	☐
'Do you know' checklists	☐	☐	☐
Tutorial questions	☐	☐	☐
Examination-standard questions	☐	☐	☐
Content of suggested answers	☐	☐	☐
Quiz	☐	☐	☐
Test paper	☐	☐	☐
Structure and presentation	☐	☐	☐

	Excellent	Good	Adequate	Poor
Overall opinion of this Kit	☐	☐	☐	☐

Do you intend to continue using BPP Study Texts/Kits?   ☐ Yes   ☐ No

Please note any further comments and suggestions/errors on the reverse of this page.

Please return to: Kate Machattie, BPP Publishing Ltd, FREEPOST, London, W12 8BR

REVIEW FORM & FREE PRIZE DRAW (continued)

Please note any further comments and suggestions/errors below

FREE PRIZE DRAW RULES

1 Closing date for 31 January 2001 draw is 31 December 2000. Closing date for 31 July 2001 draw is 30 June 2001.

2 Restricted to entries with UK and Eire addresses only. BPP employees, their families and business associates are excluded.

3 No purchase necessary. Entry forms are available upon request from BPP Publishing. No more than one entry per title, per person. Draw restricted to persons aged 16 and over.

4 Winners will be notified by post and receive their cheques not later than 6 weeks after the relevant draw date.

5 The decision of the promoter in all matters is final and binding. No correspondence will be entered into.